1-14-97

DATE DUE

12-28	JAN 28 1983	JUN 24 1998
2-7	OCT 19 1984	FEB 16
8-18	MAN 11 1984	FEB 11 '03
7-11	AUG 8 1985	JUN 26 '03
9-28	DEC 31 1985	NOV 10 '04
11-23	DEC 18 1986	OCT 10 2006
5-8	DEC 30 1986	APR 09 2008
2-15	JUL 28 87	JAN 30 '90	JAN 27 2012
6-16	APR 12 88	OCT 12 '90	DEC 05 2013
FEB 23	DEC 28 88	JUL 8 '92	
FEB 25		OCT 7 '92	
MAR 17 1981		JAN 30 1995	
MAY 8 1981		MAR 01 1995	
JUN 11 1981		FEB 21 1996	
JUN 29 1981		MAY 09 1997	JAN 13 1998
JUN 2 1982		FEB 18 1998	
JUL 15 1982		MAR 04 1998	

GAYLORD   FEB 28 '89   PRINTED IN U.S.

THE HUNTING DOGS OF AMERICA

JEFF GRIFFEN

THE HUNTING DOGS
OF AMERICA

DRAWINGS BY RAYMOND S. PEASE

DOUBLEDAY & COMPANY, INC.

GARDEN CITY, NEW YORK

This book is dedicated
to hunting dogs of all kinds.
They have supplied me with some
of the finest friends and experiences
I have ever known.

ACKNOWLEDGMENT

The author wishes to thank Clifton L. Havener Jr. of Gaines,
C. E. Fawcett of Purina and Pete Czura, photographer, for
valuable aid in forming this book, as well as Dr. Howard C.
Raven and Dr. Isidor Yasgur, two veterinarians who know
a lot about field dogs. The author is also grateful to American
Kennel Club, United Kennel Club and The American Field for
permission to quote from breed standards, for library usage
and for photographic assistance.

CONTENTS

THE HUNTING DOGS OF AMERICA

SECTION I

Introduction

Through the years much has been written about hunting dogs. Yet it is amazing how the pressures of our time, desire for the ultimate in hunting pleasure, the search for improved nutrition and the by-products of the electronic age are all contributing to new trends in field dogs. Care and feeding plans have drastically changed, training systems improved. New concepts of wildlife management and conservation have arisen. The burgeoning of the population, which daily devours more of the countryside, would tend to discount the belief that hunting has much future except on game farms and other artificial places. More people than ever before are taking up the quest of all types of game and entering into field-trial competition, and this participation is bound to increase.

Why?

For one thing, hunting is a man's world and there aren't many masculine things left that men can do and call their own. Few women can understand, let alone enjoy, freezing in a duck blind, or climbing up and down hills for grouse that whir away unseen more often than not, or tramping through swamps at night in search of raccoon. No, woman is the hearthmaker, man the hunter by nature.

Also, our cities of concrete, steel and glass may be one of modern man's great achievements, but to escape from the drive and tension they generate, from the routine of paper work, the pressure of decisions, and once more feel sunlight and wind, maybe some rain in one's face, and pit one's skill and timing against a flying bird, this makes a man himself again. Above all, to have as one's companion a dog that performs with lively purpose—points with electrifying style or dives into an icy current to retrieve to his master with loving care because his master has taught him to do so—this is the stuff of which memories are made, a tonic better than sleeping pills and tranquilizers.

The purpose of this book is to show how to gain these rewarding moments with a hunting dog. All breeds of sporting dogs and hounds are discussed so the beginner may gain a perspective of what they encompass and thus decide which is most suitable for him. And the experienced hunter can more deeply appreciate his gunning companion, perhaps even acquire another breed that he has heretofore overlooked.

The hunting characteristics of each breed will be described, as will its strong points, weaknesses, what it can be expected to do and not to do, and the type of hunting it is most suited for. The history of each breed, how it was developed, where, by whom, its original purpose, are included not only for general knowledge but for training. Because of the hunting habits of the country of origin, each breed has acquired certain dominating traits and qualities, hence must be bought, trained and hunted with these in mind. In the process will be discussed the path each breed is taking in the field-dog world. When the words pointer and setter appear uncapitalized in the text they carry a general meaning. Capitalized, they refer specifically to the Pointer and English Setter as breeds.

No book is complete without information on maintaining one's dog. Thus there are chapters on how to pick and raise a puppy, canine diet including the new self-feeding system, planning and building a kennel, training, care of the mature dog, the fun and value of field trials, worming the dog, tattooing him for identification, and many other points of importance included so one may enjoy his hunting dog to the fullest.

I shall not dwell too much on the standards of each breed. Most anyone these days can tell at a glance the variety of any registered dog. Only the expert is interested in height of withers, width of cranium, pitch of eyeballs, etc., and this principally for bench shows. Dogs of field breeding do not easily classify into standards. They run small, medium and large, and their conformation may best be described as good, average or poor. This does not mean that "looks" are to be ignored in field dogs, but it's the old story of "handsome is as handsome does." From time to time brief portions of American Kennel Club and United Kennel Club breed standards are quoted and I am grateful for permission to do so. But for the most part I shall rely for my standards upon the current field champions, most of which have surprisingly good practical conformation, balance and overall symmetry. These are the dogs that even the unpracticed eye looks at and says, "Ah-h-h."

To enjoy hunting today one must, more than ever, have a good dog. That means well bred, well trained and in sound condition. Everything that follows has been included with this end in mind.

Chapter 1

The Wonderful World
of Hunting Dogs

Each year more and more people are discovering the exciting world of field dogs. If they want to hunt pheasant or quail, ducks or geese, rabbits, raccoon, bear or mountain lion, America has the finest dogs on earth to do it. For those who don't want to hunt, there are Beagle and Basset packs to follow afoot and listen to their merry baying, or the challenge of field-trial competition for almost every breed of field dog we have. To the man who trains his own dog and uses it for hunting or in competition comes one of the most rewarding relationships imaginable, hours of patient discipline followed by years of pleasure and excitement, a treasure of memories. With its pointing breeds, flushing spaniels and retrievers, scent-hunting and sight-hunting hounds, the world of field dogs has more facets of enjoyment and challenge than any other sport yet developed by man.

If you have ever hunted over or seen an outstanding field dog in action, regardless of the breed, you'll never forget the experience.

Let me describe a brace of bird dogs that will stick in my memory forever. They worked as a team through the fields and bottoms of North Carolina in search of quail—Rex a big bold liver-and-white Pointer, Sam a strong, graceful tricolored Setter. I noticed the grin of pride as their boss loaded them into the back of his pickup one frosty morning. We hunted from foot, the boss and I, and the dogs knew what we were after. Like demons they seined the lespedeza edges and honeysuckle thickets, swung through the jack pines and sunny sides of the bottoms, cut up the pea patches and straw fields, checked every squirrel and possum scent but never lingered over them. In tight cover they worked at close range. When we came to a big field they took it apart, one along one edge, one along the other. At the far end they paused an instant to see if we were coming on or turning. No matter which way we went they swung to the front automatically or with a simple whistle and hand motion.

It was a thrilling sight to see them work the wind, stop an instant to gooseneck hot body scent, then knife boldly ahead to stab a covey. If they

Today's hunting dog, because of his field-trial background, is a stylist of great ability. Here three field champions are shown pheasant hunting with their owner, Robert G. Wehle of Scottsville, N.Y.

momentarily lost the scent, they didn't boil around in a frenzy but made a quick circle until they found it again. When one stacked up on point, the other backed on sight. If the dog on point flagged slightly, we knew he was telling us that the birds were pretty far ahead and we let him relocate. After each bit of shooting I'd turn around to look at the dogs. There they'd be, glued in their tracks. With that prideful grin the boss would say, "Fetch 'em, boys!" and they'd tear off to retrieve. Three times that day the sleeper jumped late and tried to scoot away, but we nailed him because the dogs were still standing steady behind us and hadn't run him up.

That was a memorable hunt and even if we'd come home with nothing, those two dogs would have made our twenty miles of walking worth while. Such an experience can be had with superior field dogs of any breed, be it spaniel, hound, retriever or otherwise, for the dogs that are being bred today for hunting are of higher quality than ever before, a fact brought about principally through field-trial competition. We think of our current dog breeds as being absolutely stable. Far from it. Like everything else in America, the world of hunting dogs is changing, as are the dogs themselves.

Look at what has happened in the past twenty-five years.

Several new breeds have appeared on the scene—the German Shorthair, Weimaraner, and Vizsla imported from Europe, the Basenji and Rhodesian

Ridgeback from Africa. One breed, the Boykin Spaniel, has been created here in our own country and another, the coursing hound which ranchers and farmers are breeding and using to capture coyotes on our Great Plains, appears in the process of being put together right now.

Many old hound breeds are being refined and registered for the first time in their long history. Redbones, Blueticks, Plotts, the Black-and-Tan, which traces back to colonial times, are all being registered and bred to a specific standard which in time will produce specimens of the highest type in conformation and ability.

New uses are being found for many breeds. The Labrador, Golden, and Chesapeake, great water and land retrievers, are being widely used for flushing and shooting upland game in spaniel style. Springers, whose forte this is, are seeing more and more water work. Along the great migratory duck flyways where moderately warm conditions prevail, Weimaraners, Shorthairs, even Setters can be seen fetching mallards and pintails from swamps and rivers.

Above all, the quality of dog is constantly being improved. If you ask an old-timer about the best bird dog he ever owned, he will describe Ol' Jake, an unregistered Pointer or Setter known to the trade as a meat dog. "Why, my brother and I killed sixty-eight quail over him in one day once." If you saw a picture of Ol' Jake on point, he'd be crouching in the grass, tense all right, but with head slung low and tail sagging. Jake was the product of an era when game was plentiful, people scarce, and land not posted. He learned his manners in the field right over the gun. When he became obstreperous, his teacher corrected him not with a check cord but with a load of shot in his rear end. As a dog he had only average talent, but his master hunted so much, the season was so long, the limit so large that the dog became a perfectionist in his unhandsome, sloppy way.

Today's dog is far more competently trained, possesses more talent, and is imbued with what we call class. Chances are his owner can't brag about the quantity of birds shot over the dog, but he'll eagerly relate the time he was grouse hunting and the dog, plunging full speed through some hazel thickets, suddenly leaped off the ground, did a 90-degree turn and froze, tail straight up, head turned proudly toward an old windfall. "The only bird I shot that morning, but I'll never forget it." Then he'll lead you over to a corner of the living room and show off a silver ash tray and half a dozen ribbons the dog has won at field trials and he'll talk about the famous field champions in his pedigree.

There's the change! The current dog is a product of selective breeding aimed always at producing a dog of greater ability. The owner can, if he wishes, use him for some memorable gunning throughout the hunting season and for field-trial competition at other times.

Today's hunting dog is more versatile than ever before. This Springer Spaniel, basically an upland game dog, has fetched a duck from water.

I do not mean to imply that all of today's hunting dogs are like this. There are still the $15 hound and the New England grouse setters that trot over their ground thoroughly, and the huge-running Southern Pointer that skins the edges of the 100-acre fields and can only be hunted from jeep or horseback. But more than ever is rising the dynamic yet practical field dog, a fast-moving, tail-cracking, responsive animal that hunts with a vengeance

The world of hunting dogs is always exciting. Here, two Plott Hounds have brought a mountain lion to bay.

and is a joy to watch. As a professional trainer put it recently, "Why shouldn't our modern field dogs be better! An owner thinks nothing of sending a bitch 2000 miles to be bred to a champion just because of certain character traits. The result is that every breed has been and continues to be improved."

Just about all field stock is registered today. So strong is this trend that the unregistered dog brings about one half the price of a registered dog of equal ability. In nearly every case the pedigreed dog is closely, if not directly, descended from field-trial blood. This is what has advanced the quality of the average dog so greatly.

One unfortunate trend is in the area of the dual champion, the dog which attains both his field and bench-show titles. Half a century ago the pointer and setter ranks split because show breeders concentrated only upon conformation while field breeders wanted only ability. Now this split has moved into just about every breed of field dog, especially since the rise of money stakes in field trials—$300 and $500 on up to $2500 in a single purse—demands the height of hunting perfection. The German Shorthair and Weimaraner people still crown a few dual champions each year and the Brittany Spaniel followers claim to have the only "dual dog" left, though how much longer they can make the claim is doubtful. The desire to have a field dog of fine conformation or a show dog with excellent field ability is noble but more and more infeasible each year.

To have a professional handler finish a dog on a bench these days—that is, gain his championship—costs between $1000 and $3000; the same goes for a field championship. Beyond this financial mountain lie other pitfalls. When a longhaired dog like the Brit is trained in the field he cannot be shown because the feathers wear off his legs and belly. And field trials have become so exacting that you can't enter a half-trained dog and stand a chance of winning. Thus the owner is being forced more and more to decide between one or the other even if he is miraculously fortunate enough to have a potential "dual dog." Unfortunately it seems only a matter of time before the dual dog disappears, out of both financial burden and breeding motives.

Because of game laws and the vast number of gunners today, the thrill of hunting is not how much game is shot down but the exciting manner in which it is taken. This means having a good dog.

What are the characteristics of a good field dog?

First and foremost he must have a desire to hunt. The basic difference between the vast majority of show dogs and field dogs is that the latter have an inordinate desire to hunt while the former do not. Without this trait he cannot be trained.

Then he must have keen scenting powers, or in the case of sight hounds, a sharp set of eyes. The old expression that "a hound is as good as his nose" applies to just about all field dogs. A bird dog of excellent ability can partially overcome the handicap of a short nose (weak scenting powers) but he never finds as much game and seldom locates it accurately. A retriever will lose too many cripples, while a hound will drop the line of scent too often and waste too much time at checks.

A field dog should hunt independently, yet show respect for any other dogs he may be working with. He must possess great endurance, be biddable to his handler's commands but not dependent upon him. He should have a good sense of direction—the ability to stay ahead if he is a bird dog or spaniel, the capacity to mark and locate fallen game if he is a retriever, a homing instinct if he is a hound. He should hunt with relish and not avoid briars or heavy cover. In personality, he should be bold, never excessively nervous or shy. A timid dog is extremely difficult to teach and almost impossible to polish to championship form.

A good field dog also has speed. He does not putter or trot about, but

Hunting is made up of rich memories like this, but it takes a good dog to enjoy a good hunt.

moves with as much swiftness as the cover, terrain, and his nose allow him. A good fast dog inevitably finds more game than a good slow dog because he covers more ground. Also, grouse and pheasant seem to set much better for the fast, driving dog which slashes suddenly into point, whereas these game birds tend to run away from the dog that pussyfoots into point.

A good field dog has class. He moves with sparkling style that makes him a joy to see in action. This is what makes memorable hunting and the taking of less game worth while. It also wins field trials.

Few dogs combine all these qualities but the more they have, the better they are. Great dogs possess one other attribute—an uncanny ability to find game. It is like a sixth sense. They seem to know the right places to look and are rewarded for their efforts. Of course experience is a great teacher, but this is an innate quality and outstanding dogs inevitably possess it.

Memory brings to mind a dog named Home Again Mike. This Pointer of excellent breeding was given away as a puppy because he was a little heavily marked. A small dog without much style or attractiveness, Mike grew up on a farm where he was freely allowed to hunt and chase quail, rabbits, and squirrels. He found quantities of quail and pointed them, but he ran with such abandon that the farmer on foot could never catch up with him and finally gave him back in disgust to his former owner, Clarence Edwards of Danville, Virginia. Recognizing his potential, Edwards began training the dog and soon had him country broken—that is, pointing solidly, backing, and retrieving. Turned over to professional trainer, Paul Walker, the dog was finished in three weeks and in his first field trial at twenty months of age he won the derby and all-age stakes at Pinehurst, North Carolina, a feat never accomplished before or since.

Though Mike was a scrawny little bag of bones, he had the heart of a lion. What he lacked in style and beauty he made up for with tremendous speed, wonderful vitality, and unquenchable desire to find game. A fast dog with a weak nose is useless because he will always find game too late and flush it, but Mike had a great nose and he literally dug up birds when other dogs could not. His first big win was the National Amateur Quail Championship at Hernando, Mississippi in March of 1956. The following fall he ran away with the National Open Pheasant Championship, turning in a brilliant performance at Baldwinsville, New York. That winter he captured the prized Continental Quail Championship at Quitman, Georgia, and less than two months later repeated his triumph in the National Amateur Quail Championship, this time at Orange, Virginia.

But Mike's greatest moment was yet to come. As the years took some of the fire from him, this doughty little dog began to use his head, and in the spring of 1960 Mike found eighteen coveys of quail in three hours of solid hunting at Grand Junction, Tennessee, to win the National Championship, highest honor bestowed upon pointing dogs.

As is true of all outstanding dogs, Home Again Mike not only possessed greatness but passed it on to his offspring. Before his premature death he sired many outstanding gun dogs and field-trial winners, including several champions. One of them, Home Again Hattie, won the National Championship crown in 1962.

Clarence Edwards once said of Mike, "It does your heart good to see this great little dog skim across the fields with but two things in mind—to find game and please his master." This tribute is probably the best standard ever written for field dogs. It is their true purpose in the wonderful world of hunting.

Let's move now to the various breeds and see the when and where and what and how of each one.

Chapter 2

The Pointing Breeds

It may seem strange to define the purpose of the pointing breeds but there are sound reasons for doing so. Not everyone is exactly sure what is required of a pointing dog and without such knowledge it is impossible to train one. Also, if you own a pointing dog and he does not completely fit the definition, then you might as well know he is not fully broken no matter how good you claim him to be, and you are not gaining all the pleasure you should from him.

The purpose of the pointing breeds is to find birds and point them solidly and accurately, then hold them until the hunter himself flushes and shoots the game, reloads, turns and commands his dog to retrieve.

Though it takes additional training to apply the above manners to a gun dog, there are very valid reasons why it should be done. First of all, the dog that breaks at shot will very quickly learn to break at wing, if for no other reason than to be the first to retrieve. When he develops this habit, you may one day be approaching his side-hill point. The birds will suddenly flush wild, fly low over the hilltop and he after them. If you or your hunting partner are trigger-happy or inexperienced, the dog will end up being sprayed with shot. I have seen this happen more than once and know of one occasion where a fine dog was so seriously injured in this manner that he had to be destroyed.

Also, when upland game is hunted, at least ten per cent of the time not all of the birds will flush together. This happens with pheasant and grouse early in the season, and consistently with quail. The dog or dogs bursting off in hot pursuit inevitably flush the remaining birds before you have a chance to reload.

Another reason for keeping a dog steady to wing and shot, at least while quail hunting, is that it keeps him from chasing off to hunt the singles immediately. And there is nothing more annoying than an unmannerly dog hunting quail singles. The shooting where real skill is involved goes down the drain. In the case of woodcock, the bird on its first flush will usually pitch down within a hundred yards even though shot at. If the dog takes off after the bird, he will seven times out of ten run it up the moment it alights.

Also, if your dog is steady to wing and shot and retrieves only upon command under natural hunting conditions, he can run in a field trial any time, any place and win. The reason most field trialers don't like to hunt over their dogs is that under natural conditions when the bird is shot and dropped in full view of the dog, he will not remain steady but break to retrieve. Then when he is run in a trial and a weak-flying quail is flushed he will succumb to the temptation to run fetch it and bring it back to the handler, an act which automatically disqualifies him. But I maintain this is only a matter of completing the training. Shorthair people hold shoot-to-kill trials in which the dog is required to be steady until ordered to retrieve the bird that has been flushed and shot in front of him. So there is no reason why any pointing breed cannot be trained to do the same.

I have heard it argued that crippled game is often lost by having a dog steady to wing and shot, but this is specious reasoning to me. The finest retriever on earth will occasionally lose crippled, even stone-dead game, depending upon where it falls and the scenting conditions. The advantages of having a completely finished dog (one that is steady to wing and shot and retrieves only upon command) so overpower any disadvantage that comparison is ridiculous as far as I'm concerned. The only handicap I know of is that a finished dog cannot be hunted in the company of dogs which will break the moment anything flies, otherwise he will soon lose his manners. When you run into this situation and you have the mannerly dog, don't hesitate to tell your hunting companion to leave his at home. If it's the other way around and your friend has the mannerly dog, I suggest you leave yours at home and see what class hunting consists of.

Now that we know what the pointing breeds should do, let's move on to the various kinds and see their differences, but first a small declaration.

For too long a time now it has been the habit of Pointer and Setter people to be "breed-blind." Owners, judges, and especially authors have looked upon other pointing varieties as useless upstarts. I prefer to take a different tack, for I have the feeling that we're living in such a variegated and complicated society today that there is not only room but outright need for all the pointing breeds and their widespread differences. In fact, I strongly feel that many people, because of restricted time, mode of living, and personal likings in a dog should have a Shorthair—Brittany, Weimaraner, or Vizsla—rather than a Pointer or Setter.

The Pointer and Setter have long symbolized bird dogs in America. They were the first two pointing breeds here. Field trials were built around them. Later when other pointing breeds were brought in, the Pointer and Setter people laughed, even scorned them because they were not as wide-ranging, not as speedy in getting around, not as dramatic on game. Thus it was assumed that these lesser breeds (and I say lesser in the sense of quantity, not quality) would soon die off and be abandoned in the face of Pointer and Setter supremacy.

Quite to the contrary, they have flourished. Each has a national association. Each supports a monthly news magazine. Each has an enthusiastic group of followers. True, the Brits, Shorthairs, Ymars, etc., seldom compete against Pointers and Setters but hold their own trials instead, including national championships, regional and AKC championships, futurities, et al. And it can honestly be said that these breeds offer several distinct advantages that Pointers and Setters do not, as shall be described.

In my review I shall stress the strong points of each breed rather than judge them by comparison, for we are here not to decide which is the best but which will most adequately serve the needs of a particular situation and provide the most all-around pleasure.

Let's begin by examining two ancient and extinct breeds which played a key role in forming all our contemporary pointing and flushing dogs.

Two Ancient Breeds—Setting Spaniel and Spanish Pointer

The Setting Spaniel was one of the earliest established types of bird-hunting dogs on record. As his name indicates, he comes from Spain and during the Middle Ages, before the advent of the shotgun, he was used all over Europe by market and pot hunters. In those times men hunted partridges with snares, traps, and hawks, but their best success was with nets and spaniels. The dog would hunt and trail partridges until near the covey, whereupon he was trained to sit or lie down flat. The hunters would then creep up and either throw a scatter net over dog and game together or else hastily erect a funnel net into which the wild birds would be slowly driven. Without these dogs the market hunters could never have made a living. In a little while the longhaired Setting Spaniel spread all over Europe and to England, where he became the main progenitor of the spaniels we know today and, when crossed with the Spanish Pointer, most probably created the setter family as well. This spaniel ancestry accounts for the setter's sometimes dropping instinctively on point even today when he comes upon birds unexpectedly, and it is interesting to note that the pointer-setter cross produces a "dropper."

The Spanish Pointer, unlike the spaniel, who stopped in the proximity of game because of training, pointed birds instinctively with rigid concentration and in a standing position. The cross that produced him is unknown, although Spain, his land of origin, had the most highly developed animal husbandry in Europe during the thirteenth, fourteenth, and fifteenth centuries. Like the Setting Spaniel, he spread across the Continent probably as the result of gifts among royalty and noblemen, for a good hunting dog was a most valuable possession in those days. Slow-moving and possessed with a great amount of point which made him staunch on game, the old Spanish Pointer was an ideal gun dog at the beginning of the wing-shooting era, for he gave hunters time enough to reload their complicated fowling pieces. Besides putting the "point" into setters as described above, he was a forefather of the English Pointer and the German Shorthaired Pointer, and probably gave his reflexes to all pointing breeds.

Such was the breadth of the contribution these two early breeds made to our present-day dogs.

Double National Ch. Palamonium, the epitome of field Pointer style and conformation.

The Pointer

The Pointer has long been the wheelhorse of the sport of shooting birds with pellets. So it has been for three centuries and so it will probably remain for a considerable time to come, for he does his job with a persistence, a class, a speed and an energy that is the standard for pointing dogs.

Not every Pointer is perfect by any means. There are those with superior and inferior intelligence, good style, poor style, choke—bore nose, weak nose. Every breed runs this way. But when you find a good Pointer, make no mistake about it, he will give his all under any conditions. He will hunt until he drops, he will cover more ground, find more birds and do it more dramatically than any other pointing breed today. Best proof of this is that he holds the world's record for finding birds under judicial observation— twenty-six contacts in three hours by Wayriel Allegheny Sport in the 1958 National Championship.

In modern times he has dominated the National Championship, emblematic of the king of pointing breeds. This three-hour-long event is open to any dog that can qualify and in the past twenty-five years he has won the title twenty-three times, the other wins going to his nearest competitor, the English Setter. In the Free-for-All Championship, which has hour heats to qualify and three-hour final heats, the Pointer has won this stake for the last twenty-five years straight. He has won the National Open Pheasant Championship at Baldwinsville, New York, every year but one since its inception in 1933. The National Open and Amateur Pheasant Shooting Dog Championships, inaugurated in 1958, have been won on each occasion by a Pointer.

Let's go back a moment and see how this fine dog was made and what has brought him to his present dominant position.

Our Pointer comes from the English Pointer, first mention of which is made in 1650 when they were used in conjunction with Greyhounds in the sport of coursing hares. Pointers located and pointed the hares, which were flushed from their bed or thicket, then the Greyhounds were cut loose to sight-chase them. These dogs were probably pure Spanish Pointer, although some claim the original English Pointer to be a separate breed resulting from a Bloodhound-Bulldog cross, but then the question is, where did the pointing instinct come from? More likely the English, always great dog lovers and sportsmen, did not create their own Pointers but discovered such stock on the Continent and brought it back, as happened after the Treaty of Utrecht in 1713. In any event, wing shooting had become fashionable by this time and the Spanish Pointer was definitely introduced as a cross.

As firearms improved, the English noblemen wanted speedier dogs, and here began the first real improvement of the breed. Foxhounds, Bloodhounds, even Greyhounds were carefully crossed into the basic Pointer and by selective breeding speed, ability and scenting powers were all increased, though his basic conformation was scarcely altered. About this time setters appeared on the scene and Pointers of high quality were used to sharpen the pointing instinct of the longhair. In the nineteenth century the reverse occurred. The Pointer is frequently recorded as being of vicious and unmanageable temper unless taken into hand at an early age, and this time Setter blood was crossed into him to mollify his nature.

The Pointer and Setter were brought to America well before the Civil War, the Pointer gaining favor in the South because of his short-haired coat, the Setter more popular in the northern, cooler climates. In England the Pointer had been hunted from foot, but Southern plantation owners rode horses to hunt quail and needed a bird dog that would cover a vast amount of country effectively. To obtain speed and range they crossed the Foxhound into the Pointer, and to this day similarity between the two breeds is immediately recognizable.

Pointers took on plenty of steam and go, but the pointing instinct became thin, and from 1870 to 1890 American sportsmen returned to England to buy new stock to reset the breed. High prices, even for this day, were paid for Pointers of exceptional ability. Though the English dogs did not have the range and speed needed here, they had "point" and quality. These beautiful deep-chested dogs, when crossed back into American stock, produced the bulwarks of our current championship bloodlines. It is safe to say that every superior Pointer of today carries the blood of King of Kent and his son Rip Rap, Price's Bang, Mainspring and his son Jingo. Also, by establishing permanent registries, outcrossing was eliminated and the breed stabilized.

The Pointer's heartland is still the South. Here he has developed into a super quail dog, ranging over great stretches of land—fifty-acre soybean fields, hundred-acre cotton and wheat fields. Quail stay in the woods and bottoms, come out only to feed. They work into the open cautiously from a sheltered edge, leaving a strong path of scent, but seldom penetrate a field more than twenty-five yards for fear of hawks. Thus the proper way for a dog to hunt them is not to quarter every huge field closely but to reach out and rim its edge all the way around. If a covey of quail has "used" into the field (a term which means to walk along, feeding on seeds and insects), the dog will strike the scent of entry or exit, follow it up and pin his quarry. The birds are most liable to come out to feed early in the

The Pointer is a great quail dog. Here's the bobwhite limit in one morning.

With a little effort Pointers are easily made into good retrievers. Here the author's dog, a field-trial winner, brings in a nice cock pheasant.

morning and late in the afternoon, thus a quail hunter wants a dog that will cover a lot of ground when he goes gunning at those times.

The hunter enters the field, has his dog circle it and if nothing is found, he proceeds to the next. Going from one field to the next, the dog should come in and hunt the bottoms and woods and thickets at relatively close range. A good quail dog buzzes the hedgerows and skirts the edges persistently, often running a quarter to a half mile ahead. When he doesn't come around, you go hunt him up because he will probably be pointing birds.

From this type of hunting developed the major field trials in the United States today. The dogs that run at this wide range are termed all-age and are handled always from horseback. The vogue for several years was toward wider and wider-running dogs, and selective breeding, aimed at this end, developed such far-ranging Pointers that they were nearly useless in other than major championships or plantation hunting. Now the pendulum has swung the other way, to the practical shooting dog.

It is a misconception to think that all Pointers work at wide range. Most do not. In developing the big-running Pointer, each litter inevitably produced some puppies, often a majority, that had no desire or inclination to

Triple National Open Pheasant Shooting Dog Ch. Elhew Jungle on a superbly intense point.

range half a mile ahead. Such dogs were always sold to the general public for hunting, thus quality breeding was and still is pushed into circulation, which accounts for the Pointer's high quality almost everywhere. These dogs have always had the speed and bird-finding proclivities of their parents and, as stated earlier, are now dominating the shooting-dog stakes. There are two versions of the shooting dog, the Northern type which is a very close worker and the Southern kind, which is a bit more rangy and referred to as a horseback-shooting dog but may be comfortably hunted from foot.

There is little doubt that the Pointer in modern times has created the hunting standard for the pointing breeds. I say modern times because before 1915 the English Setter was king of the hunting and field-trial worlds. The tables turned and since that time the Pointer has had the best of it. Though many people who fancy other pointing breeds do not like the Pointer's standard—that of finding birds as fast as possible—it's a hard one to argue against. Other things being equal, speed is the factor which has led to his position of dominance. He simply beats slower dogs to the birds. In fact, the Setter is the only dog that can compete with any measure of success against him.

The other pointing breeds—the Brittany Spaniel from France, the Shorthair and Weimaraner from Germany, the Vizsla from Hungary—have all come to this country within the past twenty-five years and were created not to cover vast areas quickly but to hunt small parcels of land thoroughly, thus they are slow and methodical in their ways when compared to the

Pointer or Setter. The Central European breeds point upland game birds, trail hare, boar and stag in hound fashion so their style of hunting cannot be justly compared to that of the Pointer, who is an established master of his trade. For this reason the restricted breeds do not allow him to compete in their stakes although they are always welcome in his, and a good Brit or Shorthair often beats him but it takes a mighty good one.

Another fact that must be made here is that the Pointer is usually a lot of dog and it takes a lot of man to handle him. Few women ever run a Pointer in a field trial, as often happens with Shorthairs or Brits. Some people like this quality; many don't. That's why we have other breeds to choose from.

Colorwise, the Pointer is basically white and it is not unusual to see him entirely so, though generally he has patches and/or ticking of liver or orange or lemon or black. These colors are never mixed except in certain strains like the Satilla Wahoo Pete line, which often has a liver head with orange eyebrows.

Pointer conformation is a matter of balance and symmetry rather than numbers and measurements. The dog is clean-looking, lithe, muscular, with a deep and well-sprung chest, and about him is an air of confidence. It is not his nature to cower unless he has been mistreated. He should have no parts out of proportion—i.e., legs too stubby or stringy, tail too long, body too extended. The long, square muzzle which formerly marked the Pointer is not seen so much any more. Many of today's best dogs are short-headed and inclined to be snipe-nosed. Conformation in the best dogs is nearly always good; it has to be for the dog to have the style, speed and endurance to win in tight field-trial competition. The ideal Pointer is full of energy and light on his feet; on game he stands with high head and tail. The males usually weigh from 45 to 60 pounds, the bitches 35 to 50 pounds. Height averages around 24 inches. He comes in white and liver, white and orange, white and lemon, white and black, usually with ticking.

The general feeling is that Pointers, because of their short hair, are not as good around briars as Setters, but I think this is a matter of the individual dog and the amount of guts he has. Nor are they more hard-headed than any other breed, but when you get one he's a tough nut. Many claim that the Pointer doesn't retain his training as well as other dogs, that each fall he needs some brushing up. But every dog should be conditioned for the hunting season anyway. One reason that he may appear to lose his edge of training is that any long lay-up gets him all fired up and in his fierce desire to hunt he won't listen at first. But his manners can be kept up throughout the year with a minimum of effort, as will be explained later.

Pointers develop at a young age and can be trained early. Usually the

Because the Pointer is fast and covers a lot of ground, he's excellent on prairie chicken, as this happy hunter knows.

pointing instinct is highly developed in small puppies. They will often sight-point butterflies and other objects while still wobbling about on their legs at six or eight weeks of age.

One justified criticism of the Pointer is that he is a hunting machine, that his desire to please is not as strong as his desire to hunt. It's true that he goes bird hunting with such vigor and application that he becomes oblivious of his master at times, but I'm not certain this is a fault. The dog, not the man, finds the birds. How often have I seen a handler or hunter (myself included) call a dog from a cast because it was a bit out of the way, had the dog ignore the command, continue on and find a bird.

The Pointer is sometimes called a cold dog, but I don't think this is true. He is not as demonstrative with his feelings as the Setter or Spaniel, but like all dogs he needs love and affection. When given this he becomes a deep and reliable friend and always the valiant hunter.

The English Setter is a fine pheasant dog.

The English Setter

Possessed of a mild and affectionate disposition, beauty and intelligence, the English Setter is one of the best-liked and serviceable gun dogs on earth. He is a cover dog deluxe whether flitting through the grouse woods or bouncing through the goldenrod haunts of pheasants or plunging into honeysuckle thickets and swamp bottoms for quail. Equally proficient on woodcock, prairie chicken and Hungarian partridge, he will dig up birds and handle them with an aristocratic elegance that is his heritage. For these reasons he has long been a favorite gunning companion and pal of American sportsmen, particularly in northern United States and Canada, as his heavy coat provides automatic protection against the cold.

It is difficult to unravel the origin of the English Setter accurately. Many claim the breed to be 400 years old because of an ancient engraving, "Partridge Shooting and Partridge Hawking," by Hans Bols, dated 1562, in which two partridges are being pointed by a long-tailed dog lying flat.

Triple Grouse Ch. Sam L's Rebel shows the magnificent style and intensity of the modern English field Setter. He is owned by Sam Light of Punxsutawney, Pa.

on the ground. Behind the dog, men are about to shoot the birds on the ground with crossbows and lead slugs. Nearby, falconers are using spaniels to flush birds for their hawks to attack. The trouble is that the scene is Flemish, not English, and the dog if it is a setter is a disgraceful one or else the artist was. Actually, by sheer logic the English Setter could not be 400 years old because the pointing breeds were of little use until firearms were perfected enough to bring about wing shooting, in the early eighteenth century. Thus he is more like around 200 years old and arrived upon the scene after the Spanish Pointer.

The claim by many including the late great Edward Laverack that the setter is merely an improved spaniel may well be true, but in the early days of every breed outcrosses of all kinds were resorted to and legitimately made in an effort for betterment. Most likely a setter of sorts appeared on the Continent long before it did in England. It was almost certainly a cross between the old Setting Spaniel and the Spanish Pointer, for the Setter even today has the happy, ebullient nature of the Spaniel, and from the Spanish Pointer would come the instinct to stand up and point birds. The English took an immediate fancy to the dog, for by 1775 setters of all three breeds—English, Irish, and Gordon—were well established and by 1800 were more popular than the Pointer, and so it remains there today.

Edward Laverack of Whitchurch, Shropshire, England, was the great pioneer of the modern English Setter. In 1825 he obtained two good specimens from a friend, bred them together, bred their offspring together, then bred these back to the original two. By such line breeding he developed a strain of Setters which led the country through the nineteenth century. These were long-feathered, large, blocky, rich-coated dogs, one of the most beautiful animals we have today though used for show and house pets now, but in their day they were also great field dogs. Orange-belton and blue-belton colors still predominate, although white-and-lemon, white-and-orange, white-and-chestnut and white-and-black are not uncommon.

Along about 1875 Mr. R. L. Purcell Llewellin of Pembrokeshire, South Wales, went to Laverack and bought some of his best show dogs of the original Dash-Moll and Dash-Hill lines. These he outcrossed with some setter blood from North England known as the Duke-Rhoebes strain and the offspring swept every field trial in sight. These are the smaller, highly animated Setters seen in the field today. They have fewer feathers, less of the pendulous lips and sleepy eyes and heavy block heads, are inclined to be tricolored—that is white, black and brown, the brown being restricted mostly to the face and front legs. Other colors are white-and-black, white-and-orange, white-and-lemon, white-and-chestnut and once in a while a belton. Occasionally they throw back to the Laverack Setter in type and this is when the beautiful, long-feathered field dog of considerable size and with the floating stride appears.

Both strains of Setters were imported into the United States, but it was the Llewellins that took the seat of glory. Gladstone and Count Noble were the two great Setters, imported from Llewellin, which formed the pillars of the breed here in America. Their offspring, when crossed together and with native strains like the Gildersleeves of Maryland and Delaware, the Mortons of New Jersey, the Ethan Allens of Connecticut and the Campbells of Tennessee, won every National Championship from its inauguration in 1896 until 1908, losing only four to the Pointers until 1918. Such immortals as Count Gladstone IV Sioux who won twice, Geneva, Mohawk II, and La Besita whose courage alone brought her the crown when she was nearly overcome by pneumonia, brought fame to the Setter ranks. After 1918 they lost their grip on the national title to the Pointers.

Some speak of the decline of the Setter. Actually it has been more the

General Skyrocket's Delight stands fast in an exhibition of perfect manners as professional trainer Carl Beattie flushes pheasant in field trial.

rise of the Pointer, but certain basic facts are involved. The Setter doesn't seem to mature as fast as the Pointer and doesn't take rigid professional training as well. He tends to be less wide-ranging by nature than the Pointer and when a Setter is a big-running dog he often becomes a renegade in later years. But as a shooting dog, which is our interest in this book, he will hold his own any time, any place, against any dog living. And in the grouse woods he is far and away the champ.

In recent years several men have engaged in serious breeding and training programs to bring the Setter back into all-age competition with the Pointer. Their efforts have produced some outstanding winners, but the road is a rough one for they have to beat the best, and quantities of it.

The English Setter is a dog of great character and beauty. This is Sky Streak, a field-trial winner owned by Cliff Havener of Paterson, N.J.

To this day there are a few people who claim to have straight Llewellin Setters. I wouldn't argue with them, neither would I be bothered about it. The Llewellins did their part long ago. They added the speed and dash and merry way of going which our current Setters have, also the high head-and-tail carriage which is so dramatic. In recent years too many of the field Setters have been high-strung and nervous; conformationwise they have been little more than a bundle of hair stretched over a bunch of bones, thin-chested and gaunt-legged. These dogs must be trained with kid gloves, but thank goodness this is not typical of the breed.

There are many types of Setters today. The slow, plodding New England grouse dog seldom moves faster than a brisk trot but is deadly on grouse and woodcock, he is generally a large dog of the Laverack looks. The meat-dog Setter, usually unregistered, has for decades been part and parcel of the farm, friend to the kids, hunting dog for the farmer in the fall, not stylish but a friendly, happy dog that is rock-steady on his pheasants and woodcock. There is the field-trial Setter of shooting-dog range, a stylish individual with a snappy gait and a gay brush tail that bounces with every plunging stride. There is the bigger-running grouse-trial Setter which literally tears up the woods, a most dramatic and specialized dog. In my opinion he's the best grouse dog there is, for he strikes his game with such swift decisiveness that the bird will freeze and stay put rather than run off or flush, as often happens with a slow, extra-cautious dog. Lastly, there is the big-running Setter which hunts quail in the South and on the major field-trial circuit. These barrel-chested, he-man dogs like Ch. Commander's Big Coon, Ch. Rudy's Wonsover, and Briardale Pensive are worked always from horseback.

Depending upon his height, which averages around 25 inches, the field English Setter weighs anywhere between 35 and 60 pounds. His most frequent color is white-and-black, although white-and-orange, white-and-chestnut, and white-and-lemon appear frequently, as do tricolored dogs—white-and-black with tan on the face or front legs. Beltons are very rare among field stock.

The Setter usually has a most delightful personality. He will jump up and down and bark when he sees his master, almost stand on his head when he thinks he's going hunting. And one wonderful trait almost invariably found in the foot-shooting Setter is a desire to please, more so than in any other pointing breed. He'll hunt to the gun, check with you frequently, go where you motion him.

The wide-going quail dog is different. Like the Pointer, he takes his own way and you have to look for him when he doesn't show—usually, that is. I hunted quail once with a giant of a man in both height and girth, but an all-day walker. He owned one of the biggest-running Setters I ever saw, a whale of a bird dog too. We hunted from foot in hilly country and when old Doc would flash by once in a while, we'd head in the direction we last saw him. Finally he was missing for about fifteen minutes and my friend decided to wait for him. "We can't do that," I objected, "he may have birds somewhere." "Don't you worry. If he has, he'll come and get us," he answered, settling over a big pine stump. Presently Doc tore up, bouncing and whining. "Let's go," my friend said confidently, and I snickered under my breath.

Well, we followed the dog nearly half a mile through fields and bottoms, the Setter stopping every little while to look back and see if we were coming. Finally we got to a big plum thicket. The dog pointed, we went in, and the birds were there. I wouldn't believe it the first time, so I went back the next day and got a repeat performance. The dog had not been trained to do this. It was a case where he thoroughly enjoyed finding and pointing birds so his master could shoot them and he could retrieve them. When he discovered his master often couldn't locate him on point, he learned to back off and go find him. It came from loving every phase of his job, especially retrieving, which proves there is nothing in the world that will make a dog hunt harder and point stauncher than shooting the birds he has found and letting him retrieve them.

The Setter by nature is usually a natural and lively retriever, and once again this probably comes from his spaniel origin. He can take briars and tough country well too, although a lot of that has to do with where a dog finds birds as a puppy. If he discovers a covey of quail in honeysuckle or a grouse under a hemlock, you'll notice that he soon hunts those spots persistently. If he tears himself up too much in briars as a puppy, he'll soon learn to go around them.

One tough thing on a Setter is burrs. They clog up his coat quicker than anything else and can be very painful when they lodge under his forelegs and scrape at every forward step. Before I hunt a Setter in the fall, I take a pair of scissors, roll the dog over on his back and clip all the hair from this area, front and back. After a day of hunting you should take five minutes to pick the burrs from all parts of his coat. They will not only wad up the hair but in time cause skin irritations that can become infected.

As we said before, the Setter doesn't have the seriousness of the Pointer, nor is he the hunting machine. The Pointer will hunt for anybody but the Setter is more of a one-man dog who will hunt his heart out for his master. For the man who wants a real companion at home, in the field and at a trial, the English Setter is hard to beat.

Grouse Ch. Orchard Valley Skylight with his favorite bird, owned by Bob Habgood of Bradford, Pa.

The Irish Setter

The story of the Irish Setter is the story of a great breed pulled back from the brink of tragedy. The big red dog, long recognized as one of the most beautiful animals man has yet produced, has also long been known for his lack of field ability—the purpose for which he was created.

It's hard to believe that originally the Irish Setter was red and white. The all-red dog we know today was a rarity existing only in a few scattered counties of southern Ireland, and he was considered far more difficult to break. Until the 1850s the red-and-white Irish Setter was acclaimed by many to be the finest of all shooting setters. He was a smart, active animal full of courage, a bit headstrong but an untiring worker with olfactory senses equal to those of any gun dog that existed.

The Irish preferred the red-and-white as a hunter because he could be observed with half the difficulty of the all-red dog against the brown heather. And they proved there is nothing to the claim that birds lie better for a dark-colored dog.

The exact origin of the Irish Setter is obscure but he probably came from spaniel blood crossed with local Irish stock which was red in color. In the days before bench shows, dogs of all breeds were kept for their working qualities alone and the good ones were mated regardless of color or conformation. Thus the Gordon Setter was crossed into the Irish, which left a tinge of black occasionally in the feathering, the kiss of death in today's show ring. About the most outstanding Irish Setter ever bred was Plunket in the 1870s. He won almost all the field trials there were in those days, but it was admitted he couldn't have won more than a good case of fleas at a bench show for lack of conformation.

The first show for Pointers and Setters was held at Newcastle on Tyne, England, on June 28, 1859, and thus began the demise of the Irish Setter. The red-and-whites were soon banished in favor of the all-red dog, and the breed was swallowed up in the tragedy of being bred for beauty without regard for utility. By the turn of the century the Irish Setter had become the darling of the show world. But the more his fame and fortune spread, the more they bred him for beauty and the less keen became his hunting instincts, consequently his ability in the field. His magnificent head with its oval dome was certainly large enough to contain brains but it didn't, at least not when the dog was hunted. The main problem was that he had little or no desire to hunt, and this is something impossible to teach a dog. You can teach him many things about hunting but you can't teach him to hunt.

Mr. O'Leary, one of the great field-trial Irish Setters of recent years, owned by F. C. Bean of Athens, Ohio.

Also, he was misgaited. Stop a moment and think of the last time you saw a show Irish Setter run. Perhaps you never have. For nearly a century they've been bred not to run but to trot. In the show ring they move at a trot. I don't mean to be disrespectful, but the show Irish Setter in the field is a clod. He has none of the flowing grace and movement that field dogs possess. He doesn't know what to do. He doesn't know where to hunt. He is a lost soul.

For a long time he has been like this. In fact, the only two Field Dog Stud Book-approved Irish Setter field champions until the 1950s were Tom and Joe Jr. in 1875 and 1878. Just one Irish Setter made much of a name for itself in the field during the long dry spell from 1900 to 1951. That was Horace Lytle's Smada Byrd, who won some major victories in the mid 1920s but never a championship. She matured late in life, coming into her own at six and doing her best winning after that time. This has been a problem with the Irish Setter. Most hunting owners don't want to wait that long for a dog to achieve its hunting proficiency.

During the Irishman's lean years many sportsmen, some of unlimited means, some clever breeders and trainers, tried to produce dogs that would be unsurpassed for gunning. As one after another failed, the cause became known as "the purest challenge in sportsdom." Not only did they have to restore the Red Ones to their former degree of field prowess, but they had also to catch up with the great strides made by other pointing breeds.

In 1950 things began to change. Those who bred for the field and not for the bench realized that show dogs could not be expected to produce the dogs they were looking for, so they turned back to the English Setter. The Field Dog Stud Book was opened and outcrossing began. One of the most successful outcrosses was to the Mississippi Zev lines, the Setter who won the National Championship in 1947. This superb dog gave his great hunting spirit, his high-tailed style and his ability to find birds to many of the modern field Irish Setters. This does not mean that all the Irish Setters in field trials today are crossed with English Setters but plenty are, particularly the better ones like Hard Tack. It shows here and there in a cowlick of white hair on the chest, a smaller body and more animation and desire to hunt than their show cousins.

In 1951 another important change took place. A group of the breed's field-minded enthusiasts got together and formed the National Red Setter Field Trial Club, a nationwide organization with the stated purpose to improve the Irish Setter as a shooting dog. They hold a national championship annually as well as many breed trials throughout the country. As a result Irish Setters have improved to the point where they now compete most successfully in open stakes against all breeds.

Two dogs in particular contributed heavily to the recovery of the Irish

The Irishman is lovable, beautiful and kind, with a portion of the happy rogue mixed in.

Setter in recent years. First was Rusty's Jinx, the leading sire of 1953–54–55–56 and probably the greatest Irish Setter sire of field dogs to appear to date. Owned by R. C. Baynard of Dover, Delaware, this great dog produced a host of outstanding winners, including the first two field champions since 1878—Ch. Double Jay and Ch. Willow Winds Hobo.

The other Irish Setter milestone was Askew's Carolina Lady, owned and campaigned by Ned LaGrande of Douglassville, Pennsylvania, a man who has probably done more to bring back the Red One than any other person in America. Lady had twenty-eight all-age and shooting-dog wins, mostly in breed-open competition, and was the first consistent winner of her breed in decades. More than that, she was bred consistently and produced more outstanding winners than any half dozen field Irish Setter dams in history. Among them were Ike Jack Kendrick who retired after some seventy placements, and Mr. O'Leary, a consistently brilliant and winning competitor.

In Ireland, too, the Red Ones have made a stirring comeback, knocking off breed-open stakes consistently, while in England Sulhamstead Bounce d'Or won the International Gun Dog League Championship. Here in the United States imported Sulhamstead Norse d'Or has been winning left and right in both breed and open stakes.

All this proves that the Irish Setter is on the upswing and that the cause espoused so long by so many is finally paying off. If you wish to buy an Irish for a gun dog or field-trial competition, I must strongly suggest that you obtain field blood, not bench-show blood. Unfortunately there is a profound difference and whether the twain shall ever meet is a question. At this point they are practically two different breeds as in the cases of the English Setter and Pointer, regardless of the claims made. The field Irish Setters of today are like old Plunket—they wouldn't bring home more than fleas from a bench show. This is not to say they are unattractive dogs. They are not at all! But a field dog must have clean, tight, athletic conformation if he is to be of any use. He cannot be a big lazy oaf. He must be lively, show a desire to hunt and know how to find birds. This is exactly what the modern field Irish Setter does and consequently the reason he looks the way he does.

In color he ranges from mahogany-red to rich golden chestnut and, as we said before, often has a sprig of white hair on the chest. The great Askew's Carolina Lady had a few white hairs on her chin and most of her offspring carry the same trademark, although it bars them instantly from any bench show. In size the Irish Setter of field blood is smaller than his show cousin, ranging from 22 inches up to 25 inches and weighing 40 to 60 pounds, while his show cousin will begin at 25 inches and go as high as 27 or 28 inches and weigh 60 to 90 pounds.

Probably the Irish Setter will never achieve widespread popularity because his color militates against him. He cannot be easily seen in cover, either moving or on point, and one of the joys of hunting is to watch the scintillating movements of a white dog as he flashes through bottoms along hillsides and slams into point. You hurry to him with a tingling thrill. This aesthetic pleasure is somehow missed in the dark dog.

But the Irisher is ideal for those who espouse a cause. Red-setter people are among the least fainthearted in the world, a truly enthusiastic group who know and love hunting dogs. Were it not for them the Red One would be next to nothing today. He's had a long tough climb to recover his field prestige, but he now wins his share of field-trial placements wherever he goes and it's obvious that he's on his way to becoming the class hunting dog he was long ago.

Valli Hi Town, a fine young field Irish Setter, with Mrs. David J. Hasinger of Philadelphia, Pa.

The Gordon Setter

If I liked to hunt a little each fall and wanted to be sure of finding game; if I wanted a great family dog that would greet me every night when I came home, the hunting dog I'd choose would most certainly be a Gordon Setter.

The sturdy black-and-tan Setters from Scotland are in several respects among the most outstanding dogs of the pointing breed, and in several other respects they are not. First of all, they are calm, intelligent, placid dogs. They don't bounce around in joy or jump all over you as an English Setter is inclined to do. They're not big good-natured slobs like the Irishers. They're more inclined to be one-family dogs, good around children, aloof among strangers, with tremendous loyalty for their masters. They are not good kennel dogs. When locked up with dozens of other dogs they become moody and homesick, consequently they don't train easily for a professional.

Huntingwise, the Gordon is thorough to a fault. He's not a ball of fire in the field, he's a plugger, but this has its advantages because few if any Gordon Setter owners go out hunting in the fall and come back without something in the game bag, whether it be woodcock, grouse, or pheasants. On quail the Gordon is a little too restricted and slow; as a consequence, his greatest popularity is in the Northeast and Pennsylvania areas of the United States where the coverts are thick and a slow dog offers the advantage of thoroughness and easy handling. They are also growing more numerous in the Midwest and on the Pacific coast.

His outstanding characteristics are a splendid intelligence, fine scenting powers and great endurance, also beautiful color and quality of coat, good looks and a kindly family nature that is not rambunctious like many dogs but more reserved and formal, and loyal beyond belief.

The Gordon Setter is an old-timer. Some claim he was developed in the sixteenth century from black-and-tan setting-spaniel blood. More likely he came along a couple of centuries later and took the same pattern of development as the English and Irish Setters. We know for certain that Collie and Bloodhound blood were crossed into the Gordon. The hound influence shows in the heavy type of head and haw, also in the way he hunts with nose to the ground. The Collie blood was introduced by the fourth Duke of Gordon, after whom the breed takes its name. He crossed a good black-and-tan Collie hunting bitch named Maddy into his foundation stock and for generations his dogs had Collie tails, white breasts and feet, although this latter color may have come from the English Setter.

In the late 1700s the Duke took a deep interest in the black-and-tan Setter, and although other noblemen in Scotland are known to have been raising them at that time, his castle kennels became celebrated as the home of the breed and he is given most of the credit for establishing it. They were then, as they are now, substantial dogs with a heavy look, excellent legs and feet, a wealth of coat and feather, beautiful heads, strong hindquarters. Light eyes were not allowed in any account, or snippy noses. They were great workers and easy to train because they moved slowly. They hunted from dawn till dusk and seldom ever false-pointed. These traits are deeply imbedded in the dog today.

The history of the Gordon Setter in America begins in 1842 when Daniel Webster and his hunting pal, George W. Blunt, imported a brace of Gordon Setters from the Duke's kennels in Scotland, a dog named Rake and a bitch named Rachel. Undoubtedly the breed had arrived here earlier but we have this as the first record. In 1875, when the American Kennel Club began its registry, 135 Gordon Setters were initially recorded.

For many years the Gordon was the favorite of professional hunters, men who combed the woods and fields for game which was shot and sold in the markets of the big cities. For this they wanted the most reliable, foolproof dog they could find, and the Gordon was it. The breed declined before the tide of English Setter and Pointer popularity and reached an ebb around World War I. About that time importations from Denmark and Scandinavia by Charles T. Inglee, former president of the American Kennel Club, put more speed and range as well as biddability in the Gordon.

Still, the breed has never gained the widespread popularity expected of it. Today it is used primarily as a show dog, secondly as an obedience dog and thirdly as a field dog.

Had it not been for the Gordon Setter Club of America, founded in 1924, interest in the breed might have died out. The club awards annual prizes to outstanding dogs in the show ring and at field trials, also to any Gordon which obtains an obedience degree, an area in which he has had

The Gordon Setter is a great natural bird dog, and the man who hunts one seldom fails to see game.

considerable success. Each year the club sponsors a specialty bench show and field trial at which all Gordons may compete.

One problem is that most Gordon people have tended to go in for showing and not for field work. Thus there are several good bench champions which have had little or no field experience, though they are deserving of it. Show owners naturally complain that as soon as their dog is taken afield he wears his feathers off and cannot be exhibited the following weekend.

Good field-trial-potential puppies and derbies appear in the ranks of the Gordons but almost none of them are steadied to wing and shot on game so they can be run in field trials. Also the trend in show Gordons is toward the larger dog, which is awkward in the field, although to date there is no great discrepancy between show and field stock in this breed. Their hunting instincts and great scenting powers have survived despite years of breeding for the bench.

In recent years field champions among the Gordons have not been numerous. One of the best was Dual Ch. Saegrete's Lock Ridge Tibby owned by George Penterman of New Jersey. Two other outstanding ones were Ch. Page's Shuriridge Hummingbird, owned by Jack Page of Bridgeport, Connecticut, and Ch. Page's Jock MacBess, owned by Tom Page of Monroe, Connecticut. Ch. Page's Johnny Walker, owned by Peter Glass of Southbury, Connecticut, has made quite a name for himself with more than twenty field-trial wins, some of which are all-breed placements.

The Gordon Setter "Standard of Perfection," written almost a hundred years ago, reads in part:

"Stylish rather racy build, medium sized, muscular dog of clean Setter type. . . . Strong, fairly short back and short tail, expressive head, slightly wavy coat. Size: shoulder height, male 22–25 inches, female 21–24 inches. Deep rather broad head, clearly indicated stop . . . muzzle long and almost parallel . . . not pointed . . . flews not pendulous . . . nose big, broad, with open nostrils and of deep black. Eyes dark brown and wise. . . . Ears set low on head, fairly large and thin. . . . Neck long, lean, arched . . . without throatiness.

"Coat—deep shining coal black with tan markings either of rich chestnut or mahogany red. . . . Tan should be shining. . . . Border lines between black and tan clearly defined. . . . Markings—two clear spots over eyes. . . . On side of muzzle tan should not reach above base of nose, resembling a stripe around end of muzzle . . . or throat . . . two large clear spots on chest . . . on inside of hindlegs and inside of thighs . . . on forelegs from knees or a little above to toes . . . around vent. . . ."

The above description of the Gordon is completely applicable today except for height. For males it is 24–27 inches, bitches 23–26 inches and weight, males, 55–75 pounds, bitches 45–65 pounds, although most field

Gordons would conform to the old height and weight rather than the newer one—the winning Gordons, that is.

No doubt a hunting problem with the Gordon is his color which, as with the Irish Setter, has militated against his popularity afield. Though he is almost always a close-working dog, you can walk by him standing on point in a thick dark swamp without seeing him. Chances are he'll stand there all day, waiting for you to find him, too!

As a one-man shooting dog the Gordon is hard to beat. He retains his training well, will find every bird that's around if there are any to be found, and he's a good retriever. He doesn't hunt with the dramatic power of the Pointer or the merry joy of the English Setter, nor does he point game with their heart-stopping suddenness and style. He's inclined to ease into his points, and you'll have to walk with him to the end of a big field but he'll hunt out every square inch of it.

For the man who wants a mannerly, gentle hunting dog with almost fanatical loyalty for his master and family, the Gordon will most assuredly fill the bill.

Peter Glass of Southbury, Conn., prepares to flush a quail in front of his field Ch. Page's Johnny Walker.

The German Shorthaired Pointer

The German Shorthair is probably the most natural retrieving, easily trained and sharp-nosed dog of pointing breed in America today. He is a powerful, vigorously handsome dog of composure and serenity, a gentleman and a companion, and for these reasons has become the ideal of suburbia's hunting group.

The Shorthair lacks the obstreperous showmanship of the Pointer or the rampant gaiety of the Setter. He is exactly what you would imagine to be at the side of a German baron when he takes to the field for a day's hunt—a dark-colored dog of trim but heavy proportions, strong-shouldered, strong-backed, well-formed head, completely obedient and competent. And so that the baron may enjoy a variety of hunting, the dog has been bred and trained to find and handle all types of game in the prescribed manner—partridges, pheasants, snipe and hare pointed and retrieved, foxes and stags bayed and trailed until shot, ducks retrieved promptly from marsh or current. For such a wide scope of activity the Shorthair has justly earned the label of "the multipurpose dog."

Unlike the English, who developed a separate breed to handle each type of game, the Germans lumped everything into a single dog. To create it they crossed the old Spanish Pointer with the Bloodhound in the seventeenth century. This proved an effective blend for gaining variety of hunting ability. The dog could trail and point but, being of cumbrous proportions, he lacked range and persistence. To correct this the American Pointer was introduced around 1870, the latter being an English combination of Spanish Pointer and Foxhound. Thus the Shorthair of today is in theory half Spanish Pointer, quarter Bloodhound and quarter Foxhound.

First brought to this country in 1925, the Shorthair was slow to be accepted because Americans, being specialists, had little appreciation or use for the multipurpose dog. Not until after World War II did it become popular. Since then clubs have sprung up all over the country under guidance of the German Shorthair Pointer Club of America, and the dog's original purpose has changed considerably. The hound characteristics of giving voice and trailing have been thrust aside; water retrieving has been eliminated from field-trial competition; and though a rabbit may be pointed, the dog is not allowed to pursue. In other words, he has become strictly a bird dog, with utilization being made of his exceedingly well-developed pointing, hunting and retrieving instincts.

Interestingly, he is one of the few field dogs still true to type. That is, he is still very close to the standard of quality and conformation to which the Germans hewed so rigorously to establish and maintain the breed. Thus a field dog can be and often is shown by his owner, and a field trial will often have a bench show in conjunction with it, so there are quite a few dual champions. Recently there has been more and more consternation within the Shorthair ranks about maintaining the proper-sized dog. Males should be from 23 to 25 inches at the shoulder and weigh 55 to 70 pounds; bitches 21 to 23 inches at the shoulder and 45 to 60 pounds. The difficulty, as always, is that show people are breeding massive dogs that tend to be ponderous in the field, while field people are breeding smaller than the standard to produce a more aggressive dog to win trials. The dual-champion title is thus in jeopardy of extinction, as has happened in other field breeds.

Colorwise the dog can be only liver-and-white or solid liver. Generally liver is the basic color, the white being little more than spots or ticking. The exception is in the Danish strains, where the white usually predominates.

The Shorthair is strictly a foot-shooting dog and was never bred for range, drive or speed, but rather for thoroughness, so the Germans could enjoy a variety of shooting. Thus he is inclined to be methodical rather than dynamic to hunt over or watch, especially when compared to the sprightly Brittany Spaniel or the fiery Pointer or Setter dashing about in

Double National Ch. Moesgaards Dandy, owned by Dr. and Mrs. Lewis L. Kline of Orlando, Fla.

quest of game. The dog shows the practical streak of the Germans at every step. When turned loose, he goes to hunting in a businesslike manner, thoroughly quartering, checking the cover precisely, handling in almost complete obeisance to his handler. For all this plus his usually excellent nose, he is considered one of the great meat dogs we have. "If you don't find something with a Shorthair," the saying goes, "there's nothing around."

The dog is naturally endowed with a large amount of "point." The puppies are precocious and develop earlier than Pointers and Setters and they are more easily handled and even-tempered. For these reasons the dog is an ideal one for the amateur to train, particularly if his time is limited and if he lives in tight hunting country of woods and bushes and small fields. The Shorthair does not serve well in wide-open spaces because he is close-working by nature. Some field-trial people are trying to change him in this respect, hoping to develop an all-age dog that will have to be hunted from horseback, but what advantage this pretends to serve, no one really knows, because the Pointer and Setter are invincible in this category, and the Shorthair's liver color will have him lost most of the time.

Carl and Barbara Coverdale of Grove City, Ohio, with their Shorthairs and some field-trial winnings.

In fact, the great problem of Shorthair breeders has long been where to go. The breed is avowedly and admittedly different in purpose and character from Pointers and Setters, and in any comparison the Shorthair suffers. But it is not fair to compare the Pointer to the Shorthair any more than it is fair to compare the race horse to the trotter. Both are horses that go around a track, yet no one judges the time of one against the other. For this reason Shorthair field trialers forbid competition from Pointers and Setters, and yet almost any long-range development will inevitably lead the Shorthair into the ranks of the Pointers and Setters where it doesn't belong and should not try to compete.

It would seem that if water work were introduced into Shorthair trials, the dog's position of being a multipurpose dog would be considerably strengthened, especially since the need for a multipurpose dog becomes stronger and stronger as our country grows. In fact, the dog's great appeal and support has come primarily from people of suburbia, young men and women who want a dog for more than a house pet and companion and guardian, who want the thrill of participating and winning at bench shows and field trials and perhaps coming up with a champion. The man in his restricted time wants a dog he can hunt easily and effectively without too much training, one that will point pheasants and grouse and woodcock and quail and rabbits and almost never fail to retrieve them, maybe pull a few ducks from the water also—not the world's greatest stylist, but efficient and loyal and handsome anywhere. Such is the German Shorthair, and offhand I would say its future is very bright.

Field Ch. Kay v. d. Wildburg, owned by Richard S. Johns of Benton, Pa. and Joseph Eusepi of Oswego, N.Y. Imported from Germany as a derby, Kay has many outstanding wins in all-breed competition.

A beautiful head study of three dual champions, Oxtans Lieselatte Von Greif, Madehen Braut Von Greif and Schoene Braut Von Greif, all owned by Mr. and Mrs. E. E. Harden of Salinas, Calif.

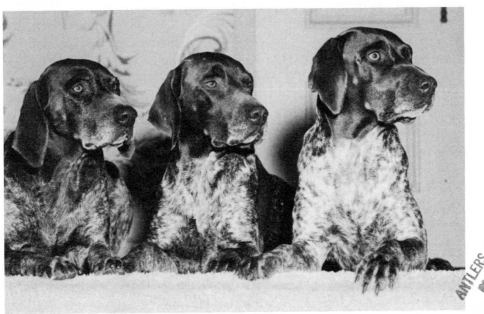

The German Wirehaired Pointer

Basically there are three types of coats among the various breeds of pointing dogs—the shorthaired coat as on Pointers, Weimaraners, and Vizslas, the longhaired coat as on Setters and Brittany Spaniels, and the wirehaired coat as on the German Wirehaired Pointer and Wirehaired Pointing Griffon.

These last two breeds, which we shall now discuss, are both relatively young, having been developed on the European continent during the last quarter of the nineteenth century, an era characterized by enthusiastic experimentation in animal husbandry. As man's mind sought to unlock the laws of heredity, interest sprang up everywhere involving height, color, coat of animals, their dominant and recessive characteristics. Gregor Mendel, the Austrian monk and naturalist, was the most celebrated theorist, but everyone had ideas, and those men whose interest lay in dogs began creating new breeds of all sizes, descriptions and purposes.

Field-dog men visualized the most ideal animal that could exist and tried to create him. They reasoned that a wirehaired coat an inch and a half to two inches long with a thick waterproof undercoat was the most

Field Ch. Haar Baron's Mike.

protective in any type of cover, on land or water, heat or cold. The heavy growth of eyebrows and beard on the dog's face would protect him from laceration in any situation. Next they planned a dog that would shed its dense undercoat in the summer to be cool, then regrow it in the fall for winter protection.

In their experimenting they bred the Poodle to the English Pointer and came up with the *Pudelpointer;* they crossed the Pointer, Foxhound, *Pudelpointer* and Polish Water Dog to produce the *Stichelhaar;* they crossed the ancient Griffon with the Setter, Spaniel and Otter Hound and came up with the Wirehaired Pointing Griffon discussed in the next section.

By combining the Griffon, *Stichelhaar, Pudelpointer* and German Short-hair they created the *Deutsch-Drahthaar,* literally the German Wirehair.

Developed in Germany, the *Drahthaar* or German Wirehaired Pointer, as he is officially known here in America, made rapid strides because of the simple fact that he was a good dog. He outdid the breeds from which he sprang, and as time went on he challenged the dominant position of his half-brother, the German Shorthaired Pointer, more often than not defeating him in the complicated German field trials although his ranks were considerably fewer in number.

Were it not for his wiry coat, he would be almost identical to the Short-hair in appearance. His lines are about the same, he is big and strong, with plenty of substance. He is about the same height and weight: 24 to 26 inches and 55 to 70 pounds for males, bitches slightly smaller but not under 22 inches. He is the same color: liver-and-white with ticking and roan-ing, or sometimes solid liver. Any black in the coat is *verboten.*

The head is moderately long, skull broad, medium stop, muzzle medium-long with beard and bushy eyebrows. The neck should have no dewlap of the hound; in fact, the entire skin is notably tight to the body. The body is a shade longer than it is high, back short, straight and strong with perceptible slope down from withers to croup. Chest is deep, hips broad, tail docked approximately two fifths of its original length. His outer coat is rough, the hairs being as tough and stiff as wire or wild-boar bristles, but it lies quite flat so the outline of the dog is not lost. The undercoat is dense in winter, almost invisible in summer.

The German Wirehaired Pointer was first brought to the United States in 1920 and has established himself with considerable popularity in the Middle West. Like all of the German breeds he was originally a multi-purpose dog, but over here he has been used only for upland game and occasional duck hunting along marshes and rivers of the Central Flyway. Because he contains little or no Bloodhound in him he is not slow or ponderous in the field, but an energetic worker, intelligent and lively in action, a lot of solid bird dog. He quarters thoroughly at ideal foot-shooting range, is proficient on all upland game, although not preferred on quail or prairie chicken where wide range and speed are an advantage.

Around the house he makes a good pet and watchdog, is inclined to be somewhat aloof with strangers but not unfriendly.

In field trials for German pointing breeds he has done extremely well for himself. For a breed to hold its own in competition, its winnings should be in the same ratio as its entries. For example, if, over a year's period, five hundred Shorthairs compete in open stakes against a total entry of five thousand, then the Shorthair should win ten per cent of the placements. In the case of the Wirehaired Pointer, he has won more than his share of placements. In 1961 Haar Baron's Tina, owned, trained, and handled by amateur Cliff Faestel of Wisconsin, won the National German Pointing Dog Championship in Ohio against Shorthairs and Weimaraners, the two breeds the Wirehaired most generally competes against. Mr. Faestel, like other owners of the breed, often competes in Open Shooting Dog stakes and wins his share against Pointers and Setters as well, proving that a good dog is good anywhere.

Dual Ch. Haar Baron Gremlin, owned by Cliff Faestel of Brookfield, Wis., is the first dual champion of her breed in this country.

The German Wirehaired Pointer is not a strikingly handsome dog because of his coat, practical though it may be. I have the feeling that were it not for this he would have gained a much wider popularity. But his growth has been steady if not meteoric in both the field and on the bench. The breed was not accepted for registration by the American Kennel Club until 1959, at which time it was also granted separate show classification. Today dual champions are beginning to appear and undoubtedly this sound hunting breed will continue to grow as more people discover its sterling abilities.

Wirehaired Pointing Griffon

Historically, biologically and practically, this bushy bundle of bristles is a most interesting though rare member of the pointing breeds. He was created in 1874 by E. K. Korthals, a Hollander with a passionate interest in experimental dog breeding. Korthals wanted to see if he could produce the perfect combination dog with a unique coat, a dog that would be equally at home on land or in water, work fur or feather and possess a coat that would be impervious to any situation from ice water to the thickest of briars and reed grass.

Starting with six pointing dogs of dubious origin, all oddly coated but supposedly containing Griffon blood, Korthals bred with two ends in mind —over-all hunting ability and rough, wiry coat. After an argument with his father, a highly successful cattle breeder who could not fathom his son's nonsensical interest in trying to create a new breed of dog, Korthals left home and went to Germany, later to France. In each place he continued his breeding activities, using the best of local blood to cross into his strain whenever it suited his needs. In France, Korthals worked for the Duke of Penthièvre, came in contact with many noblemen and at every opportunity enthusiastically espoused the cause of his dog. Here it was most widely received, thus this country is generally considered to be its home.

During the process of creating the Wirehaired Pointing Griffon Korthals is said to have used spaniel, setter, and Otter Hound blood to cross into the basic blood of the six dogs with which he started. At lease one cross of German Shorthair blood is known to have been made, also the ancient Griffon hound from which the true Griffons descend.

The Korthals Griffon, as he is called in France, was introduced into this country by the late Louis A. Thebaud of Convent, New Jersey. Around 1900 he imported several outstanding specimens from France and conducted a breeding program which for a time successfully promoted the dog as a close-working hunter. Gradually interest in the breed waned and today they are rather few and far between, although the owner of one will never fail to extol him, proving that the qualities which the persistent Dutchman put into his dog still remain strongly imbued even today.

The dog is smaller than his first cousin, the German Wirehaired Pointer, and not as active afield. Because of this he is almost never run in trials but used strictly for gunning.

The standard describes him as follows:

"The Wirehaired Griffon is a dog of medium size, fairly short-backed, rather low on his legs. He is strongly limbed, everything about him indicating strength and vigor. His coat is harsh, like the bristles of a wild boar, and unkempt-looking in appearance . . .

"Head is long and furnished with a harsh coat, forming a mustache and eyebrows, skull long and narrow, muzzle square. Forelegs are very straight and muscular; hind legs furnished with rather short stiff hair, the thighs long and well developed. Tail is cut to two-thirds of its normal length.

"Coat is hard, dry, stiff, never curly, the undercoat downy.

"Color: steel gray with chestnut splashes, gray with chestnut splashes, chestnut, dirty white mixed with chestnut, never black.

"Height and weight: males 21½ to 23½ inches, 50 to 65 pounds; females 19½ to 21½, 45 to 60 pounds."

That Korthals succeeded in developing a practical dog cannot be denied. Followers of the breed claim it can be trained to handle any type of game, fur or feather, and retrieve it proficiently from land or water. Certainly its tough, wiry coat provides the ultimate in protection against cold, dampness, briars and thorns, reed grass, even heat. Though the dog is not particularly attractive because of his beard and bushy eyebrows, nor does his bristle coat encourage fondling or petting, still he's a sound hunter all the way through. He possesses a considerable amount of point, has an excellent nose, handles easily, works closely and always to the gun. He is rather slow afield, goes into any cover whatsoever, is a great swamp dog and superior on woodcock. Once again, his color provides nearly perfect camouflage, making him difficult to see at a distance or when buried in a thicket on point. But his range is so close that this seldom happens.

Wirehaired Pointing Griffon.

Personalitywise, he is inclined to be somewhat aloof but not unfriendly. Because he's a mannerly, tractable dog he trains with relative ease. He's ideal for the man getting along in years who likes to do a little preserve shooting and wants to get all the birds he pays for. Or the man who goes jump-hunting for a couple of hours of an afternoon—that is, drive to a small area that he knows is a hot spot for birds, perhaps a swamp bottom or the edges of a cornfield, hunt it thoroughly, then go back to the car and jump to the next spot. For this kind of hunting a man wants a close-working dog that is nearly foolproof, and the Wirehaired Pointing Griffon, Korthals' handmade dream, certainly qualifies. He's no raving beauty or dramatic firebrand afield, but he seldom makes a mistake.

The Brittany Spaniel

One of the most rapidly growing breeds in the country today is a brisk little bangtailed rascal called the Brittany Spaniel. Also referred to from time to time because of his size as the vest-pocket gun dog, stunted setter with a sawed-off tail, overgrown Springer, he is to his admirers just plain Brit. For the uninitiated, confusion arises because the Brit does not spring game in true spaniel style. Instead he points it as do the Pointer and Setter —upright, steady, for the gunner himself to flush.

There are many sound reasons for the Brit's popularity, which we shall discuss later. Right now let's look at his history, and an interesting one it is because he's the only breed in the entire pointing family to have been developed generally by a people rather than specifically by an individual or elite group. Every breed began from crosses of utility or necessity, but at a key point some highly intelligent person, usually of wealth and nobility, took hold and began a selective breeding program which carefully set the type. Soon thereafter standards were established, and all the breeders worked toward a specifically chosen goal.

No such thing with the Brittany Spaniel. He was developed by the French peasants of Brittany strictly as a hunting dog. All sorts of crosses were made—whatever was handy. The only criterion was that the outcross be a good hunting dog, which more often than not strengthened the stock, otherwise it would never have become a breed.

What kind of a dog did the French peasant want? Generally he wanted a playful, friendly dog that would be good around his home and add a touch of brightness to his dreary life. Specifically he wanted a hunter that would find all types of small game to fill the pot—rabbits along the hedgerows, woodcock and duck in the marshes and beside the creeks which laced through Brittany, partridge and pheasant in the grain fields. He had to have a dog that was close-working and ever obedient, because the vast majority of his hunting was poaching. Great noblemen owned all the land, and to shoot the woodcock and partridge which brought good prices in the market place you had to sneak on some duke's land, running the risk of being caught and punished. Your dog had to be particularly good, particularly obedient, point surely, retrieve quickly, because you might have to run a few moments after you shot something.

How did the French peasant of Brittany put his dog together? Noblemen always had the best stock, so if you had a good hunting bitch you cultivated the acquaintance of his gamekeeper and maybe that way you bred to a blueblood. Also, the Welsh who came to the seacoast ports were forever bragging about their spaniels and if you talked fast you might trade a sheep for a couple of puppies. Then, too, in the tides of war when everything was in upheaval, a good hunting dog might often be found running wild through the woods. And when the English ruled Brittany they brought their own hunting dogs. Spaniels, setters, pointers, hounds, all served the cause at one time or other.

The peasant dog was not pretty, but practical. Why not? Who could afford gamekeepers and purebreds with pedigrees except a duke or a viscount? Let him laugh at the peasant dog and call him anything he will— "Dog with a short tail. Coal man's dog. Dog with no name!"

"But try one and see how they hunt."

"Try one of those crossbred mongrels!" the duke would chuckle disdainfully. "They lack elegance. They lack everything. What right do they have to exist?"

"Because they are good," the peasant would chide. "That is their reason for existing."

And good they were, whether inbred or outcrossed. Along the rugged coast, people wanted a big, tough dog so the Irish Setter (the red-and-white one) was bred into him. Consequently the Brittany Spaniel in this area was longer-legged, took on the Setter look in head and body. Inland

Brittany National Ch. Towsey.

the peasant wanted a smaller dog because it ate less, was more incon-
spicuous when you sneaked into some forbidden field or marsh. Through
the centuries a breed gradually emerged—spaniel in type, knee-high, sharp-
nosed, always quick and obedient, ever busy and bustling when hunting,
a rustic kind of dog that trailed a rabbit like a dart, retrieved from land
or water, had the courage to penetrate any cover. He had a downhill
build—strong shoulders and chest and front legs, stout back that sloped
down to a solid rear end and short hind legs. No beauty but a stout little
worker all the time.

When did this occur?

Dutch artists of the seventeenth century graphically portrayed several
small white-and-chestnut spaniels with short tails. Jean-Baptist Oudry, the
great eighteenth-century French naturalist and animal painter during the
reign of Louis XV portrayed a liver-and-white Brittany Spaniel pointing a
red-legged partridge. At the beginning of the nineteenth century Jouy
wove a Brit with all the principal characteristics of today into one of his
famous tapestries. All this would seem to support the claim of many peo-

Ch. Warrior's Duke de Triumph, owned by Clarance J. Goering of Newton, Kansas, shows beautiful style pointing quail.

ple that the Brit is a very old breed whose size and type were attained long before the setters of England.

One of the best descriptions ever written about the Brittany comes from the memorandum book of French Major Gran-Chavin. It reads:

"In 1906 I arrived in garrison at Pontivy and a little while after, I classified horses from confines of three provinces: Morbihan, Finistere and Cotes du Nord. In traveling through many villages I noticed the presence of many small spaniels. Almost all had short tails, the ears looked pretty much the same and they were colored white-chestnut, white-orange and white-black. The white-black very often had spots of red on the cheeks and over the eyes. These small animals were fascinating due to a lively physiognomy, a short gait and intelligent looks.

"Everywhere they would tell me they were excellent hunters, fearless of the thicket, would point very well and especially well did they hunt the hare, sometimes up to three-quarters of an hour.

"I was not surprised to find this infatuation. Their endurance and rusticity were often revealed to me during the course of the long hunting days in a country very much intersected with rivers and canals and often very woody."

Another very accurate description comes from the pen of M. Lefournier, writing in *L'Eleveur* [The Breeder] of May 3, 1908.

"The Brittany Spaniel of good origin is a very rustic dog who points instinctively, tracks at a small gallop, is always in motion, ferrets everywhere, needs no urging. He is a bundle of nerves, enduring in all trials which no thicket can stop.

"Very intelligent, he loves his master, listens to him, has always an eye on him, waits for only a gesture or a sign to obey, seems to anticipate the wish of the one who employs him.

"His nose is good, and as the dog knows how to use it, one is surprised to see the results obtained from so small a dog. The Brittany dog excels in hunting the woodcock in the wood and thicket. As for his courage he would not be a Breton if he did not have a heart. He retrieves with pleasure and is excellent in the woods as well as the marshes.

"When I have told you that by his very nature he is a faithful companion of his master and the friend of the children, I shall have depicted his disposition."

The Brit developed with the people of Brittany and, like them, his final form was the result of local conditions and outside influences. But the form was not consistent from village to village because there was no standard. Not until 1907 was he recognized as a breed in France, thanks to the efforts of Arthur Enaud, a French sportsman. His interest in the Brit came just before 1900, at which point the dog began to degenerate because of too much inbreeding. Once the breed was recognized and a club established, then the standard was written, which included the following: Size, 19½ to 22 inches, low set with short back, round head, rather short ears with comparatively little fringe, short coat on the body, feather waved but not curly, rather cob-like, tail naturally always short 4 to 6 inches . . . although stocky he has the aspect of a cob or a hunter, the look of a resourceful and vigorous ragamuffin.

Since the beginning the peasants had docked the Brit's tail so it would not be injured in the great fields of furze, a thorny scrub pine. Then one of the numerous outcrosses produced dogs with short tails or no tail at all and it was thought that these were the most desirable dogs, consequently the original standard contained the words "naturally short tail." After much debate the word "naturally" was dropped and today many if not a majority of the Brits' tails are docked to four inches.

In those days around 1900, white-and-liver was the predominant color. There were also many tricolored dogs as well as white-orange and white-black ones, but since then the color standard has changed. Today the

American standard calls for "dark orange and white (the most popular color) or liver and white. Some ticking is desirable but not so much as to produce belton patterns. Roan patterns or factors of orange or liver shade are permissible. The orange and liver are found in standard parti-color, or piebald patterns. Washed out or faded colors are not desirable. Black is a disqualification."

Today's height is "17½ to 20½ inches measured from the ground to the highest point of the back, the withers. Weight should be between 30 and 40 pounds. The hair of the coat is dense and can be either flat or wavy. Furnishings are not profuse. Long, curly, or silky hair is a fault and any tendency toward excessive feathering should be severely penalized as undesirable in a sporting dog which must face burrs and heavy cover." In conformation the dog stands a mite higher than he is long.

The first imports to this hemisphere were made to Mexico by M. J. Pugibet. Later in 1931 Louis A. Thebaud, the same man who established the Wirehaired Pointing Griffon here earlier, made several successful importations to the United States and helped found the Brittany Spaniel Club of North America which later became today's American Brittany Club. His nephew, René Joubert, scored the first important field win when his good bitch, Fenutus, beat a group of pointers and setters in 1937.

Soon thereafter Kaer de Comouaille, owned by Alan R. Stuyvesant, began making a name for himself as a field winner and sired Dual Ch. Allamuchy Valley Uno, a great Brit and producer of many great ones. Through the years Mr. Stuyvesant contributed mightily to the Brittany breed here by importing foundation stock from France for himself and others.

The American Brittany Club, founded in Detroit in 1942, boasts more than 35,000 members today. Its creed is to preserve the Brit as a "Dual Dog"—that is, having the field dogs good enough in type to win their bench championships, and vice versa. The club has more than thirty regional clubs sponsoring AKC licensed field trials and bench shows as well as informal activities for their members such as fun trials, picnics and meetings.

The national organization also sponsors the National Trials for Brittanies every year at the famed Crab Orchard Wild Life Area, Carbondale, Illinois. This championship stake establishes the Brittany National Champ each year. Also run at the same time are the National Amateur Handler's Stake and the Brittany Futurity. In conjunction with all this is held the National Specialty Show, in which most of the dogs competing in the field also enter the bench show. A highly coveted Dual Dog Award is given to the Brit compiling the greatest number of points in the field and on the bench.

This extraordinary photo of a rare occurrence shows Ch. Ti-War Andre de Triumph pointing a quail while in the process of retrieving one.

Certainly the Brittany Spaniel is one of the last of the pointing breeds, if not the last, successfully to claim the title of "the dual dog." But because of the vast difference between breeding motives of show people and field people plus, as explained earlier, the vast expense of gaining a championship title, it would appear that the dual dog cannot survive much longer. Brittany followers have gone to the greatest lengths yet seen in field breeds to preserve this worth-while title, however.

But to get back to the Brit, no other breed is quite like him. He's not pretty, not a graceful or colorful performer, but he is tremendously alert, always on his toes, ears cocked, a lively expression on his face that says, "I'm ready whenever you are, boss."

His greatest attribute is his natural affection, and this is probably what has endeared him to so many followers. In the field this trait takes the

A Brittany Spaniel makes an excellent pheasant dog.

form of a great desire to please and tends to shorten his range, as he checks back frequently with his handler. It also prevents him from running off to self-hunt.

In his field training the Brittany must be approached differently from the Pointer and Setter and Lab. He is not a strong-willed dog, consequently cannot tolerate too much forceful correction. Training must be taught to him, not pounded into him as so often is the case with tougher dogs. Such is the desire to please in the Brit that a single slap or a harsh word will usually prove ample punishment for a mistake. This does not mean that you should put up with a lot of nonsense because he is sensitive. In fact, this is the real problem that most amateur trainers of Brits run into. They are afraid to correct their dog at all, consequently he is never broken to the degree that he should be.

Since the Brit is usually a natural retriever, early training should not emphasize this trait because it will make the dog want to fetch game rather than point it. Thus his training program should be laid out so he is taught to find and point birds first. After the dog has thoroughly mastered this, the owner may then concentrate on retrieving.

Because the Brit is a friendly, likable fellow and easy to handle, he's a great favorite with women. Some amateurs have had fine success with them, and the only woman professional field-dog handler that I ever met or heard of, Nicki Bissle of Oregon, works exclusively and most successfully with Brittanies.

A word that you hear frequently in Brit circles is "cobby"—he's not cobby enough, or she's a good cobby type. It means compact and short-legged, not rangy or massive.

When the Brittany Spaniel first came to this country his enthusiasts claimed he would replace the Setter and Pointer. This has not happened yet and it's not likely to, but there are some situations where I would take a Brittany over any other pointing dog. If size meant anything, either around the home or apartment or in transporting him, the Brit is the best compact model there is. If I wanted great affection and devotion in a dog, the bouncy, joyful, plucky kind, I'd choose a Brit. If my livelihood required that I move about considerably, to different areas of the country or particularly to different parts of the world, I'd have a Brit because, in my opinion, they can find and handle all kinds of upland game better than any other pointing breed. By their type of busy, bustling hunting at close to medium range they find birds, maybe not as many quail as a wide-going Pointer or as many grouse as a slashing Setter, but take the specialist out of his element and he's usually lost, whereas the Brit is not. He adapts easily, learns quickly, which makes him about the best jack-of-all-trades pointing dog we have. He'll handle ptarmigan in Iceland, chukars in India, valley quail in California and ringnecks anywhere; he'll fetch ducks and geese from water or marsh, point woodcock, all in a way that would delight the heart of the best French poacher!

The Weimaraner

Of all the various types of hunting dogs brought to America in the last 300 years none has received more fanfare and publicity, none was organized more exclusively or sold at higher prices than the Weimaraner.

Oddly enough, all the people involved from the original importer, Howard Knight of Providence, Rhode Island, in 1929 to Jack Denton Scott, who started the publicity campaign of the Weimaraner about 1947, and subsequently the editors, magazine writers, newspaper columnists, radio commentators, television and even movie studios who ballyhooed the animal into a "colossal" "astounding" "sensational" myth were all sincere men with no ax to grind. But everything was so overplayed that no dog on earth could possibly have lived up to the wild boasts and impossible claims made of the "Gray Ghost." Consequently it has taken considerable time and quiet effort on the part of many conscientious breeders to bring real progress to the breed here in America.

The Weimaraner (pronounced Vi'-mar-honor and often called Ymar for short) has a scanty factual history. Though reams have been written on the subject, each author after presenting his own pet thesis, be it the Great Dane theory, the German Shorthair theory, the Bloodhound theory, the Pointer theory or the Bracke theory, inevitably admits that no positive conclusion can be reached. World Wars I and II destroyed too many records and people for us ever to know the entire story.

The breed was first brought to light around 1810 in Weimar, capital of the province of Thuringia, now in the southwest section of the Russian zone of Germany. Grand Duke Karl August dreamed of Weimar as a German Athens culturally and politically. Field sports of all kinds flourished, particularly hunting in the thickly wooded hills surrounding the city. The nobility took great delight in collecting fine guns and breeding superior dogs.

Like the rest of Europe, German nobility found it most fashionable to use English hunting dogs, to the point of being scornful of their own native breeds. Somehow a large gray dog came into being around Weimar, used for hunting wolves, boar, deer, bear, and later for upland game as the big game disappeared. One story says that the Grand Duke, an avid hunter, brought the original stock from Bohemia after shooting over the dogs there at the estate of Prince Esterházy, but this doesn't make sense because it ignores the big-game origin of the dog.

More than likely the Weimaraner had long existed in the area. In 1631 Van Dyke painted a portrait of Prince Rupprecht von der Pfalz with one of his favorite hunting dogs of a breed known as *Huehnerhund* (chicken dog). With its silver-gray coat and pendant ears the dog closely resembled the Weimaraner of today except for his uncropped tail.

One German writer around 1900, calling himself "Fama," wrote:

"The ideal hunting dog in olden times was the *Leithund* [Leading Dog] . . . who would trail the scent of a chosen stag or deer in a herd. From this they developed the '*Schweisshund*' brown in color.

"They had Pointers for smaller game, for birds, rabbits and the like. Then came the idea to cross these two to meld the qualities of both. The result of this noble experiment was the Weimaraner, a dog that points with an exceedingly good nose."

Unfortunately no one knows who Fama was or how he reached his conclusions, logical though they are. We know the *Schweisshund* existed in several varieties and colors and was closely related to if not descended from the Bloodhound.

Another writer named "R. F." claimed in the late 1930s that brown dogs by withdrawal of or lack of Vitamin D changed to silver-brown to gray to silver-gray, and since many German Shorthaired Pointers (*Deutsch Kurzhaar*) were solid brown or liver, the Weimaraner undoubtedly rose from this source.

Major Herber, generally accepted father of the modern Weimaraner until his death in 1939, scuttled this theory by pointing out that, color aside, the German Shorthair contains none of the conformation of the Weimaraner—a very true observation. His theory was that the Weimaraner origi-

Weimaraner head study.

nated from the Bracke, an ancestor of the *Schweisshund,* and earlier called St. Hubert's Hound, a black dog that turned gray by mutation to form the Weimaraner. He did not support the Great Dane theory which was advanced by reason of the Weimaraner's yellow, sometimes blue eyes, gray coat and often hefty size.

One has no idea of the vehemence with which the Germans argued these insoluble points month after month, year after year, in books and magazines, always concluding that there was no positive answer. From the great mire of supposition it seems fairly safe to assume that the Weimaraner existed long before 1810 when the Grand Duke and his nobles took interest in the dog. Perhaps he was never mentioned by early writers because he was not considered a breed, only a color variation of the St. Hubert's Hound. Perhaps as his usefulness as a big-game dog diminished he was crossed with the Spanish Pointer, fine examples of which had been brought from Spain to Germany again by nobility. Perhaps this supplied the pointing instinct. Perhaps, perhaps, perhaps. . . .

In any event we know the nobles of Weimar took a great liking to the dog around 1810 and began breeding it for their own private hunting use. The breed was kept so exclusive that a hundred years later few Germans, a dog-conscious people, had ever heard of a Weimaraner or Weimar Pointer.

There is little doubt that certain outcrosses were made during the nineteenth century. The town of Apolda, not far from Weimar, beginning in 1860 sponsored what was called a "dog market." Actually it was a dog show held at the Whitsuntide festival each year until World War II. In 1882 the Weimaraner was strongly represented and the Thuringia Club for Breeding Purebred Dogs suggested to owners that they cease crossing the Weimaraner with other types of German Pointer (there were several besides the Shorthair) because the color and characteristics were being lost. The Gray Ghost was becoming reddish-brown, gray-brown, even flat brown and was taking on too much of a Pointer look.

The breed was in the throes of a decline and might well have passed from view had it not been for the forming of the now famous Weimaraner Club of Germany at Erfort, Thuringia, on June 20, 1897. The club specifically stated that it had no intention of publicizing the breed for general use, only of refurbishing and perpetuating it and above all returning it to the field where it rightfully belonged. No more than 1500 dogs were ever wanted (they never reached 1000) and every owner had to be a club member. The Weimaraner was never intended to be an everybody's-dog, rather a gentleman's hunting dog and companion.

A year earlier, in 1896, the Weimaraner had been recognized as a distinct breed and at the start of registration the club accepted only those dogs which met the highest standards of color and conformation. Though many were barred, it set the breed back on its feet quickly. Dogs or puppies could not be sold or given away to other than club members, who had to promise to keep the Weimaraner pure and destroy all culls, mutations, throwbacks or unworthy examples of the breed.

By 1915 the Weimaraner had become known among gunning circles for its ability and unique color, chiefly through Major Herber's efforts to

Field Ch. Fritz von Wehmann, winner of seven championships and 86 field-trial placements, one of the great field Weimaraners of all time, owned by Gil Wehmann of New York City.

establish it as a sound hunting dog. During the Hitlerian era all dog clubs, even stud books, came under government control. Registration grew more stringent, membership more restricted, non-Aryans were barred. World War II so decimated the ranks of the Weimaraners that not more than 300 survived, but the Weimaraner Club of Germany was reorganized in 1951 and is now affiliated with the German Hunting Dog Club.

The first Weimaraners were brought to the United States by Howard Knight in 1929. He had to join the German Weimaraner Club to do it. Even then there was considerable opposition to any of the breed leaving the country and the two he imported were later discovered to have been rendered sterile before shipment. In 1938 he obtained some additional stock, an outstanding male puppy named Mars aus der Wolfsreide, a bitch in whelp, Aura von Gaiberg, and Dorle von Schwarzen Kamp, all of whom became foundation blood here.

Mr. Knight never sold any Ymars, only gave them to a few friends with the understanding that they never be crossbred and that any with markings other than white star or blaze on the chest be destroyed. He was the first president of the Weimaraner Club of America, founded in 1941, and was instrumental in having the breed recognized in 1943 by the American Kennel Club. When he retired, Mr. Knight gave his Weimaraner stock to Mr. and Mrs. A. F. Horn of Grafmar Kennels, who carried on the pioneering and produced many early champions. Grafmar's Swingtime won her C. D. Obedience title in three consecutive shows with scores of 95, 97 and 99, and a short while later Grafmar's Ador won his C. D. at the age of six months and two days.

These and several other incidents during and shortly after World War II got the Weimaraner publicity barrel rolling to the extent that the breed took off on a price spiral never before known in dogdom. As tales grew more fantastic, from hunting mountain lions to pointing and retrieving quail with no training to tracking down a lost child on a three-day-old trail, prices for puppies soared to $500 and up. Inevitably the fast-buck breeders took over, sold anything that was gray; even the blue-black and longhaired Weimaraners (both appear in litters of gray parents from time to time but are not acceptable) were sold at higher prices as "oddities" of the breed.

Originally the Weimaraner Club of America made every prospective buyer furnish character references, join the club and swear on a stack of Bibles that he would use the dog for hunting. This galled a lot of Americans who had fought a war to defend freedom of choice, but the main reason the restrictions failed here was that in the field the Weimaraner did not live up to his ballyhoo. It was claimed he could run 38 miles an hour, but while bird-hunting he was one of the slowest, most pottering dogs ever seen. Unattractive too, because he ran with his nose on the ground like a hound after a mole. Beyond that he had a penchant for wetting on every second bush he passed. Incredibly it seemed a trait of the dog and in field trials he looked awful. I say all this without disrespect because in the last fifteen years the Weimaraner has made tremendous improvement.

First of all, the Weimaraner Club abandoned its restrictions, realizing that the proper way to promote breed improvement is not through force but through the incentive of competition—show ring and field trial. In their thirst to win, breeders will aim at the highest standard. As one succeeds, another will try to outdo him, and somewhere along the line is always the person who wants to buy the best, so the breeder will be well rewarded for his efforts. By dictating what must be done, not nearly so much is gained, at least not among Americans.

Another vast improvement took place among those who wanted to win field competitions. The more the Weimaraner was laughed at, the more determined became certain fanciers to produce good field dogs that would be primarily bird dogs instead of a little bit of everything. Again, I have no intention of slandering the all-purpose dog, but he does not represent the methods of hunting indigenous to our country. To show what I mean, the following is the program of the Major Herber Memorial Trials, roughly speaking, the German National Championship for Weimaraners. Sixteen areas of judging comprise the points which name the winner. They are as follows:

1 – Seeking (coordination and endurance receive preference over speed and distance. Author's note: this is just the opposite of what we desire in the United States.)
2 – Pointing
3 – Rabbit trailing
4 – Nose
5 – Viciousness toward prey
6 – Viciousness toward man
7 – Retrieving from deep water
8 – Flushing ducks
9 – Blood trailing (injured deer, etc.)
10 – Trail of bloodthirsty animal on prey trail
11 – Retrieving of fowl (Handler lets dog seek in direction of fowl without giving command to "fetch" and not approaching fowl closer than 60 yards.)
12 – Retrieving over hurdle
13 – Retrieving according to weight (14, 11, 9, 6 pounds)
14 – Delivery (of rucksack with handler out of sight)
15 – Bark on command
16 – Cooperation with handler (All other 15 exercises to be considered.)

For all this, complete obedience to the handler is obviously imperative as is thorough, close quartering, both factors which we do not stress here and generally try to avoid. Also, to train the all-purpose hunter requires a considerable amount of time, which very few of us Americans have.

An old German hunter I've known for a long time put it another way. "When I was in the old country I hunted over the all-purpose dog and thought he was the greatest. He was a good mechanical worker but never breathtaking. The longer I am here in America the more I like the specialist, hound, retriever or pointing dog that knows how to do one job perfectly. I like to see him work independent of his handler but in accord with him, a dog that has been trained, yes, but one that is dramatic. This is a joy to see. This is what makes for hunting memories."

I think the old man came pretty close to the center of it. Certainly the Weimaraner is a good dog, but over here he had two pitfalls. He had first to overcome his ballyhoo, then adapt himself usefully to the needs of our particular country. This he has done remarkably well in the last ten to fifteen years. Improvement in Weimaraner field stock has been remarkable. The pottering and the constant wetting have been bred out of them, entirely by selective breeding, not by outcrossing because if there is one thing sacred among Weimaraner people it's keeping the blood pure and straight. In the field now, the dog gets out and hunts. He doesn't slide along the ground in a fast trot or slow lope that originally earned him his nickname of the Gray Ghost.

Although he is essentially a bird dog now, the Ymar remains a great retriever. The Weimaraner National Championship, which is a shoot-to-kill trial held alternately in the East, Midwest and Far West, requires that the dog have received his water certificate (double retrieve from water, with or without decoys) to be eligible to run.

Ymars are such good water and land retrievers that they would hold their own in the best of retriever circles and probably do a better job in many cases, but they haven't been permitted to compete against Labs, Chessies and Goldens for two good reasons. First, the American Kennel Club feels that a breed should compete only in the area of its purpose and the Ymar is classified as a pointing dog. Secondly, the retriever people don't want him beating them. The two make a rather formidable barrier. One drawback against the Weimaraner as a retriever is that he doesn't have a double coat, hence should not be used in ice water. But in reasonable weather he is hard to beat, being a fast swimmer, smart at catching cripples and very tender-mouthed generally.

The Weimaraner today is used two thirds for showing, obedience and tracking, one third for field hunting. As with most of the other pointing breeds, a deep split has arisen between show and field stock, the former

A Weimaraner points a pheasant for two gunners.

Zouave's Miss Cuca, Weimaraner National Open Champion, 1962.

breeding for coat and looks, the latter for ability. Dual champions exist but they are not numerous. The real Weimaraner field-dog fancier runs not only in his own trials but in restricted breed trials against Shorthairs, *Drahthaars,* Brittanies and Vizslas, also against Pointers and Setters, and each year his successes increase.

The Weimaraner Futurity is the big money stake, with some $1500 to $2000 going annually to the winning owners and breeders. This derby stake is sponsored by the Weimaraner Club of America which also puts out an excellent monthly magazine.

The most outstanding characteristic of the Weimaraner is his color, a real eye-stopping gray. The standard calls for a short, smooth and sleek coat in shades of mouse-gray to silver-gray, usually blending to a lighter shade on the head and ears. A white spot no larger than a half dollar is permissible on the chest or throat but not on any other part of the body. The nose is gray, lips and gums flesh color. The head is rather long and aristocratic, with a moderate stop and without the arched bridge of the Shorthair. Ears are long, lobular and set high; eyes must be light in color, either light amber, gray or blue-gray. (All pups are born with startling blue eyes and gray-white zebra stripes, both of which change after a couple of months.)

The Weimaraner is called a medium-sized dog, but I've seen some mighty big ones and would say that they generally run on the large size. Males should be 25 to 27 inches at the withers; bitches 23 to 25 inches. The average weight is 60 to 75 pounds but it isn't unusual for them to reach 85 or 90 pounds. Being formerly a big-game dog, he is not penalized for having too much size. A more serious fault is the coat color being anything other than gray, eyes being off-color, the mouth black or mottled.

There has been much discussion about the Weimaraner temperament, some claiming that they have a vicious streak, others that they do not make good kennel dogs. Neither of these seems to be true although there are individuals within every breed that express these traits. Generally the Weimaraner is an excellent family dog which instinctively protects his own, and this has perhaps been misconstrued as viciousness. I know that I wouldn't barge into a house that harbored a Weimaraner without knocking first, but this is only common sense and I like the protective trait myself.

As for their not being good kennel dogs, I think this came from the claim that the German Weimaraner was always a part of the family, a hearth dog and pal to his master, therefore in a kennel, isolated from human companionship, he became restless and unstable. If this was true once, it is not true now. Most field Weimaraners are kenneled and it's done without difficulty. But to take a dog of any breed which has been brought up in the freedom and family surroundings of a home and suddenly lock him up in a kennel is asking for trouble, and the Ymar is big enough to give it. Generally though, he is not a nervous or high-strung or mean dog. He's composed and friendly, loves children and will retrieve any stick they throw for as long as they care to throw it.

Professional trainers strongly recommend that Ymars be worked early and heavily in the field before they are yard-broken. If the desire to hunt is developed first, the dogs will not be inclined to become overdependent on the handler. The other way around they may. The claim that they gain and lose weight easily, hence are more difficult to condition, doesn't seem to be valid either. The Ymar is a powerful dog and carries his weight well. Any dog that is not properly conditioned will give out when hunted or run in a field trial.

The East was the original stronghold of the Ymar. Probably the highest quality of field dog still remains there, although surpassed in numbers by the Midwest and West Coast. California has come a long way with the Weimaraner, as have Illinois, Indiana and Ohio. In fact, in all parts of the country the Gray Ghost has outlived his fanfare and settled down to the task of proving himself, and is succeeding in doing so on all fronts.

The Vizsla

This newest addition to the pointing breeds was brought to the United States in 1950 and in a relatively short time has proceeded to establish himself as a darned good bird dog and a fine family dog.

The Vizsla (pronounced Veesh'-la) comes from Hungary, where it was a nobleman's dog of the highest quality and was used basically for hunting birds on the great wheat plains which for centuries formed Central Europe's breadbasket. The breed is very old. Some say it was used by Magyar hunters with falcons to take small game a thousand years ago. Earliest written references, in the thirteenth century, mention a "Yellow Pointer" which was possibly the same dog, more likely an early form of it. During the 150 years of Turkish occupation of Hungary to 1686, the Vizsla is frequently mentioned in correspondence. By that time the term "Yellow Pointer" had been dropped and the currently accepted name of "Hungarian Vizsla" was in use.

We have no clues from what breeds or types of dog the Vizsla evolved. Any discussion of the dog invites comparison with the German Shorthair and the Weimaraner. In conformation he resembles the Shorthair only he's more refined, not so heavily chested or thickly muscled, neck a little longer, and head very similarly formed with prominent skull, moderately accentuated stop and straight muzzle that often has a slight arch on the bridge of the nose, as does the Shorthair's.

The main comparison to the Weimaraner comes in the coat. Though entirely different in color, gray versus golden rust, one could easily be a mutation of the other, or both could have come from the same source.

All this is guesswork, of course, but if I had to hazard an opinion I would certainly say that the Vizsla didn't have its origin from dogs brought to Europe by the Magyars or Huns. These peoples had unsettled cultures that never produced animals of high quality, whether it was horses, dogs, or whatever.

The Magyars and the Huns bred rough dogs like the Komondor and the Kuvasz, the former a roly-poly, moplike dog used for herding sheep, the latter a huge tough guard dog for nobility. The Vizsla on the other hand is a distinguished and beautiful animal. In my opinion he is the result of great thought and careful selectivity, whereas the Magyar and Hun dogs just sprang up and they show it.

We know that the dog was raised by noblemen just as the Weimaraner was. The Hapsburgs who ruled the Austro-Hungarian Empire were Germanic in their tastes, thinking and associations. Undoubtedly they knew the Gray Ghost of Weimar and they fancied a different-colored dog to be used for a slightly different purpose. Where the Weimaraner was originally a big-game dog and later became a bird dog, the Vizsla was probably always a bird dog first, on pheasant, partridge and quail, which abounded in the grain fields of Hungary, secondly an all-purpose dog for rabbits and fetching ducks from water.

We don't know what this early "Yellow Pointer" was, but not by the wildest stretch of my imagination can I call the Vizsla yellow. He is burnt gold or rust. It's conceivable that a Yellow Pointer existed at an early period in eastern Europe, and the noblemen, looking around for a distinctive color, crossed a red hound like the *Schweisshund* into him. A single glance at the Vizsla will tell it contains hound blood but in a much more refined way than the German dogs. Consequently it was probably not Bloodhound but a lighter, more active type of red hound.

Possession of the Vizsla was always limited to nobility, who gave the dog as a highly prized gift to their hunting cousins, consequently none fell into the hands of commercial breeders or the general public. As a result of such limited circulation and two world wars in this century the breed was almost wiped out. After World War I and the dissolution of the Austro-Hungarian Empire a few Vizslas appeared in Czechoslovakia, Austria and Rumania.

Ch. Ripp Barat, owned by Mrs. Betty Kenly, Phoenix, Arizona.

After World War II a couple pairs of Vizslas slipped out of Hungary into Vienna. It was the descendants of Czech and Austrian dogs that arrived in the United States first. Yugoslavia possesses some of the breed. Tito's private physician gave one as a gift to an American doctor friend. Some people claim there are a few in Turkey, although I never saw any in the two years I was there.

The Vizsla came to the United States in 1950 almost by accident. An American attached to our Rome legation sent a pair to a friend of his, an insurance salesman named Tallman in Kansas City, Missouri. When the dogs arrived, Mr. Tallman didn't know what he had and mistook them for Weimaraners. He telephoned Jack Baird, well-known dog authority in Poughkeepsie, New York, who referred him to a friend in Kansas City who identified the dogs.

A couple of weeks later Mr. Charles Hunt of Cottage Grove, Tennessee, a long-time Pointer and Setter man, saw the male dog, Rex, work beautifully on land and in water and became a convert immediately.

During the spring of 1951 Mr. Tallman created interest in the new breed by exhibiting his dogs at shows. Mr. W. A. Olsen and Mr. J. A. Hatfield, both of Minneapolis, arranged to import some puppies from Vienna. Meanwhile, Mr. Hunt and Dr. I. S. Osborn of Le Sueur, Minnesota, unbeknown to each other, both imported Vizslas from the same kennels in Czechoslova-

Two Vizsla puppies sight-pointing.

kia. Mr. Hunt teamed with a friend of his, Fritz Barthel of San Diego, whose wife was Hungarian and knew something of the breed.

In 1954 the Vizsla Club of America was formed with seventeen members, Dr. Osborn as president and Mr. Hunt as secretary-treasurer. That same year the dog was accepted for registration by the Field Dog Stud Book. The American Kennel Club recognized it in 1960.

Dr. Osborn's Rex Selle was the first Vizsla champion in the United States. Peter von Chinook, owned by Mrs. Paul F. Stewart of San Francisco, was also an early champion.

Probably the most outstanding Vizsla to appear in this country to date is Ripp Barat, owned by Mrs. Betty Kenly of Phoenix, Arizona. Ripp has won the National Vizsla Championship three years running, 1960–61–62. He has also competed in open stakes and won consistently against all breeds. The dog went to the Canadian prairies for three summers, where professional trainers of Pointers and Setters still go to break their young dogs and finish the older ones. Each year trainers from all parts of the United States make a pilgrimage to the "Big Country" of Manitoba and Saskatchewan, last frontier of the sharp-tailed grouse, better known as the prairie chicken. Each trainer leases ten to twenty sections of prairie land from the Canadian Government (one section contains 640 acres) and in three months, July, August and September, they can change a raw recruit into a hunting and pointing genius if he has what it takes. Most of our finest field-trial dogs are broken here, a typical example being Ripp Barat, who was under the developing hand of Illinois trainer Paul Sabo, himself a Hungarian and lover of the Vizsla. Most of the time Mrs. Kenly handles Ripp herself, and campaigning him has taken her to most of the West Coast and Midwestern states. In 1962 Ripp Barat was named runner-up in the Pacific Coast Championship for German Pointing Dogs, missing the title by a whisker.

Vizslas have established themselves as particularly sound hunting dogs wherever they have appeared in field-trial competition. They have done it by merit, not by fanfare. They compete on a limited scale in their own trials, but because the dog is not yet numerous Vizslas run mainly in open trials against German Shorthairs, *Drahthaars* and Weimaraners and they've won their share or more of placements. Originally puppies were high-priced, but more extensive breeding has brought the price down to $75–150, that of the average good puppy of any breed.

As a field dog the Vizsla is finding a wide following in the Midwest, Southwest and Far West. Slowly he is working his way eastward. The dog hunts at comfortable foot-shooting range, up to 150 yards. He is light-footed, moves with grace, speed and application. He's a crackerjack on all types of upland game—pheasant, quail, grouse—and makes an excellent water dog for retrieving ducks in moderate climates.

Personalitywise the Vizsla is lively, gentle-mannered and demonstratively affectionate, makes a loyal family pet, the male being fearless and definitely on the protective side. The dog is a highly intelligent and sensitive animal, trains easily without extreme pressure and has a lot of "point" in him. Though medium-sized and lightly built, the Vizsla is robust and sporty to look at with his tail docked to one third its length and his striking color. The standard describes it as always solid and "rusty gold or rather dark sandy yellow in different shades, with darker shades preferred. Dark brown and pale yellow are undesirable. Small white spots on chest or feet are not faulted."

Males stand 22 to 24 inches at the withers and weight 45 to 60 pounds; bitches, 21 to 23 inches shoulder height, 40 to 55 pounds in weight.

The dog has an aristocratic bearing about him. Because of this and his attractive coloring as well as his excellent disposition, he is developing a following in the show ring which will certainly increase as time goes by.

Vizsla—the golden Pointer! He has established himself well in his new home.

Chapter 3

The Flushing Breeds

As the hunter crosses the field, the little stub-tailed dog scurries back and forth ahead of him like a windshield wiper, sweeping 35 yards to one side, turning and sweeping across the front to 35 yards on the opposite side, then back again. In the thick goldenrod the dog cannot be seen, but his path is easily followed by the swaying stems. He scampers back into the open, darts through a blackberry thicket, skirts the edge of a swamp, the hunter eyeing him carefully.

Suddenly his stub tail begins to flutter with excitement. He dives into the swamp bogs, breathlessly trailing. The hunter hurries forward, snaps the safety off his gun. An instant later a big cock pheasant comes boiling out of the thicket, cackling his displeasure at being flushed. The hunter fires, drops the bird on the far side of the swamp. The dog, sitting on his haunches from the moment the bird flew, has marked the fall. At the command of "Fetch!" he bounces off joyously and brings the heavy bird in safely to his master's waiting hand.

Such are the actions of the flushing breeds, better known as spaniels, of which several varieties exist—the Clumber, the Cocker (American and English types), the Field Spaniel, the English Springer, the Welsh Springer, the Sussex Spaniel, the American Water Spaniel, and an American newcomer, the Boykin Spaniel. Of these spaniels, far and away the most popular for hunting are the English Springer, the Cocker and the Boykin. The Springer outnumbers the Cocker about four to one in field trials and for general hunting, although as a house pet no purebred dog is more loved or popular than the Cocker with his contagiously good-natured disposition. The Boykin Spaniel, native of the southeastern United States, where he is used for hunting wild turkeys, retrieving ducks and doves, is strictly a hunting dog, about forty years old as a breed and unrecognized to date by any registry. But we shall include him here because he is a hunting dog on the American scene and may some day become a blueblood.

Spaniels are among the oldest varieties of dog on record, dating back more than 600 years to Chaucer's time. In 1340 the celebrated English medieval poet wrote in the Prologue to the *Wife of Bath's Tale*, "For as a

Spanyel whe wol on him lepe." The effervescent disposition was part of the dog even then.

A few years later in 1387 Gaston de Foix, a French count vitally interested in all kinds of hunting dogs and, reportedly, owner of more than a thousand at one time, wrote of the devotion of spaniels to their masters, their merry tails and ability to find and flush partridge.

He also described as faults their being fighters and great barkers who often led the Greyhounds astray. The count lived near Spain, the country we suspect to be the origin of the spaniel. I say suspect because there is no proof beyond implication of name. Some claim that Caesar brought spaniels to the British Isles in 55 B.C. when he invaded. The word "spaniel" derives from the Roman or Latin word *Hispania,* meaning Spain. Dr. John Caius, Cambridge University professor who wrote a most scholarly and authoritative treatise on all English dogs about 1575, stated that the name came from *Hispaniolus,* but it might also have come from the French *Chiens de l'Espagnol,* meaning "Dog of Spain." Because of this connection between the word spaniel and Spain, the generally accepted theory is that the Spanish, outstanding in all aspects of animal husbandry in the twelfth, thirteenth, fourteenth and fifteenth centuries, either created the dog themselves, possibly from a European hound and herd-dog cross, or else developed it from animals brought in by the Moorish invasion in the eighth century. Ancient Egyptian tombs have revealed models of dogs with almost identical conformation, nevertheless Spain still seems to be the land of their origin.

Though the spaniel appeared in almost every part of Europe, England has been considered its home for the last three centuries. Here the family was developed into the many variations we now have. Every spaniel breed recognized in the United States today but one (the Brittany, a Pointer from France) comes from the British Isles. Throughout English history there is constant mention of the spaniel. Shakespeare refers to him frequently and Henry VIII had a special Spaniel Keeper. In fact, a Cocker Spaniel may have changed the entire religious life of England. Henry VIII wanted a divorce and sent Lord Wiltshire to Rome to obtain the Pope's permission. Lord Wiltshire took his pet spaniel with him. When Wiltshire knelt to kiss His Holiness's toe, the Pope extended his foot as a convenience, but the spaniel mistook the gesture as an attempt to kick his master in the face. He leaped forward and bit the toe. After the riotous scene which followed, Lord Wiltshire left Rome in haste. When Henry VIII could not obtain his divorce he disassociated himself and England from the Catholic Church.

By the end of the sixteenth century the spaniel family had branched into the water and land varieties. In the water group was the English

Water Spaniel, now extinct though a heavy contributor to the modern retriever, and the Irish Water Spaniel, so similar to the Poodle.

Dr. Caius, the Cambridge professor, divided the land spaniels into two groups—setting spaniels, which crept forward and pointed their game so a net could be used, and springing spaniels, which sprang pheasants and partridges for the falcons and rabbits for the coursing Greyhounds. The former developed into our contemporary English Setter and from the latter came all our modern-day flushing spaniels.

With the development of the shotgun, and consequently the rise of wing shooting after 1700, various-sized spaniels were used for different types of hunting. Where they were all called springing spaniels before, now the larger ones were called Springers and the smaller ones Cockers because they were used primarily for woodcock. Size alone was the difference and often both appeared in the same litter.

Also from the smaller size emerged the Sussex Spaniel, the Field Spaniel and the English Toy Spaniels like the King Charles and the Blenheim varieties which were bred as "comforter dogges" for the ladies of the English court to hold in their laps and keep their hands warm in the winter.

A spaniel and a Mastiff were the first two dogs brought by the English to America, on the Mayflower in 1620. In the early days game was so abundant that a spaniel darting about at close range and springing everything before it was a most effective dog. Even market hunters used them because they were fine retrievers on both crippled and dead game, required little training and were very very biddable by nature. As game grew scarce in the Northeast and great sections of the South were opened up, the pointing breeds came into better use. They covered more ground and with the pointing dog the gunner could station himself before flush so as to be better prepared. The spaniel all but disappeared from the American hunting scene by 1850, though it was crossed into other breeds like the American Water Spaniel.

In the 1880s the Cocker began the groundwork for his meteoric rise as a show dog. The very first spaniel registered in America was a liver-and-white Cocker named Captain in 1879 by the National American Kennel Club, the present-day American Kennel Club.

Shortly after 1900 rich Americans living around New York took a fancy to pheasant hunting with English Springer Spaniels, as done by the wealthy of the British Isles. Scottish gamekeepers with strings of Springers were imported to the large private shooting preserves and estates on Fishers Island, Long Island and elsewhere. Thousands of wild and semiwild pheasants were maintained for the pleasure and sport of owners of these "game estates."

As naturally happened, the sport of shooting pheasants was not enough.

Spaniel was pitted against spaniel, Springer and Cocker too, and soon field trials developed along the pattern established around the turn of the century by the English. The first American spaniel trials were held in 1924 on Fishers Island and Verbank, New York, on native birds in natural cover. Gradually, with the passing of the great estates where the trials were first held, the system of planting birds on a course ahead of the working dogs was devised. Though the technique was artificial, spaniel trials have spread across the country since that time.

But the spaniel is at his best as a hunter with his master gunning over him. From the hayfields and weed patches of New York, New Jersey and Pennsylvania to the brome grass of Illinois and Ohio, from the cornfields of the Dakotas to the rice stubble of California the spaniel provides the finest sporting hunting there is. Perhaps this sounds like a bold statement, but the spaniel flushes his game, thus the hunter is never as completely prepared as he is with a pointing dog, and the bird has an even chance of escape. Spaniels are not quail dogs but they are superb on pheasant and woodcock; even on grouse they are hard to beat.

I think the reason they aren't used more widely for upland gunning is because it takes a crack shot to bring home much meat with a spaniel. You've got to be quick and handy with a gun. You're walking along in a field or swamp and all of a sudden Brrr-p-p-p! There goes a bird. You must keep an eye on the dog and have quick reflexes to boot, but this is what makes spaniels the sporting dogs they are!

Their training is simpler than that of a pointing dog. The principal requirement is that he flush his game within gunshot. Thus he must quarter at 25 to 35 yards to the sides and forward. His tail is his signal that he has struck game. Once that begins to buzz, look out!

Spaniels are great cover dogs. They plunge into thickets, bustle through swamps, are undaunted by briars.

Spaniels are great natural retrievers. Because they are proficient on land and water they double ideally for the man who hunts pheasant and woodcock, then takes on a few ducks.

Spaniels are great family dogs—lovable, obedient, frolicking, always responsive to affection, great stealers of human hearts.

The Clumber Spaniel

In size the Clumber is the biggest of all Spaniels and also the slowest, although the first Spaniel Field Champion of record in England was of this breed. In those early days the Clumber dominated field-trial competition, probably because, being slow, he was easier to handle, hence more mannerly.

The Clumber is not of English origin. He came from France about 1760 as a gift from the Duke of Noailles to the Duke of Newcastle, who lived at Clumber House, Nottinghamshire. The dog, built long and low, may be the result of a Basset Hound cross with the old Alpine Spaniel. His head is heavy and well hawed like a St. Bernard. Though he was crossed with other varieties of spaniels he still retains his length and size.

The Clumber has often been referred to as the "retired gentleman's shooting dog," and if there is such a thing, he is it. His popularity in England from 1850 to 1910 was chiefly among the retired military men and civil servants living in cities. A comfortable house dog, the Clumber could be taken to small vegetable gardens surrounding cities for a bit of shooting. The retired gentleman sat on his walking stick while the heavy spaniel poked about among the turnip and potato patches for game and he would retrieve anything that was shot.

The dog has never been popular for hunting here in America because of his slowness, although some were used in the East and Midwest during the 1930s. Though cumbersome, the Clumber is impressive and dignified in appearance, possesses a sure nose and is a reliable retriever. He is usually almost solid white except for a few lemon markings about the head and once in a while on the body. He stands 17 to 18 inches tall and weighs up to 65 pounds.

Today the Clumber is a rare bird, seen occasionally at the larger bench shows. But he still has his natural hunting instincts and those who own him often use him to gun over. Perhaps as our population grows more dense and the demand for a more thorough and methodical hunting spaniel increases, the Clumber will draw more followers.

Clumber Spaniel.

The Cocker Spaniel (American and English)

The smallest of the sporting dogs, with floppy ears, large, soulful eyes and joyful disposition that always responds to affection, the Cocker Spaniel is one of the most lovable and popular dogs on earth. In fact, because of all these qualities, the vital little Cocker has been taken over primarily as a house pet and show dog to the vast neglect of his hunting prowess, which was originally his reason for being.

Certainly his beauty and disposition and convenient size all militate in favor of his present uses. Children love him as a playmate and at a bench show he is one of the most beautiful little dogs ever developed by man. In the old days when he was a bird dog, bouncing across fields, charging into thickets, scampering through swamps in true spaniel style, such was his proficiency at pushing woodcock and snipe into flight that he gained the name of Woodcock Spaniel, then Cocking Spaniel, finally Cocker Spaniel, the name by which he is known the world over today.

In the early development of the English land spaniel from which our flushing breeds now descend, a litter of puppies was liable to include dogs of two or three different sizes. The larger ones were called Springers and

National Field Trial Ch. Berol Lodge Glen Garry, an immortal field Cocker owned by Henry Berol of Chappaqua, N.Y.

used for partridge and pheasant shooting; the smaller ones were called 'Cockers and used for woodcock hunting; the long-bodied ones were called Sussex Spaniels and were favored by those hunters who wanted a slower, more methodical working dog.

The early spaniel classes at bench shows in England were marked by confusion and arguments because of the lack of distinction between the emerging breeds. Springer puppies were often shown as Cockers one year, then as Springers the next year when they grew up. By 1883 special classes were provided for the Cocker at English shows; in 1892 he was recognized as a separate breed by the English Kennel Club and much of the confusion cleared up.

The modern Cocker Spaniel is generally considered to have started with Obo, whelped in England in 1879, weighing 22 pounds and standing 10 inches high. Obo produced many fine dogs which were sent to Canada and the United States, especially Obo II, often called the father of the American Cocker because just about every winning show Cocker today traces back to him. Other great early names were Rivington Signal, Rivington Red Coat, Rivington Blue Gown and Rivington Sam.

The Cocker Spaniel took a different course in America from the one it took in England. Here he was bred for the bench show and as a house pet; in England his hunting proficiency was maintained at no sacrifice to the show ring. As the American variety became smaller and more beautiful, the English version grew rangier and stronger. Today the difference is so pronounced that they are two separate breeds at shows, though in field trials they compete in the same events in the exact same manner, hence we have classified both groups together in this analysis.

For the sake of comparison, the Cocker Spaniel (this is the official name for the American type) weighs between 22 and 28 pounds, has a maximum height of 15½ inches for males, 14½ inches for bitches, while the English Cocker Spaniel (official name) weighs 28 to 34 pounds with a 17-inch maximum height for males, 16 for bitches. The American type is the gorgeous animal. He has a pronounced stop, rounded skull, large, prominent eyes and long ears. His chest is broad and his body covered with a profuse coat and long feathering. Both American and English Cockers come most often in black although other self colors (solid) like buff or red appear and parti-colors are very frequent, especially in field breeding.

The English Cocker resembles a small Springer more than the American type, which is a distinctive showpiece. Both have the merry spaniel disposition, but in recent years the American show Cocker, from too much inbreeding, developed shyness and hysteria to a serious degree. This did not appear to any extent in the field-trial bloodlines because such dogs are valueless afield and are immediately destroyed regardless of their looks. Cockers by nature are mild dogs that cannot take much pressure or hard training, but they must have a certain amount of boldness and initiative and hunting desire to make them serviceable in the field.

The first field trial for Cockers was held in 1899 in England, after which such competitions grew in size and popularity.

Spaniel trials came into vogue in the United States during the 1920s and the first championship was held at Verbank, New York, in 1924 under the auspices of the Cocker Spaniel Field Trial Club of America. Cocker trials prospered, thanks to the efforts of Ralph Craig, Elias Vail, a great field-dog trainer, Herman Mellenthin, one of the foremost Cocker breeders in history, Leonard Buck, Colonel H. S. Nielson and Ella B. Moffitt, about the first American woman to espouse the cause of field-trial spaniels. Ch. My Own High Time from Mr. Mellenthin's kennels was the first dual champion, but soon there were Miller's Esquire, Rowcliffe Hill Billy and others. Today dual champions among Cocker Spaniels are unheard of because once again the bench-show people breed for something entirely different from the field people.

For many years now American Cockers have not been crossed with English Cockers, as frequently occurred at one time. It took many years of researching pedigrees during the 1930s by Mrs. Geraldine R. Dodge and the English Cocker Spaniel Club of America to establish the latter breed so it could be recognized by AKC in 1946.

The field Cockers we have today are a far cry from only a few years ago. They have improved tremendously. They are peppery little fellows, zipping here, bouncing there, with stout hearts and a keen desire to hunt. Not enough people use them to gun over. A field Cocker is a dandy little dog. I think the trouble is that most people expect too much of him. He's a light dog, consequently can't pound the brush and heavy cover all day, and too often Cocker owners fail to condition their dogs well enough, if at all. Considering their size, Cockers are best hunted in pairs. In this manner two hunters can have some fine shooting at a reasonable pace. Cockers are particularly effective for the jump hunter—that is, the hunter who has limited time and goes by car to several different spots like swamps for pheasants or a special grouse cover—and of course they are great in a flight of woodcock. This is their true forte because they work thoroughly.

Rabbits can be shot over a Cocker but it isn't advisable because he may develop the habit of taking off after one when in the middle of a retrieve. He will retrieve almost anything naturally, although I wouldn't advise using him as a water retriever. In a field trial he has to retrieve from water but that doesn't mean he's adequate for duck shooting. The dog is just too small, although his heart is big enough, to haul in cripples under other than simple conditions. He is primarily a land retriever and even the big four-pound game-preserve pheasants are a load for him.

If you want a Cocker for hunting, I strongly advocate your obtaining field-trial bloodlines, not show stock regardless of the sales pitch. Good hunting Cockers come from pet-shop breeding once in a while, but your best bet is with proven field-trial blood. Such a dog will make a fine house pet for the wife and kids, yet still be able to go out and do his duty in the field if you take the trouble to develop him.

As always happens in competition, whether it be field or show, the losers

The Cocker is a good calm water retriever.

begin searching around for something to win with. In the case of the Cocker Spaniel trials it was the English Cocker, which had been maintained far better for field work than the American Cocker. Shortly before and ever since World War II, English Cockers were imported extensively to the United States to compete in field trials and they soon dominated the scene. Rivalry between the two groups has always been keen, but it took a lot of doing by die-hards before the American Cocker was brought up to the quality of his English brother. People like Mr. and Mrs. Henry Berol, the Garvins' Dungarvan Kennels, Mr. and Mrs. Charles Greening, Mr. and Mrs. Dean Bedford and the Winslows went to no end and effort to refurbish and maintain the Cocker Spaniel as a hunting dog in our country.

The East has always been the hotbed of Cocker activity, although in recent years the Midwest and Far West have begun to participate more actively. Many women handle Cockers in field trials. These joyful little fellows work well for them. The 1962 National Champ, Ru-Char's High Jinks, was handled to his big title by owner-handler Mrs. Ruth Greening.

The annual Cocker Spaniel National Championship, held usually in Ringoes, New Jersey, attracts around twenty dogs handled by both professionals and amateurs. Clark Gable's Camino's Red Rocket, an English Cocker, won the title in 1958. The trial consists generally of five land series and two water retrieves. The Cocker Spaniel, as stated earlier, is required to have the proficiency of fetching from water or carrying a dead bird across water, if the necessity arises, while hunting afield.

One of the greatest spaniel stories in the past few years—of all time, for that matter—concerns a little buff Cocker named Prince Tom, bought for twenty-five dollars as a birthday present for Tom Clute, a jukebox salesman in Adrian, Michigan. The dog seemed bright, was registered but had no champions of any kind or shape on his pedigree. At first Clute began teaching his dog parlor tricks—how to shake hands, roll over, hold a cigarette and holder in his mouth. The pair tried their luck in obedience classes at dog shows from knowledge Clute had gained reading books on the subject. Soon the little buff Cocker had bested Shepherds, Poodles, Collies and all the other canine bright boys to win his CD (companion dog), CDX (companion dog excellent) and UD (utility dog) titles.

One day Clute met a hunting friend who liked his little pepper pot of a dog and suggested that perhaps he could be trained for field work. Clute had never hunted in his life or even heard of a field trial, but he began reading up on the subject and training his dog. By all accepted rules, obedience work ruins a Cocker for field trials because the early discipline suppresses most of the resourceful qualities and initiative, but field work lighted a fire in Prince Tom. The little dog, born a dynamic ball of nervous energy, quickly found a wild joy in hunting, swimming, retrieving. As it turned out, obedience was the only way Clute could have trained his dog.

While making jukebox calls, Clute carried a basket of pigeons around in the back of his car. Whenever he and his dog passed a nice-looking field on the way home, Clute would jump out and plant a pigeon and train his spaniel a little. A good-looking swamp or weed field was also worked and the Cocker soon learned to bounce up pheasant and quail adroitly. When he made a mistake, like chasing, Clute could stop him cold from his obedience training. Gradually the field-trial manners sunk in as the little spaniel's desire and joy for hunting grew.

Clute sent the dog to a professional trainer for finishing and after that Prince Tom began to win field trials throughout the Midwest. He qualified for the Cocker National Championship in New Jersey and Clute was undecided about going for the big one until his mother talked him into it, then she went along to see the little dog run.

Arriving at the trial, Clute realized he was in mighty high cotton and up against the most skillful professional handlers in the country. Cocker Spaniel field-trial people generally don't suffer from the lack of money and they hire the best dog men available to win. Clute suddenly saw the odds he was facing. No American Cocker Spaniel had ever won the National, no amateur handler had ever won the National, no Midwesterner had ever won it. The Cocker stronghold in the United States is the New York-Connecticut-New Jersey area and the Bucks County region of Pennsylvania. Clute was facing the best of it right now.

In the first series Tom was braced with the great champion, Berol Lodge Glen Garry. On the very first bird which had Garry flushing and Tom sitting to honor, Garry took off like a fire ball and ran smack into a tree, dazing himself. Meanwhile the shot pheasant had come down not more than five feet from where Tom was holding. The wounded bird kicked

Especially good on woodcock, the Cocker can handle pheasants adroitly too.

and flopped at Tom's feet while Garry staggered around, unable to grasp the bird. Tom shuddered, trembled, whined—but held fast. One move and he would have been disqualified.

Such incidents are the supreme test of training versus desire. In spaniel field trials the dog must remain under complete control of the handler, yet exhibit constant desire, zest and enthusiasm to do his job. It's a mighty thin line, which often stretches the emotions to a near-breaking point.

At the end of each series the judges announce the dogs they wish called back for the next test. The first day completed and half the trial over, Clute and Tom were the only amateur entry remaining. If they went the rest of the way conservatively he would win the coveted Amateur title. But Clute's mother, who had talked him into coming, now told him to go for all the marbles with a vengeance.

One Cocker after another was knocked out through the second day. Late in the afternoon as the final series came up, a water test, only two dogs remained, Greatford Meadowcourt Pin, a snappy English Cocker import, and Tom.

The large gallery surged tensely to the edge of a pond to see who would win.

The first duck went to Pin. The crowd grew silent. The handler nodded his readiness. The judge waved a signal. Far across the water the bird was flown from a boat and shot. It fell with a splash and Pin was ordered to fetch it. He dashed to the water, hesitated, looked at his handler, then ran back and forth along the edge, summoning up the courage to jump in. His handler ordered him the second time to fetch and he dove in to complete an excellent retrieve.

Now it was Tom's turn. The duck was flown and shot, and plummeted to the water. The little buff Cocker was keyed up beyond belief. He whined and trembled on line, on the verge of breaking, but Clute could not send him without permission. Finally the judge nodded and Clute said, "Go, Tom."

Everyone in the huge semicircle behind the dogs, handlers, and judges held his breath.

The little dog shot off like a cannon ball toward the water. At the edge he sprang up and out, hurling himself fifteen feet across the water before splashing in and swimming for his duck. The gallery let out an unrestrained roar and the rest is history.

I tell this rather long story not only to give some insight into the thrills of field trials in general and Cockers in particular but because several of my pet beliefs are substantiated.

First, *anybody* with patience, persistence and enough know-how can train his own dog. Whenever you get stuck, a dog man, even a professional, will help you.

Second, if the owner happens upon a good one and applies his training thoroughly he can take the dog right to the top, because all his efforts are applied to one animal and because he will take the time to do certain things that professionals just can't do when they have a big string.

Third, the lively, animated rogue is the hardest to train but the best in the end, so if you get one, don't give up on him. I venture to guess that there are hundreds of dogs of all breeds that are house pets, yet could have won championships if they'd had the chance.

In any case, the Cocker Spaniel of field bloodlines is a stouthearted little dog that has made a great comeback. Don't expect everything of him, but pound for pound he'll give you more than your money's worth. He certainly deserves to see more use among hunters who look for a real sporting dog afield and a loyal, joyful companion at home.

The Field Spaniel

The origins of the Field Spaniel trace back to the old land spaniel which appeared throughout England in the fifteenth, sixteenth and seventeenth centuries. Later, as various breeds within the spaniel family began to emerge—the Cocker, the Sussex, etc.—the Field Spaniel was an early name given to the Springer. The Springer gradually became a liver-and-white or black-and-white dog, and this left a lot of spaniels of the same size or a shade smaller floating around with no classification. Most of these were solid-colored dogs, particularly black, and they soon came to be called Field Spaniels.

Unfortunately a small group headed by Mr. Phineas Bullock, who raised Sussex Spaniels, began crossing Sussex and Cocker blood into the Field Spaniel with the aim of producing a "distinctive" spaniel. What they came off with was a dog of tremendously long body, very low to the ground and with abnormally heavy bone structure—a silly caricature of a spaniel. Later Mr. Mortimer Smith went to great effort to improve the breed and succeeded in developing a well-balanced, practical and handsome sporting spaniel.

Probably the spaniel which came over on the Mayflower was a forerunner of our contemporary Field Spaniel. This same early blood supplied the numerous spaniels that hunted here in America before the pointing breeds came into vogue after the Civil War. Our own land spaniel disappeared before the onslaught of "pedigreed" blood, but not before he left his mark in many of our breeds here.

The modern Field Spaniel is used occasionally for hunting in the United States, but his popularity is nothing compared with Springers and Cockers. He is generally about 18 inches in height, weighs 35 to 50 pounds, has plenty of speed, endurance and nose but is not as attractive in appearance as the Cocker or Springer. Generally he is black in color but can be liver, golden liver, mahogany-red or roan. Parti-colors like black and white, liver and white, orange and white are frowned upon because this makes him too similar to the Springer.

The Field Spaniel has plenty of intelligence as well as hunting and retrieving ability. Probably the two reasons he hasn't gone farther in this country are because he hasn't the "prettiness" of the Cocker and Springer, and he has no national organization behind him to promote his interests. This last point may sound silly but national clubs have become the backbone of every breed. Publicity is disseminated, a monthly magazine published in which breeders have a place to advertise, show and field-trial winners are reported, breed standards discussed. All are vastly important.

Despite his lack of an organization, the Field Spaniel remains a sound dog, deserving of wider use.

Sussex Spaniel.

The Sussex Spaniel

Deriving his name from that part of England where he was first bred and developed, the Sussex Spaniel is a long-bodied, short-legged dog with plenty of strength but not much speed. The breed was developed by Mr. Fuller of Brightling, who possessed the first and most important kennel of Sussex Spaniels. Later, Mr. Phineas Bullock, also of Field Spaniel fame, did considerable work with the Sussex.

The reason for the dog's slowness is his long torso, similar to the Clumber and on the Basset Hound proportions. He has a beautiful golden-liver coat that makes him an attractive dog; consequently he has avid followers in the show ring. Height is 17 to 18 inches, weight from 35 to 45 pounds. The dog is a conscientious worker and generally has a most pleasant disposition. He often gives tongue (barks like a hound) on scent when afield, this trait undoubtedly belying some elements of his past.

The dog loves to hunt, is easily trained and makes an accomplished retriever, but here in America the game is a bit too far apart for such a slow-working spaniel, hence he has never been popular in the field.

The Welsh Springer Spaniel

Undoubtedly one of the oldest, if not the oldest, member of the spaniel family is the Welsh Springer. He dates back to medieval times when very possibly hardy Welsh sailors may have brought him home from Spain or from the Continent. His first mention is in the Ancient Laws of Wales codified by Hywel Dda 1000 years ago.

The red-and-white Welsh Springer, a shade smaller in size than the English Springer yet larger than the Cocker, is consistently shown in old prints and described in writings as one of the best hunting and shooting dogs ever produced in the British Isles. Certainly he played a prominent role in the development of the Brittany Spaniel, perhaps also in the English Setter, Welsh Setter and in all the modern spaniels of England.

A tough, stouthearted fellow by nature, the Welsh Springer is a hard-working, willing hunter, regardless of the cover or weather conditions. He has successfully been shipped to many countries of the world, both tropical and temperate climates because he can withstand the extremes of heat and cold. His naturally flat coat with a soft undercoat provides excellent protection in thick cover and water. Possessed of a superior nose and endurance, he is also a first-rate retriever. Often though, if not trained early in life, he becomes a self-hunter and consequently hard to handle. Thus the training rules are broken in his case and he is best taught obedience and retrieving before his field work. One nice thing about him is that he has a strong temperament, which allows him to take training better than most spaniels. No cowering softness here, only vigorous desire. As a family dog he is of handy size, gentle around children and a good watchdog too.

The Welsh Springer has seen far too limited use in the United States, mainly because, like the Field Spaniel, he lacked a national organization behind him. He was a favorite of the late Theodore Sturgis for upland game hunting in New England. Also the late Hobart Ames, famous president of the National Field Trial Championship Association, loved the Welsh Springer as a retriever to work with pointing dogs.

Since World War II several have been imported, and in 1960 a club was formed. To date most of the activity has centered around the show ring, but several owners are using their dogs most successfully to gun over, so they may yet catch on in this country.

As we stated earlier, the Welsh Springer Spaniel is always red and white in color. His height runs up to 19 inches, weight up to 45 pounds. Obviously built for endurance, he has a strong, compact appearance. A real sporting dog that, like the Welsh mountain pony, is vigorously healthy through centuries of rugged living.

This may seem like a lot of praise for a rather obscure dog, but if you ever hunt over one or own one, chances are you'll shout far louder.

Welsh Springer Spaniel.

The American Water Spaniel

This hustling, hunting little brown dog, boon companion of old-time hunters and as American as huckleberry pie, has been earning his keep in the United States for well over a hundred years now. In the early days, around 1875, he was called simply the Water Spaniel and most hunters who hunted ducks or birds in the Middle West had one or had a buddy who did.

Applejack legend has it that Christopher Columbus originally brought the dog to this country. That's not so, although we don't know the dog's true history. Before the Civil War many people began to move into the West, which was then Illinois, Ohio, Missouri, Iowa—an area in which game of all kinds abounded. In those days settlers valued a dog that could put meat on the table, and the Water Spaniel did just that. He sprang rabbits, flushed quail and partridge, fetched ducks and geese from water. He was the nearest thing to an all-around dog this country has ever produced—

small enough so he didn't eat much or take up much room, friendly enough to be a house pet, clever enough to do anything connected with light hunting.

We don't know what blood formed him, probably the now extinct English Water Spaniel which, along with hounds, was one of the earliest dogs brought to the American colonies. Many believe the Irish Water Spaniel and the Curly-Coated Retriever were used because their coats so closely resemble the American Water Spaniel of today. If so, the crosses were made at a later date, possibly in the 1860s to the 1880s, and what scanty records we have on the American Water Spaniel tell us he was breeding pretty much true to type by 1865. His small stature tends to belie such a cross, although he has more of a retriever head than a spaniel head.

The Water Spaniel saw widespread use in the United States up to 1900, especially in the Middle West. After that time the specialists began to arrive, and shooting habits changed from the fire-at-whatever-you-see kind to hunting a particular type of game. Retrievers handled ducks and geese; Pointers and Setters worked quail and other upland birds. Soon came the flushing spaniels and the European pointing breeds, all pushing our native Water Spaniel farther into the background.

Several attempts were made to organize a club for the dog, the first successful one finally appearing in 1937 and called the American Water Spaniel Club. In 1939 the breed was accepted for registration by the Field Dog Stud Book and in 1940 by the American Kennel Club.

At first glance you might think the dog a small retriever instead of a spaniel. Actually, he's in between and is equally at home on land or in water, but he was classified as a spaniel mainly because of his size. On land he works in the spaniel manner, flushing pheasants to the gun, marking the falls, then retrieving. But some people teach him to point and hold quail rather than spring them. In his early training, the dog tends to stop as he closes in on hot game scent and he can be easily encouraged to stand still until the gunner moves up and flushes the quail himself, thereby providing better shooting. For pheasants it is a simple matter to urge him on to spring them, same with grouse and rabbits.

In water he works just like a retriever, handles himself better than any of the other spaniel breeds, loves to ride the prow of a skiff through marshes, fetching in mallards, teal, pintails, whatever such sneak hunting produces. In a duck blind along a river or in a wheat field, where the birds will settle to feed, he blends in perfectly with the surroundings, learns almost immediately to sit still at the approach of birds and has great ability at marking falls. The little fellow is a highly intelligent and skillful dog with a flypaper memory. Hence he adapts easily to a variety of situations. Though game as any retriever alive, he is a little light for

American Water Spaniel.

rough coastal waters, and this is probably the reason he was developed as an inland dog and has so remained.

In appearance the American Water Spaniel is medium-sized, standing 15 to 18 inches at the shoulder, not too compactly built—that is, his body has a little length to it but is well developed and sturdy with strong loins and well-sprung ribs. His head, quite broad and full like a retriever's, does not have the pronounced stop of any of the spaniel family and never a snippy nose. He does have spaniel ears, on the wide, pendulous side and covered with curls. Eyes should be hazel or dark brown, never yellow which is a disqualifying point in the show ring.

The coat is the outstanding feature of this dog. It's solid liver in color with a closely curled wave that is dense and thick enough to protect the dog in water and all types of cover. In fact the whole dog from his ears to the tip of his tail is one gleaming chocolate-colored marcel wave after another, so perfect that a woman swoons in envy. Legs and tail have medium to short curly feather, the tail is full-length and never ratlike like the Irish Water Spaniel's, although both dogs have shorthaired faces. A little white on the toes or chest is permitted. Males weigh 28 to 45 pounds, females 25 to 40 pounds.

Their temperaments are typically spaniel, the dogs being gay and lively in manner and action. They make wonderful pets around children and in the home, learn quickly and are always anxious to please.

Among those who have championed the cause of the American Water Spaniel have been Driscoll Scanlon, first president of the American Water Spaniel Club in 1937, John Scofield, secretary-treasurer of the club, Carl Hinz of Milwaukee, Louis Smith of Holliston, Massachusetts, John Sherlock of Kenmore, New York, and Thomad Brogden and Paul Bovee, both of Wisconsin.

The breed has appeared in the show ring in fair numbers, and several champions have been crowned, but I have never seen one at a field trial or heard of one so competing. This accounts in part for the breed's being so slightly known. If a dog can win a few field-trial placements he soon has the public looking at him and develops a following in time.

As far as I'm concerned, the American Water Spaniel is one of the most overlooked dogs on the American hunting scene. He's ideal for the man who wants everything a spaniel can do on land plus more powerful water work but doesn't want as much dog as a retriever. Why the breed has not become more popular in recent years is one of those unexplainable things. But then popularity among dogs is a social phenomenon that has always puzzled me. I guess it is composed of beauty, timing, publicity, snob appeal and sometimes ability. If this last means anything, some day the American Water Spaniel will gain his just recognition. Meanwhile I recommend him highly for inland water work and upland game hunting of all kinds.

The Boykin Spaniel

Ask any duck or dove hunter along the coast or inland low country of North and South Carolina, Georgia or northern Florida what a Boykin Spaniel is and he'll shift his wad of chaw, spit a string at a lazy hound and say, "Best damn retriever they ever was!"

If he has one to show you, it'll be a cocky little fellow, full of bounce and energy, deep liver in color with a wavy or curly coat and a docked tail. It'll have the spaniel "look" in body but a touch of retriever in the head. To prove his point, your friend will insist you go with him to a nearby pond, whereupon he will throw a stick as hard and far as he can. The little dog will tear into the water gleefully and fetch it.

In fact, there's a story about a fellow who trained his Boykin to fetch a silver dollar no matter where he scaled it—out into the mule pasture or over into the cornfield or right clean across the river into the honeysuckle thicket. One day, while demonstrating his trick, the man threw the coin into some woods and a boy passing by saw it fall and grabbed it, but that didn't stop the Boykin. He retrieved the boy. That's how he got his name!

The above is told only around big fireplaces in hunting lodges after the white lightning's been flowing for a while, but in case you've never heard of the Boykin Spaniel, it's an unrecognized breed indigenous to the southeastern section of the United States. We include it here for two reasons. First, it's a darn good dog—fine natural retriever; secondly, some day it will probably be recognized as a breed.

How did the Boykin really come into being?

It seems that about forty years ago a raunchy brown pup wandered into a Spartanburg, South Carolina, church during the Sunday service. He was deposited outside and afterward Mr. A. L. White took him home out of sympathy. The puppy was of undetermined breeding (polite phraseology for the Heinz 57-variety kind) but he grew into a smart little busybody that would retrieve anything. Mr. White gave the dog to his hunting pal, the late Whit Boykin, a well-known sportsman from near Camden, South Carolina, who developed the dog into an exceptional retriever and turkey hunter. Now the dog that hunts wild turkeys, like the man who hunts wild turkeys, has to be a keen operator. The idea is to slip around silently through the woods until you come upon a flock. A wild turkey has better hearing and sight than all the men in the world put together, but that doesn't stop a good turkey hunter. Once he finds a flock he sends his dog out to scatter it, hastily builds a blind, then proceeds to call them up. Boykin's dog soon became known for his rare ability to find flocks of wild turkeys and scatter them, also to retrieve ducks, doves and quail under any and all conditions.

Old-timers who remember the dog say it contained considerable Cocker Spaniel blood, and a brown spaniel bitch was mated to him, producing the foundation stock of what is now called in that locality the Boykin Spaniel.

The dog today looks similar to our American Water Spaniel only quite a bit smaller. In fact, it's very possible that the original dog White found had American Water Spaniel blood in him rather than Cocker, because a liver-colored Cocker is rare enough to be zoo material. In the early, formative years Boykin stock was inbred considerably and some say that Chesapeake blood was used as an outcross at one point, which seems quite possible from the head, which is spaniel-like but with something added.

In size the Boykin weighs between 30 and 38 pounds and stands 15 to 17 inches at the withers. They breed true to type now, being generally dark liver with occasionally a white star on the chest. In action they are very quick and brisk, and they always love water.

Whenever you see a spaniel riding the bow of a duck boat through a southern marsh or sitting beside a gunner dropping doves at the edge of a big wheat field or scampering ahead of a hunter gliding silently through a patch of turkey pines, you can bet it's a Boykin Spaniel, America's newest hunting spaniel.

The Boykin Spaniel—a great water dog.

The English Springer Spaniel

If I lived north of the Mason-Dixon line and particularly liked to hunt pheasants but also went for grouse, woodcock and ducks a few times during the season, I would never be without a well-trained Springer Spaniel. He's just about the finest sporting dog for upland game on the American scene today—sporting in the sense that the hunter finds his ability to take game most highly challenged.

No dog will do everything, but the Springer comes about as close as any in handling a variety of circumstances in his most exciting and sporting manner. Because he has more size than a Cocker, a good Springer is a real cover buster. Because he springs his game rather than pointing it, the gunner must be skilled in all phases of shooting, from quick reflexes and perfect timing to knowing the proper leads, for all his shooting will be done with little or no preparation. I have always said that my idea of a sportsman is a man who hunts grouse with a 20-gauge shotgun and a Springer Spaniel. I have known two such critters and they were about the finest shots I've ever met.

The Springer is at his best on pheasants. Here he is a real deadly dog that will push the wily ringneck to flight no matter what the circumstances. So often a pointing dog establishes point only to have the bird run off before the gunner can get there. Relocation is not always successful or may end in a bump of the bird out of range. Of course the good pointing dog on pheasants learns to loop ahead, cut off the running bird, and pin it between himself and the gunner. I have often seen this done, but it takes a lot of experience and even then only one dog in ten ever learns it.

With a Springer there is no need for all this. Once he hits pheasant scent he tracks it down until the bird flushes and that's that. The only thing he must do is stay within gunshot range, and this is a matter of training.

The Springer is particularly effective in heavy cover. He is short enough to hustle under things that often block the taller dog. Among swamp bogs where pheasants love to hide he can invariably root them out. In a cornfield where a pointing dog cannot be seen and is relatively ineffective, the Springer really shines. He pushes the scurrying pheasants aloft in a hurry.

In areas thick with pheasants, like the Dakotas, the Springer is preferable to any pointing breed. Ten or twenty running birds will drive the pointing dog insane. As he roads one he runs into another, whereas a Springer offers the perfect method of hunting for the situation and a well-trained one will provide some outstanding shooting.

There's no great trick to hitting a pheasant with a shotgun, and when its location is clearly indicated by a pointing dog, you haven't much reason for missing unless the circumstances are unusual. With a Springer it's another story. You know when the dog is on game but you don't know when and from what direction the bird will flush. This uncertainty and the necessity for quick, accurate shooting mean the difference between merely knocking pheasants down and real sporty shooting.

The one situation where a Springer is not adequate is on quail, which is the reason why I qualified his use to areas above the Mason-Dixon line. Down South, or any place where quail are hunted, a dog that steps out and swings widely will find the most birds.

Springers, if they are allowed to hunt with pointing dogs, will soon begin swinging far beyond gunshot range and prove useless. And they are too good to restrict at heel merely to do the retrieving. For singles hunting the Springer might be used, but here again he would serve little purpose until the area where the birds had pitched was located (not always as easy as it sounds), then a close-working pointing dog is preferable.

Many claim the Springer to be the nearest all-purpose dog in America because he is an excellent retriever from land and water. He is great for snagging crippled ducks along the edges of marshes, also for fetching them

The Springer Spaniel is a beautiful dog. This is Ch. Rostherne Hunter, owned by Mrs. R. Gilman Smith of New York City.

from swamps and rivers and lakes, even for coastal duck hunting when the water is not cold. Naturally he must be trained for this but he loves the water if introduced to it properly. For this ability to double as an effective water retriever the spaniel has become particularly popular in the Midwest and Far West where he can be utilized in this capacity, especially by the hunter who goes for upland game 75 per cent of the time and takes on the Mallards for the other 25 per cent of his shooting. If the percentages were the other way around, then a retriever would be better; it takes a heavy-duty dog to fetch ducks, crippled or otherwise, from cold, rough water or across heavy currents for even half a day.

When we said that the Springer was particularly adaptable to the Midwest and Far West we didn't mean to imply that he is not widely used in the East. He most certainly is. In fact, this area is his home. He was first brought to the United States for use on the great pheasant preserve estates in Long Island, Fishers Island and elsewhere along the eastern coast. In the early days before the dog spread across the northern latitudes of our country, it was the East that first imported him, bred him, trained him, promoted his use in field trials.

In the East today, where the retriever has long been the popular duck

The Springer is a dynamic, hustling hunter.

dog, the Lab and Golden are being trained and used to hunt upland game. This is also true in other sections of the country, particularly in California, and of course where this happens it cuts into the work of the Springer.

The Springer still stands, however, as the best sporting dog obtainable for a day of mixed shooting of pheasants and waterfowl in swamps and low-lying coverts. Many will come forth with honest claims for their German Shorthairs and Weimaraners, but these are pointing dogs and for sporting work on the pheasant nothing beats a flushing dog.

The Springer has a long and illustrious but complicated heritage which begins we don't know when. Some say with Caesar, who was fascinated by the British method of hawking. Whether the Britons at that time used spaniels to work with their falcons, or just any old pooch, is not known.

We do know that the Springer is descended from the old land spaniel family of England and is the third-largest of the four groups which finally emerged—Toy Spaniels or "Comforters," Cockers, Springers and Setting Spaniels or our modern-day setters. After 1700 setters were no longer associated with the spaniel family, and by 1800 all spaniels over 28 pounds were called Springers, English Spaniels or Field Spaniels. The Field Spaniels were of solid color while the others were black-and-white and liver-and-white, colors which we associate with the Springer today. The word "Springer" was first used to describe a spaniel's action in the presence of game rather than as a description of a breed.

Originally Springer and Cocker came from the same litter, size being the only distinction between the two. Even after a century of discriminating breeding, the English Cocker and English Springer are almost identical except for size. Oddly enough, the best field-trial Springers are on the small size and light-boned; thus they resemble their brother the Cocker even more than the show strains.

Spaniels were brought to America early in our history and used to hunt game up until the Civil War. These were the old English Spaniels, liver-and-white, black-and-white, the forebearers of the Springer and Cocker here. Their use declined after 1850 as the great spaces of the Midwest were opened up. Market hunters wanted pointing dogs then. Some of the early spaniels undoubtedly helped form other breeds here like the American Water Spaniel, and a few were around to be registered in 1879 when the first Stud Book was published in St. Louis by what is now the American Kennel Club. The first spaniel registered was a liver-and-white Cocker. We don't know his height but from the sound of it he might better have qualified as a Springer.

In the early 1800s a few English kennels began keeping personal records on the breeding of their spaniels because outcrossing to Setters and Beagles was becoming common practice. One such notable case was the Boughey family, whose Aqualate Kennels in Shropshire, England, began a stud book in 1813, oldest on record. To them goes much of the credit for standardizing the Springer Spaniel breed. Many of our contemporary Springers trace back to Mop I, Mop II and Frisk, not illustrious names but early standout spaniels. At that time in other sections of England, Springer-type spaniels appeared, of which the Norfolk Spaniel, later absorbed into the Springer, was an example.

In the 1880s Springers began to enter the English show ring, but it was not until 1899 that the first field trial was held for them by the Sporting Spaniel Club. Clumber Spaniels won most of the prizes, but this was soon reversed by the speedier and more effective Springer.

In 1902 the English Kennel Club recognized the Springer as a separate and distinct breed, though it had been so in the eyes of hunters for centuries. Registration was begun at that time and soon the British Isles were being combed for all dogs resembling Springers, regardless of lineage, so they might get on the band wagon. Despite such shenanigans most all of the good modern field Springers in England and America are descended once or many times over from six great dogs: Ch. Denne Duke, E.F.T.C. Rivington Sam, Caistor Rex, Dash of Hagley, Ch. Velox Powder and Cornwallis Cavalier. (The prefix Ch. denotes a bench champion, while E.F.T.C. means English Field Trial Champion.)

The real support of the Springer in the British Isles came when the great shooting estates in England and Scotland changed their mode of hunting from the "walk-up" type of shooting to the "drive." For the "walk-up," Setters and Pointers were the ideal dog. They ranged ahead of the walking gunner, located and pointed the game. At flush and shot they dropped flat to the ground, at which point retrievers or spaniels were sent to fetch the fallen game. For the "drive" the gunner was stationed more conveniently and comfortably in a butt and men "beaters" walked in a line toward the stationed gunner, flushing grouse from the moors and driving them over the butts. For this type of shooting only a retriever is needed and the Springer was ideal because after the shoot some gunners always wanted to do a little "walk-up" shooting and here the Springer was at his best, providing the sporting form of gunning so dear to an Englishman's heart. Thus was the Springer trained and used on a practical scale as well as in field trials.

Some of the great English kennels which have produced field-trial champions in the British Isles, here in the United States and Canada as well as in India and elsewhere in the world are: Rivington Kennels, producers of both Springers and Cockers including the immortal Rivington Sam, founder of a great line of Springers though he was a Cocker; Horsford Kennels of Mr. William Humphries who was one of the early pioneer bench and field-trial judges in England and the United States; O'Vara Kennels which, under the guidance of one of the world's greatest professional trainers and handlers, T. J. Greatorex, has won the English National Championship Trials six times; Staindrop Kennels, owned by the late Edgar Winter who was a professional dealer in super gun dogs and shipped more winners to America until his death than any other kennel; Saighton's Kennels, owned by Talbot Radcliffe, supplier in recent years of a number of brilliant field-trial Springers.

The rise of the Springer Spaniel in America followed the successful introduction of the Chinese and English ringneck pheasant to the Western Hemisphere, a point which speaks highly for the dog's finesse on this game bird. The first "planting" took place in 1790 when an Englishman, married to Ben Franklin's daughter, imported some English ringnecks for his New Jersey estate, but they all died the following year. The first really successful planting was in Oregon in 1881 when twenty-eight Chinese ringnecks imported from Shanghai were released in the Willamette Valley. Eleven years later Oregon hunters, during the first open season on this great game bird, shot an estimated quarter to half a million of them. Continued plantings spread the pheasant to California and across the entire northern

The Springer's forte is pheasants.

latitudes of the United States, where today he is a part of the landscape.

In 1924 the first Springer Spaniel field trial was held in the United States at the Fishers Island estate of the Ferguson brothers, Walton, Jr., Henry and Alfred, all early supporters of the Springer in America. The trial was sponsored by the English Springer Spaniel Field Trial Association, organized the year before by a group of enthusiastic sportsmen. Mr. William Humphries, who had come over from England to judge the Springer bench class at Madison Square Garden, won with a field dog he'd brought along.

Another important promoter of the breed at this time was Eudore Chevrier of Winnipeg, Canada, who, after shooting over a fine Springer in 1920, became so enthusiastic about the dog that he began a mail-order business selling show and field Springers which he imported from England. Through Mr. Chevrier's efforts thousands of people heard of Springer Spaniels for the first time and many bought good examples of the breed from him.

Even in the early days of the Springer, dual champions were rare, fewer than ten having appeared during the entire history of the breed in the United States. It was the same old story. Show people and field-trial followers bred for different purposes. In breeding for beauty, the show people have gradually produced a Springer that is heavy-boned and on the massive side, often in excess of permitted requirements and of limited value in the field. Meanwhile the field-trial people, in aiming to produce

When properly trained, the Springer is a fine water dog.

the best field dogs possible, have leaned toward those which had power, were quick and agile, highly intelligent and could absorb training. This happened to be a medium-sized dog 17 or 18 inches tall instead of the bench-show 20-inch maximum or higher. The field dog is light-boned and consequently weighs closer to 40 pounds instead of the usual 50. He is inclined toward a wide head and a snippy nose, whereas the show Springers lean to the long, boxy setter head. In America, as in England, the show strains and field strains are considered two separate breeds. Many have tried to cross the two in hopes of bringing them closer together, but this merely reduces the quality and vitality of the field bloodlines. It has never proved worth while.

Through the years support for the Springer Spaniel as a hunter and field-trial competitor has come from men in all parts of northern United States. Women, too, have taken interest in ever increasing numbers, to the extent that in 1956 they organized LASHA, meaning Ladies Amateur Spaniel Handlers Association. This organization boasts members from Connecticut to Oregon and has Cocker and Springer challenge trophies for which the ladies compete.

When the hunting season ends each fall, many Springer owners keep right on running their dogs through the winter and spring in field trials. For this a well-trained dog is necessary, for competition is keen, even among amateurs. Spaniel trials, unlike Pointer and Setter trials that may have a jackpot of $1500, involve very little money. Trophies are the major portion of the prizes. It's strictly a sport and you get this feeling by attending a trial. One of the real fun classes is the Amateur Gun Dog stake in which the amateur handler works his own dog and shoots his own birds. In all other stakes official guns do the shooting.

The National English Springer Spaniel Field Trial Association is the parent organization, boasting twenty-seven active member clubs with the bulk of the activity in the East, Great Lakes states and on the West Coast. In 1947 the first National Championship Trial for Springers was held at Crab Orchard Lake near Carbondale, Illinois. It has since become an annual event of great significance where professionals and amateurs fight through five land and two water tests to gain this most coveted crown of the Springer world.

In the National two dogs are put down at a time, each with a separate course to work. The courses adjoin so each dog and handler sees and must respect the work of the other. Pheasants are planted a few hundred yards ahead of the dogs as they work. Judges watch to see how well they seek out the birds, flush them within gun range. The moment a bird is flushed by either dog, both dogs must sit, the flushing dog marks the fall while the other honors. Three official guns following close by the handlers

Rilson of Ranscombe retrieves a pheasant to Luke Medlin in a field trial. Springer field trials in the last two decades have mushroomed.

and judges do the shooting. When a bird is dropped, the dog that flushed it is sent to retrieve. The honoring dog is called to heel by his handler. The retrieving dog must mark the fall accurately or take handling (hand signals and whistle directions from the handler) to locate the shot pheasant which, when found, must be brought back to the handler quickly and tenderly.

If the guns (official shooters) miss a bird, as often happens, the dogs are moved on by their handlers. Judges have the prerogative of keeping the dogs down as long as they choose, but they usually see enough after two or three birds have been shot to decide whether to keep the dog for the next series or drop him. Judges alternate on the dogs and rate them according to a standard of performance. During the final land and water series, dogs are handled one at a time so both judges can see each work.

A dog is eliminated if he chases a flushed bird or breaks from his hupped or sitting position to retrieve before his handler has sent him. Flushing out of range or passing a bird on the course are serious mistakes, but not too many blunders are seen at the National. Dogs have to qualify to gain the right to run, so they're the cream. Running style, method of working the wind, manners on game and polish of retrieves usually decide the winner—also Lady Luck!

But any dog that completes all the series in the Springer National is a good one, and when an amateur handles his dog through to the end he can be, and is, justly proud. A special award goes to the best amateur-handled dog at the National and it is a valuable win.

SPRINGER NATIONAL CHAMPS

	Dog	Owner	Handler
1947	Russett of Middlefield	Dr. C. G. Sabin	Roy Gonia
1948	Stoneybroke Sheerbliss	Mr. & Mrs. P. D. Armour Jr.	C. H. Wallace
1949	Davellis Wager	David B. Silberman	Martin J. Hogan
1950	Whittlemore George	Mr. & Mrs. P. D. Armour Jr.	Steve Studnicki
1951	Fliers Ginger	C. Malone Kline	Arthur Eakin
1952	Stubblefield Ace High	W. T. Gibson	Stanley Head
1953	Mickelwood Scud	Mr. & Mrs. P. D. Armour Jr.	Steve Studnicki
1954	Ludlovian Bruce	Col. Joseph C. Quirk	Lawrence MacQueen
1955	Ludlovian Bruce	Col. Joseph C. Quirk	Lawrence MacQueen
1956	Mickelwood Scud	Mr. & Mrs. P. D. Armour Jr.	Steve Studnicki
1957	Staindrop Breckonhill Chip	Mr. & Mrs. R. D. Chapin	Elmore C. Chick
1958	Staindrop Breckonhill Chip	Mr. & Mrs. R. D. Chapin	Elmore C. Chick
1959	Brackenbank Tangle	Ernest W. Wunderlich	Elmore C. Chick
1960	Carswell Contessa	Mr. & Mrs. P. D. Armour Jr.	Mrs. Julia Armour
1961	Armforth's Mickelwood Dan	Mr. & Mrs. P. D. Armour Jr.	Steve Studnicki
1962	Kansan	R. E. French	P. L. Scales
1963	Waveaway's Wilderness Maeve	W. E. Lane	C. L. Wingate

In addition to the above event, a National Amateur Championship for Springers was inaugurated in 1963. Held in Ohio in early December, this stake promises to gain great popularity in the future years, for the Springer Spaniel has always been a favorite among amateurs.

In recent years more and more British imports have appeared among the ranks of Springer field-trial competitors and they are winning more than their share of prizes. It is not unusual to see half the dogs in an Open All-Age stake listed in the program as bred in England. This is particularly true at Eastern trials though it also involves other sections of the country. British imports have consistently won or placed second, third or fourth in the Springer National. Thus it would seem that we are not breeding the really top-quality Springer here in America as consistently as are our English cousins.

Many people feel there is more to it than that, however, claiming it is more a matter of environment than of heredity. British dogs have early experience on wild game the like of which is not easily found here in this country. In using artificial methods, especially pigeons, to train the Springer here, we do not bring out the full hunting instinct that displays itself in every action of a real hunting dog. Whether this is true or not is hard to prove. The fact remains that English dogs are being imported and are winning consistently. If they are better dogs in any way, certainly our Springer bloodlines will be improved as they are absorbed. Whenever field-trial competition forces fanciers of any breed to search harder and farther for new blood in order to win, it is bound to lead to improvement in the long run.

English trainers have long employed rabbits to bring out the "hunt" in Springers, and this may be a key to their success. Rabbits teach the Springer to trail and spring game instead of pointing it. Springers can be taught to point with little or no effort. In fact, many have to be broken of the habit because they are disqualified for so doing in a trial and are not of much use afield as pointing dogs because they work too close.

A Springer can be used effectively for rabbit hunting. He loves to start and run them but should not be allowed to work the trail beyond gunshot. Otherwise some very bad habits will form.

A good Springer in action is a joy to watch. He is under control at all times, moving as though his handler had an invisible string on him. Though he is ever obedient he hunts like a demon, and surely no game bird whose scent he comes across will escape being flushed. The field dogs are easy to train, absorb commands readily and make wonderful house pets besides. They have friendly, affectionate dispositions and become great pals with their masters as well as with children and people of all ages.

The Springer Spaniel has come a long way in a relatively short time in this country. He has done it on a very sound footing not based on commercialism or fanfare but on the fact that he's a great little hunter.

Chapter 4

The Retrieving Breeds

Throughout the ages dogs that could retrieve have been held in great esteem by hunters. There are three prerequisites to taking game. It must be found, then killed or wounded by some means, and finally it must be located and brought back to the hunter. It is this last phase of locating and returning dead or crippled game that makes the retriever worth his weight in gold. The frustration which comes from not finding a rabbit or quail or pheasant or duck or goose or whatever after you've shot it is maddening. If you doubt me, just ask any bird hunter who doesn't use a dog. A grouse can be stone-dead and you walk within a foot of it and never see it.

Early writings and sketches indicate that in olden times dogs were trained not only to retrieve game that the archer had plunked but to bring back arrows from land or water when the shot was missed. From the time of the Greeks to the eighteenth century retrievers were any kind of dog that could do the job. Looks meant nothing. Intelligence was what counted. They had to be especially alert to mark the location of the fallen game, and biddable so they could be sent to a certain spot to retrieve if necessary. Beyond that it made no difference. If any special types of dogs were developed and used for the art of retrieving we have no record of it.

We know that the early spaniel family in England separated into two divisions, land and water, mainly because of a difference in coats. The former developed into our modern light-coated flushing breeds discussed in the previous section; the latter contributed strongly to our current heavy or double-coated retrieving breeds.

The retrievers officially listed as such in America today are the Chesapeake Bay, the Labrador, Curly-Coated, Flat-Coated Retrievers, the Irish Water Spaniel and the American Water Spaniel. These will be discussed in this section along with the Poodle, which in recent years has seen surprising use as a duck dog.

From the mere interplay of words it is obvious that the Water Spaniel is nearly synonymous with retriever, and that all spaniels and retrievers have a lot in common even though their looks are quite different. In the past ten to fifteen years, as shall presently be described, the two breeds have become so closely allied in the work they do and the ways they do it that when this book was first outlined we planned to include the flushing and retrieving breeds in the same section. Both are trained the same. Both operate the same way on land or water. The only difference is that one specializes in water work, the other in land work.

Like so many of our breeds, the retrievers came from England originally. The two that are native to the United States, the Chesapeake and the American Water Spaniel, were developed from stock that was undoubtedly of English origin.

The great breeds of dogs in the British Isles were for the most part created by men interested in a particular phase of shooting. The men who hunted grouse on the moors of North England and Scotland developed the pointing breeds. Men who loved to hunt pheasant and woodcock in dense cover perfected the spaniel breeds for this work. Those who hunted the marshes, the coastal and tidewater lands, for ducks, snipe, and the like, needed an expert water retriever. The spaniel was adequate, but they wanted a heavier-bodied, double-coated dog. The added size and strength would provide the power to swim through rough water, break through heavy marsh grass. The double coat would shed water and give protection in any kind of weather. When no such dog was available, they literally made one—the retriever.

Though the original purpose of the retriever was as a water dog, his proficiency on land was soon recognized. As the different hunting breeds became entrenched, the English used them in various ways. For example, on the grouse moors, the classic idea of hunting was to have pointing dogs—Setters and Pointers—range ahead of the walking hunters while the non-slip retrievers (dogs that walked at heel, marked the fall and retrieved only upon command, but were not permitted to find or flush anything) followed at heel. When the pointing dogs located game and established point, the gunners flushed the birds and shot, whereupon the pointing dogs fell flat to the ground and the retrievers, who had been sitting in line behind the scene watching and marking the fall of the birds, were sent to fetch them.

This was considered the epitome of hunting as late as the 1930s in both England and America. And this was the origin of our pointing-dog manners of being steady to wing and shot. When the dog dropped to the ground, he was out of danger of being shot, but at the same time could not mark the fall of the birds. Thus if he was allowed to stand at flush and shot he could easily mark the fall of the birds and be used as a retriever.

The retriever in the old days was called upon to work only after shot. This is the origin of the so-called "line" in retriever field trials, where two dogs sit side by side and mark the fall of birds shot 50 to 100 yards away.

Since hunters often dropped three or four birds at a time, even more, the retrievers had to be taught to follow a line to a blind retrieve that perhaps was not marked.

The reason that this team combination of pointing dog and retriever never caught on was that it required the use of too many dogs, all of which had to be highly trained and mannerly. Only the wealthy could afford to hunt in this style, so someone developed a method of force-breaking a dog to retrieve. Then Pointers and Setters could be taught perfect field retrieving so there was no need to tote along a specialty dog merely for this work.

The retriever became tremendously popular in America after 1800 because of the abundance of waterfowl here at that time. No-limit duck shooting existed right up until 1900 and high limits remained until the early 1930s. In just one of those "good old days" it was simple for a gunner to drop fifty to a hundred ducks. For this he needed a reliable, tireless water retriever that could plow back and forth in any kind of weather, and that was smart enough to nail the cripples first, then fetch the dead ones. Here the retriever in the form of the powerful Chessie had no equal.

The retriever was also an essential part of the market hunter's life. When you earned a living shooting wild fowl you hated to waste a shell by missing a bird, but if you only crippled the bird and it escaped, the shell was wasted the same as a miss. Thus a good retriever that could nail crippled ducks was a most valuable asset.

In the last thirty years, since about 1935, we have seen a vast change in the retriever's pattern of life. First of all, the great droughts of the 1930s dried up many of the marshes where ducks bred, found refuge and food. Eventually the water returned, as did the ducks, but their numbers were so vastly depleted that we had to apply stringent waterfowl regulations which limited the take in some lean years by as much as one quarter of previous allowances. Obviously when duck limits are cut the retriever is put out of business. Why should a man with a four- or five-duck limit keep a dog all year to pick up what he knocks down during the season? It's far wiser for him to shoot and shoot until five dead ducks either float to shore or fall over land so he can pick them up by hand. To hell with the cripples. Besides, he'll have more shooting that way.

Another thing that hurt the retriever was the elimination of shooting on the northward or spring migration. Hunters who usually had a crack at the ducks going and coming now were limited only to the southern migration. Justly so, for the sake of the waterfowl, but it nevertheless meant less work for the retriever.

In recent years the rise of high-class game clubs where members or well-heeled hunters go duck shooting has brought about another practice detrimental to the retriever. Instead of bothering to maintain well-trained retrieving dogs, the club uses the more profitable guide system. At twenty-five dollars per day, the guide takes hunters to supposedly favored spots, then slips downstream and waits in a sneak boat. As the hunters drop birds, the dead ones drift downstream to him and he merely fishes them out of the water. The cripples he doesn't bother with but simply tells the gunners to keep banging away until they get their limit in dead birds. Everybody is happy and nothing is wasted but game.

One of the things that kept the retriever going through the late 1930s and early 1940s was field trials. Here a man could work his dog and have some fun during the rest of the year, and the good blood was also maintained and improved.

Even more important was the employment of the retriever for flushing upland game in a manner identical to the spaniel's work. Retriever authorities writing as late as 1945 said it couldn't be done—above all, shouldn't be done. On land the dog was a non-slip retriever and that was that. But the pressure of the times and the ingenuity of people changed all this. Rare is the gunner nowadays who hunts pheasant and ducks and can afford the luxury of a setter for one and a retriever for the other, also keep both in proper training. Because of this, people who had retrievers began teaching them to quarter and spring game within gunshot range.

Today the retriever is an outstanding example of the trend in America to make the hunting dog serve more than one purpose afield. From the swamps and buck brush of the East Coast to the rice fields and wheat stubble of California and Oregon, Labradors and Goldens are pushing pheasants into flight in the traditional spaniel manner, flushing them to the gun, marking their fall when shot, then hustling off to retrieve, which is their speciality.

The way duck and goose shooting declined for a time, it almost seemed that the retriever was destined to fade from sight as a utility dog. The lot of preserving him fell to field-trial fans and those avid hunters who enjoyed the ultimate in waterfowl shooting, who took pride in owning a great duck dog and watching him perform, and who, above all, possessed the desire to conserve game. It is estimated that ten to fifteen per cent of the wild fowl shot down is lost even with a crack retriever. Without a dog the percentage is as high as forty to sixty—all this game a total waste, left to die at the hands of predators or rot in the marshes and along the shores.

In a matter of ten or fifteen years the retrievers of America have taken on a new phase of hunting that will definitely guarantee their future use as gun dogs. Who knows, perhaps someday retriever field trials will include quartering and flushing tests similar to those of the spaniel. Some breeds are much better than others at it. Let's move into their analysis and see which ones are the hot shots on the scene at the moment. But first a glance at an ancient breed which is a fountainhead for nearly all retrievers.

The St. John's Newfoundland — An Early Breed

One of the greatest water dogs man has ever possessed was developed here in North America, in and around the isolated fishing center of St. John's in Newfoundland.

Newfoundland was discovered by John Cabot in 1497, and St. John's, because of its splendid horseshoe harbor that could accommodate the largest of ships, was settled as a British colony in 1583. Within seventy-five years, fishermen from France, Spain and Portugal were regular visitors. What scanty information we have indicates that the Indians had no dogs, though some historians feel that early Norsemen may have brought some. Most likely the original stock came from European sailors and settlers— probably the black St. Hubert's Hound and the massive Great Pyrenees.

In time two distinct breeds arose—the large and powerful black Newfoundland, which pulled carts and carried burdens like a mule, and the St. John's Newfoundland, a black water dog about the size of a Pointer with a heavy, oily coat that shed water like a greased balloon.

Many claim that the large Newfoundland, about the same as the dog we know today, was a great swimmer, noted for his rescue work around wrecked ships. I find this hard to believe of so massive and ponderous an animal. In a high sea I think he would be clobbered, and suspect that in the confusion between the two breeds they have credited the wrong one.

We shall never know, but in any case the Newfoundland of St. John's, the smaller version, was a most practical dog. During the fall and spring when great masses of migrating ducks and geese clogged the island, he worked tirelessly with gunners as a retriever. By and large, though, he was a fisherman's dog, working around the nets, on the boats, recovering anything that fell overboard, fetching a cod that slid back into the water as the fish were being transferred to the pier, swimming from ship to shore with a hawser line. In those days a ship dog was a handy asset, not only for companionship but for practical use.

From 1750 on, these Newfoundlands from St. John's rode the ships to England and the Continent. They were a captain's pride and joy, friend of the crew and general handyman. When a port was reached, the captain would take his dog ashore with him. Kids would pet its thick black coat and squeeze its heavy otterlike tail, and the port inspector or company official would chide the captain. "Now, why do you give bunk space and good food to a black devil like that? You'd do better skinning him and selling his hide as a pelt." Whereupon the captain would explode, "Ha! That black devil, as you call him, is worth five of your lazy stevedores, he is! And he's saved the company a year's wages for the stuff he's hauled out of the water for us." "Oh, a retriever, eh? D'you think he could fetch a duck if he had the chance?" "A duck! He'll haul the blighters in faster than you can shoot 'em!" "Is that so-o-o? Well, suppose we have a little go this afternoon and see."

And much to the gentleman's surprise the dog was outstanding—better than a spaniel in water because he had power, better around marshes because he could bull through the heavy cover to cripples. For a nice sum of money the dog changed hands that day. The captain made himself a good bargain and the hunting owner had a fine duck dog.

Since an outstanding specimen of the big Newfoundland was carefully measured (6'2" nose to tail) in 1779 by the famous English naturalist and engraver, Bewick, we can assume that the St. John's dog was also in England at that time. We know that an English brig foundered off the coast of Maryland in 1807 and aboard were two St. John's pups which were saved and went on to establish the famous Chesapeake Bay Retriever. We know that Lewis on his expedition west with Clark in 1802 had a Newfoundland, probably of the St. John's type because it retrieved game, chased buffaloes out of camp and kept watch for grizzly bears. Scannon was his name and when the Indians stole him at one point, Lewis and Clark's camp went on the warpath until he was recovered. All of which only goes to prove that the breed was well known.

By 1800 the St. John's dogs had established such a reputation as water retrievers in England that duck hunters regularly visited the seaport of Poole in southeastern England to buy them off the Newfoundland ships.

As a brisk trade in dogs developed around the English port of Poole, so did the confusion between the Newfoundland from St. John's and the much larger, almost ponderous Newfoundland cart dog. More than likely some English noblemen placed orders for the smaller ones as hunters and received the larger ones, which were useless as such but worked out famously as house pets.

Colonel Peter Hawker tried to clear up the matter by calling the smaller dog the St. John's dog or Labrador because it had spread up the coast of Labrador. In his book *Instructions to Young Sportsmen*, written in 1814, he described Labradors as "by far the best for every kind of shooting." His description of them continues:

"Oftener black than of another colour, and scarcely bigger than a pointer, he is made rather long in the head and nose, pretty deep in chest, very fine in the legs, has short or smooth hair, does not carry his tail so much curled as the other (Newfoundland breed) and is extremely quick in running, swimming and fighting. . . . Poole was till of late years, the best place to buy Newfoundland dogs, but now they are become scarce owing to the strictness of those . . . tax gatherers!"

Lord Malmesbury who lived near Poole and Colonel Hawker bought several of these dogs in the early days, as did four other noblemen, and soon all had well-established kennels of the Newfoundland from St. John's. They valued these dogs so highly that each went to great effort to keep the strain pure. This was most fortunate because the dog tax increased in Newfoundland and Labrador to such an extent that natives could no longer afford to keep dogs in any quantity.

The final blow came in 1885 when, to encourage sheep breeding, a law was passed allowing but one dog per family, thereby bringing an end to dog breeding on the island for all practical purposes. In less than a decade the Newfoundland of St. John's became extinct in the land of its origin, but the contribution he made will never be forgotten, for this fisherman's dog which was such a sturdy swimmer has passed on his water qualities to every major retrieving breed we have today.

The Curly-Coated Retriever

The first retriever to appear in an English bench show was the Curly-Coat in 1859, and thus he is considered the earliest breed among our modern retrievers. No records exist which reveal the origin of this fine but increasingly rare dog. Stonehenge, the great English canine authority, wrote in 1860, "This variety of retriever is always a cross between the St. John's Newfoundland and the water spaniel which is generally Irish." Others claimed it was a product of the old English Water Spaniel and early retrieving setters crossed to the St. John's dog for refinement and, later in the 1880s to the French Poodle for the tight curl of the coat which they have today.

The cross to the Poodle certainly worked, because not only does the Irisher strongly resemble him but he is about as curly-coated as any dog living. He looks as if he just escaped from a beauty-salon operator who went mad, giving a permanent wave. A mass of curls flows from the dome

Banworth Artison, English field trial and show winner recently imported by Horace Merwin of Southport, Conn.

of his head to the tip of his tail. In fact, this is probably the chief reason he never grew popular in this country. The curly coat picks up burrs and all sorts of twigs and grasses beyond belief, requiring that the dog be thoroughly combed out after each hunt.

It's too bad, too, because the Curly-Coat is a sound, reliable worker with excellent endurance, a soft mouth and superior scenting ability. Also his gentle disposition and high level of intelligence make him easy to train. He loves water, can take the cold, will even dive after crippled ducks, and generally makes an excellent land dog for flushing and re-trieving.

Of all the retriever breeds the Curly has the longest legs and the lightest body. He is almost square in his looks, with a wiry strength rather than a burly, massive strength, which would seem to indicate speed but in this case doesn't. The Curly lacks the animated style and punch of the Labrador. He seeks out his retrieves with thoroughness and completes them at a comfortable trot, not the gallop so common in our modern field-trial retrievers.

The Curly-Coat reached its peak of popularity in England during the latter half of the 1800s. He was heavily exported to New Zealand and

Australia in 1889, where today he is still a favorite retriever on land as well as water.

A few Curlies were brought here before the Civil War and thereafter, but then never attained much of a following in the United States. In the marshlands and tidewater bays where duck hunters wanted a power dog, the Chesapeake overshadowed him. Later, in field trials where speed and animation made a difference, the Labrador overshadowed him. His big moment came in the late 1930s when J. Gould Remick, a well-known New York sportsman, espoused his cause. Sarona Sam of Marvadel and Sarona Jacob of Marvadel, both owned by Mr. Remick, and Carbon of Marvadel, owned by F. Royal Gammon, gained several worth-while wins in field trials, though vastly outnumbered by the other retriever breeds.

In color the Curly-Coated Retriever is either black or dark liver. The standard does not limit the breed to minimum or maximum heights or weights, but he runs about 24 inches at the withers and weighs 60 to 70 pounds.

Today the Curly-Coat is a rarity on the American hunting scene and surprisingly, though he is a beautiful dog, he has never gained much support from the show world. There are fewer than a dozen specimens in the country at the moment, but some recent importation by his followers promise to bring him back into the limelight.

The Flat-Coated Retriever

Though the ranks of the Flat-Coated Retriever have been thin here in the United States, he has always been regarded as a sound and effective dog. Long known as the gamekeeper's assistant on the moors and estates of Britain (which speaks highly for him) the breed was called the Wavy-Coated Retriever when it appeared for the first time in the Birmingham Dog Show in 1860. That dog's name was Wyndham. Owned and exhibited by R. Braisford, he caused quite a stir among retriever fanciers because they recognized real merit in him immediately.

As so often happened in those days, a dog breeder or often three or four would work together for several years to produce a distinctive type, then appear at a dog show with it and leave the aroused public wondering what blood was used to create the dog. In the event that he proved himself in the field, as Wyndham did, he quickly developed a group of followers who soon wrote up a standard and organized a club to support the dog's interests. Breeders then had a direction to follow, and in time, as the dog produced offspring true to type, the Kennel Club of England recognized it as a legitimate breed.

The Flat-Coat is at home on land or water.

In the case of Wyndham it is doubtful that even his owner knew his true origin, for dogs of this type had been used by gamekeepers for some time. It is believed that the Flat-Coat was a cross between the St. John's Newfoundland and the Gordon Setter. Authorities also indicate that crosses to the Irish Setter and Golden Retriever were used later to bring out quality of coat.

Probably Dr. Bond Moore of Wolverhampton, England, deserves more credit than anyone for developing the Flat-Coated Retriever into the form we know today. He insisted it should follow the Labrador in color, conformation and purpose—that is, be a black, heavy-coated water retriever, for a cross between a Gordon and a Lab could just as easily have been steered toward the pointing breeds or even become a land retriever serving like an oversized Springer.

Such was the Flat-Coat's immediate popularity in England that four years after his first show he had special classes, and by the end of the nineteenth century enjoyed wide use throughout that country as a working retriever and top field-trial dog. Then came the overpowering rise of the Labrador around 1905 and the Flat-Coat fell from use, never to recover from his decline though he is used in many parts of England today as a working retriever.

In the United States he appeared from time to time after 1870 but with very meager support. Never did he have a club to back his interests here, nor did he crash onto the field-trial scene with the sensational winning efforts of the Golden Retriever. The Flat-Coat has always been more of a reliable than a flashy dog in temperament, color and actions.

Because of his setter blood, the Flat-Coat is considered to have an outstanding nose and a particularly good aptitude for marking fallen birds. It has also made him one of the best land working dogs as well as water dogs among the retrieving breeds. He is black in color, solidly made with a heavy, dense coat, and weighs 60 to 70 pounds.

One of the best Flat-Coated Retrievers shown in public trials—there haven't been many of them—was Blackdale Ben of Wingan, a good-looking import owned by Barbara Field Bliss. He did well in Retriever Trials in 1940 and 1941 and sired some excellent Flat-Coats. In fact, just about all those now in the United States except the few recently imported carry his blood.

Occasionally these days a Flat-Coat appears in field-trial competition, mostly in amateur stakes. However, Rab of Morinda placed fourth in an open all-age stake in 1959, the first such open win for the breed in three decades.

The Flat-Coated Retriever Society of America, first ever organized here, came into being in 1961 under the direction of Mrs. Dorothy Moroff of Aroma Park, Illinois, and Homer Downing of Lyndhurst, Ohio, both field-trial fans, and Mrs. Sally Terroux of Morrison, Colorado, a show dog and obedience follower. Mrs. Terroux's Ch. Bramcroft Dandy, UD, became the first American Flat-Coat bench champion and is a top obedience dog. A Flat-Coated Retriever specialty show is now being held annually which, along with the other club activities, is certainly stimulating interest in the breed for showing, field use and obedience. In the obedience ring the Flat-Coat is beginning to excel, turning in consistently superior scores.

Whether the Flat-Coat, reliable dog that he is, will ever rise to challenge the other retriever breeds is questionable. The road back will certainly be an arduous one but he's capable of doing it and, with a little more backing, may soon begin the try.

The Golden Retriever

The most beautiful of all retrievers, the Golden is also the youngest—only about a century old in England and slightly over thirty years here in the United States—but in the time he's been around, this good-natured, lovable lad has established some amazing records.

As so often happens when something extraordinary or unusual appears in the world a myth grows up around it, and in this respect the Golden Retriever is no exception. History had it that the breed was started by Lord Tweedmouth (formerly Sir Dudley Majoribanks—names that sound like a Sherlock Holmes mystery) who went to the circus at Brighton, England, in 1860 and saw a troupe of Russian performing dogs. These dogs were so intelligent, so beautiful, so this, so that, so everything, that Tweedy bought the whole troupe on the slim possibility that they might be made into retrievers "for popping a few duck and the like" at the family estate in Scotland.

Anyone with much sense would know that circus performers don't sell their means of livelihood very cheaply, if at all. The price would have thinned anyone's wallet and in Tweedy's case he would certainly have had to know in advance that they would make good retrievers, but he blithely took a gamble.

Then lo and behold! Five years later, in 1865, there was the Golden doing just scrumptiously as a retriever and the canine world ate up the bizarre origin of the dog, even added many interesting facets to the story. The circus dogs were supposed to be Russian Trackers, guardians of the sheep flocks in the Caucasian Mountains where roaring winters dropped temperatures to 10 and 20 degrees below zero and icy winds swirled snow into gigantic banks. So intelligent were these dogs, says one authority in all seriousness, that the Russian peasants merely turned them loose in the fall with a flock of sheep and a cache of food. The dogs carefully tended the sheep through the unbearable winter, rationed out the food to the sheep and themselves, kept the wolves away and provided serene comfort for the flock while the peasants retired to the village on a diet of bread and cheese, with vodka and women to keep warm. When the terrible winter ended and the birds and flowers of spring arrived (by that time the vodka had run out and the women had run away) the peasants would return to the mountains and there would be the dogs with the sheep which had all had little ewes, and the flocks were twice the size. What I would like to know is why, with a setup like that, would anyone want to join the circus!

Anyway, the circus story, given backing by the late Arthur Croston Smith was told and believed by everyone, and still is in many retriever circles. Gradually, however, researchers began to pick holes in it, and eventually Croston Smith admitted it was nonsense, but by that time it had become so popular that everyone wanted to believe it.

The final devastating evidence came out just a few years ago when Lord Tweedmouth's grandnephew, the Earl of Ilchester, revealed the original records, written in Tweedy's own hand. So there!

Truth of the matter is that Tweedy started the breed all right, but the dog he used was Nous (Greek for Wisdom), the only yellow pup in a litter of black Wavy-Coated (Flat-Coated, today) Retrievers. Nous was bought from a cobbler by Tweedy who wanted to create a breed of yellow retrievers.

Now Tweedmouth gained his name by living at the mouth of the Tweed River in southeast Scotland. Along the river and in the area was a tea-colored dog called the Tweed Water Spaniel, probably similar to a Springer only a bit more leggy. Nous was mated to one of these in 1868 and the result was Ada, Crocus, Primrose and Cowslip, laconic names destined for immortality. They probably had some black brothers that were drowned, but anyway Tweedy proceeded to line-breed, outcrossing once in a while to a Tweed Water Spaniel or a Wavy-Coated Retriever but preserving only the yellow or golden dogs for his stock. Experimental crosses were made once to an Irish Setter and once to a Bloodhound at Tweedmouth's famous Guisachan Kennels, but they proved of no substantial value. Once Tweedmouth had his color, which was the main objective of his breeding program, he concentrated on conformation and ability.

As his dogs began to run true to type he gave some to his closest friends, and in time three other great strains (actually kennels) arose to match Tweedmouth's Guisachan—Ilchester, Ingestre, and Culham. Thus the four pillars of the Golden Retriever. Unfortunately Tweedmouth and Ilchester failed to register their dogs, probably because they were irate to have them first classified as Wavy-Coated Retrievers. Ingestre and Culham, both of whom used a yellow Labrador now and then as an outcross, did register theirs and a majority of our Goldens today trace back to these original kennels. In 1913 the Kennel Club of England recognized the dog as a separate variety of retriever, calling it a "Yellow or Golden Retriever." Finally in 1920 the word "Yellow" was dropped.

In England the Golden Retriever quickly established itself not only as a beautiful show dog but as a standout water worker and a real wing-ding on land as a springer of game and as a retriever.

The first Goldens to reach the Western Hemisphere were brought to Vancouver Island and Victoria, B.C., by British army officers around 1900. These dogs never received recognition by either the Canadian or American Kennel Clubs but they spread along the West Coast as far north, some say, as Alaska.

The first kennel of Goldens in North America was established by the late Bart Armstrong of Winnipeg, Manitoba. Through his efforts the breed was finally recognized by the Canadian Kennel Club in 1927, and by the American Kennel Club in 1932.

Because of the many natural qualities—beautiful coat, strong hunting instinct, tractability, hence easily trained—the Golden Retriever began to catch on among show and field people as well as house-pet owners. Right from the start great Goldens appeared in the United States. International Champion Speedwell Pluto in 1932 became the first Golden bench champion in this country, also the first Golden to go Best in Show. So good was his conformation that his photo is still used as the standard for the breed over thirty years later! Carrying on this new-found fame in the show ring was Ch. Toby of Willow Lock in the late 1930s, another great one.

In 1938 the Golden Retriever Club of America was founded to direct the destiny of the breed here in this country and, though the club never went out of its way to overpublicize the breed, the Golden outperformed the fondest dreams of his admirers.

Imagine if you will, the field-trial world for retrievers at that time. Begun December 8, 1934, it was well established by 1939 but completely dominated by the Chesapeake Bays and Labradors.

The Golden is a good water retriever.

Out of the blue, from the Middle West, always a hot spot for the Golden because he is a great land dog, came in the late 1930s a Golden named Rip, owned, trained and handled by amateur Paul Bakewell III of St. Louis. Rip was a big devil and Paul didn't know much about field trials. Rip won the first open all-age stake ever taken by a Golden in America and the judge said he was the greatest natural retriever he'd ever seen. Rip became the first Golden to win his field championship, December 1939. That same year he won the coveted *Field and Stream* trophy as the outstanding retriever in the country.

Wherever Rip and Paul went they were the combination to beat. Sometimes he was edged into second or third but almost never out of the money. Time and again his fond owner would buy him in Calcutta Pools for high sums and seldom did Rip ever let his master down. In 1940 he won the *Field and Stream* award again; in 1941 he was on his way to winning it for a third time—a feat that would have been a goal for retrievers through the ages to shoot at—when he died.

Ask any old-timer who saw Rip perform and he will say unstintingly, regardless of his own personal feelings about retrievers, that never was there a better one than Rip and darn few equaled him. In the rather short span of his field-trial career Rip brought in 236 consecutive birds without a miss.

No sooner had the immortal Rip passed on to retrieving ducks for angels than along came King Midas of Woodend to cop the first running of the National Retriever Championship in 1941, another major boost for the Golden in its formative era. At that same time the first Golden Utility Dog came along in Goldwood Toby UD.

In 1944 another Golden, FTC Sheltergrove Beauty, won the National Championship, making it two Golden wins in four starts in this most highly prized of all retriever field events. During the second half of the 1940s dual champions began to appear in the breed. Dual Ch. Stilrovin Rip's Pride, grandson of old Rip, earned his in 1946 as did Dual Ch. Tonkahof Ester Belle, shortly followed by Dual Ch. Stilrovin Nitro Express.

Big names among the Goldens in the 1950s were 1950 National Ch. and FTC Beautywood's Tamarack; Dual Ch. Squawkie Hill Dapper Dexter; 1951 National Ch. and FTC Ready Always of Marianhill; FTC, AFTC Oakcreek's Freemont; FTC, AFTC, Canadian Dual Ch. Rockhaven Raynard of Fo-Go-Ta; FTC The Golden Kid; and FTC, AFTC, 1952 Can. National Ch., Can. FTC Oakcreek's Van Cleve, all-time high point-scoring Golden (78½ open all-age points, 46½ amateur all-age points). Then there was a triple winner—in the field, on the bench and in the obedience ring—AFTC, Ch. Lorelei's Golden Rockbottom UD.

In recent years many Goldens have won their fair share of titles. To name a few: AFTC Happy Thanksgiving; FTC, AFTC Macopin Expectation; FTC, AFTC Fairhaven Donner; FTC, AFTC Nicholas of Logan's End; and AFTC Stilrovin Tuppee Tee.

Today the Golden Retriever is spread from the rocky coastline of Maine, to the humid swamps of Florida, across the country to the rivers of California and Oregon. Neither heat nor cold affects this dog much. He is not built for icy waters like the Chesapeake Bay Retriever, but he's a good swimmer, particularly effective in lakes and rivers and swamps of the Middle West. Here is his heartland, as it has always been. Here he is particularly effective.

In this field-trial scene, Golden on left is coiled and ready to retrieve as pheasant falls in distance. Lab on right must honor by sitting and watching.

Given a line, the Golden streaks off.

Proudly the Golden delivers his pheasant after a 150-yard retrieve as judges watch and Lab drools with envy.

The Midwest is a great game area. The Mississippi Flyway brings ducks and geese in abundance. The wheat, barley and corn fields of Ohio, Indiana, Illinois, Michigan, Wisconsin, the Dakotas supply feed for pheasant, thus they are found in great quantity. Hunters from these states want a land-and-water combination dog and here the Golden fills the bill perfectly. Because of his Gordon Setter ancestry he has a great nose, possibly a shade better than the Labrador or the Chesapeake. He loves to

Mark!

spring game and, when given the opportunity, puts up every living thing, fur or feather, in front of a hunter. And his nose seldom allows a cripple to escape.

Though the rivers get cold and the lakes freeze over in the Midwest, you don't get the icy brine of the Chesapeake or other coastal waters which numbs all but the most rugged dog. Here he has found his ideal place and will certainly continue to grow.

The Golden's personality can be characterized by one word—affectionate. He is a wonderful family dog, a great pet for kids, with a joyful disposition similar to the spaniel. Because he is nearly always tractable, he is probably the easiest of all the retriever breeds to train. But to obtain the last degree in polished manners required in field-trial work is sometimes difficult with a Golden because you can't punish him very much for his mistakes. He has to be trained out of them and not chastised out of them. Because he is usually so eager to please, he often makes a fine dog for the amateur who concentrates all his effort on one dog and for the woman who likes to compete in retriever trials.

Though a lot of field-trial people don't like Goldens because they are inclined to be soft, they can never deny that some magnificent ones have appeared. In fact, it seems that the moment Labrador people begin to criticize the Golden, along comes a great one and clobbers them. There is no doubt that a good Golden field-trial dog is harder to come by than a Lab and that he cannot take the training pressure that the Lab or Chessie can. But in the hands of a sensitive and gentle person who knows what to do, the Golden will work wonders—as the records prove. He is also the most tender-mouthed of all retrievers. Like just about every breed that was originally developed for field use and acquired a show-bench following, the Golden is pretty well divided into two camps today. The last living Golden Retriever Dual Champion, Craigmar Dustrack, was killed January 31, 1963 by a falling tree. Others may appear but they will be few and far between now.

"Tam," as he was called, was just about to complete his obedience work for a CD degree when the accident occurred. (Goldens have established an enviable record in obedience work.) Tam had hunted many years for his owner, Forrest Flachman, and others, for dove, quail chukars, ducks, geese and pheasants. He often pointed the birds that held and sometimes caught alive those that hesitated a bit too long before attempting to escape. His owner described him as "first and foremost a hunter, then a gentleman, family partner, swimming companion and a good outfielder in any baseball game."

No better epitaph could be written for a dog, nor any better description of the Golden.

The Chesapeake Bay Retriever

A raw December wind slashes out of the northeast, throwing salty breakers against the icy shore. The blind is hidden by a stretch of swamp grass in front of which the stool of tightly bunched decoys bobs realistically. Two men scan the leaden skies for ducks, as does the husky chocolate-colored dog crouched on a mudbank nearby. The shooting has been poor, and to keep warm the hunters flap their arms and flog their bodies from time to time.

Suddenly a small bunch of broadbills comes trading by. They hesitate as if to settle, but one of the gunners moves too quickly. They see him, flare off and move on. The birds have been shot at so much they're shy.

Soon a pair of black ducks cruise past. They see the decoys, loop back and set their wings a little. The two gunners hold their breaths. The dog watches intently, never flexing a muscle. As the two ducks pitch in, the gunners rise up and shoot. Both birds fall, one dead 30 yards to the left, the other crippled 50 yards out.

"Get 'em, Sam!"

The chocolate-colored dog leaps from the bank into the freezing brine. He ignores the dead duck, heads for the cripple, which is paddling for deep water. As the dog closes in, the duck dives. The dog treads water a few seconds, waiting, then heaves himself up, head and shoulders out of the water, to look around. When the duck surfaces, he spots it and closes in again. The duck dives and the procedure is repeated three more times until finally the dog wears the cripple out and catches it with a lunge. Nearly a hundred and fifty yards out he turns and heads for shore. A huge swell followed by a rolling breaker catches him, engulfs him. He's dragged under, disappears completely, then reappears paddling steadily for shore, his prize still firmly gripped. Just as he gains the shore the under-tow drags him out, but he keeps trying, finally leaps from the rollback onto the beach, delivers the duck still alive at the blind, whirls and quickly returns for the dead one still floating to the left.

When sunset arrives, the two hunters head back to the car one short of the limit. All day long the big Chesapeake has been hitting the icy water and fighting the surf to make his retrieves. Going home now, he doesn't walk at heel but noses along the swamp edge until he finds a cripple, and the two gunners make him carry it back to the car to be sure he'll quit hunting for the day.

The Chesapeake Bay Retriever—greatest heavy-duty water dog America has ever seen. For 150 years he's been the wheelhorse and workhorse of the duck world, quietly receiving the eulogies of thousands of old-time duck hunters for whom he worked. He kept the Curly-Coated and Flat-Coated Retrievers from amounting to much in this country. He fought tooth and nail but finally yielded the title of King of the Retrievers to the Labrador. Now, because of the vast changes in styles of duck hunting and in shooting limits, he threatens to pass from existence.

The history of this great dog?

Story has it that back in 1807 an English brig ran aground and was wrecked off the coast of Maryland in the world-famous Chesapeake Bay ducking area. The American ship *Canton* rescued the crew and cargo, including two Newfoundland puppies, a dusty-red dog later named "Sailor" and a black bitch later called "Canton." We don't know whether the ship had sailed directly from England, in which case the puppies would have come from there, or whether the ship had stopped at New-foundland and picked up the pups with the intention of carrying them back to England where St. John's Newfoundland dogs such as these were fetching high prices as retrievers—probably the latter. In any event, the two pups were given as gifts by the crew of the wrecked brig to two men who housed them at this dire moment.

Undoubtedly the men were avid duck hunters who knew something about the famous St. John's dog and highly prized these. For when the dogs grew up they became extraordinary retrievers, established consider-

able reputation for themselves and were bred, possibly together and certainly to local retrieving stock about which we know almost nothing. Assumptions range from Curly-Coated and Flat-Coated Retriever blood to Irish Water Spaniel and Coonhound stock.

Actually the Coonhound claim is not as farfetched as it sounds. The old southern strain of Redbone Foxhound had a coarse and tough red coat. The dog, so effective on coon, possessed great bone, excellent intelligence, stamina and tremendous tenacity of purpose, all characteristics of the Chesapeake. What puzzles most people is the origin of the Chessie's famous double coat, which is so oily as to be almost waterproof and so dense that you can hardly part it to reach the skin.

There is a farcical story of an early Chesapeake bitch being tied to a tree near a swamp and being mated to an otter. Beyond this nonsense there is constant reference to the Otter Hound in early writings. In fact the Chesapeake Bay Retriever was called the Chesapeake Otter Hound at one point, so it is most likely that the old English Otter Hound was crossed in strongly. This now rare breed still possesses a hard, tight coat that is oily and he can stand almost any amount of immersion in water, which might well be the answer to the Chessie coat.

Anyway, by the 1880s the dog had emerged as a definite type and was being used in the rough, icy waters of Chesapeake Bay. Though not too attractive, he was superbly efficient at plying his trade of fetching ducks. At that time both market hunters and sport shooters gunned ducks in quantities, sometimes 200 a day or more, and a dog really earned his keep.

So effective became the Chesapeake Bay Retriever that he turned aside all attempts by the Curly-Coated and Flat-Coated Retrievers to gain even a toe hold of popularity in this country. Several early clubs sponsored the dog but the first one of national scope was the American Chesapeake Club, founded in 1918. Earl Henry of Minnesota was the first president, followed by Matt Barron of Iowa, which shows the extent of the Chessie's use in the United States at that time, though his strength remained in the east.

The Chesapeake is a steam roller of a dog. He is so big and strong, and his desire to retrieve is so indomitable, that he overpowers the situation whether it be a duck in rough water or a wild-flapping crippled goose. He never does anything in a sissy way. When he grabs hold of a bird it doesn't get away. His oily coat allows him to dive into freezing water; ice can hang on his back like marbles and never bother him. He is—first, last, and in every situation—a standout water retriever.

The dog is usually chocolate-brown, sometimes deadgrass, rarely black in color. He weighs up to 75 pounds and stands up to 26 inches high,

The Chessie is a duck dog supreme.

although occasionally a big 90-pounder or larger will come along. His yellow eyes are set wide apart in his broad, massive head and are always alert. His body is solid as a bronze bull, hindquarters as high as or a trifle higher than his shoulders, and here is where he gets his swimming power.

Since World War II other retriever breeds have made substantial gains each year, yet the Chesapeake with all his ability has declined slightly.

How is this possible?

One reason is that the dog is not noted for his beauty but for his working ability. His broad head is set on a thick, muscular neck which looks too

A Chesapeake completes a tough water retrieve. Note how hindquarters are a shade higher than forequarters.

short for his body. His feet are too large for his size but great for swimming, and down the middle of his back is a wavy mat of oily hair. Thus he's never had a substantial following in the show ring, and any mention of breeding to beautify him a little brings screams of anguish from loyal duck hunters.

Another thing, the oily coat which is so effective in water is not so effective in the living room or front parlor, particularly when the dog is drying out. It has a slightly unpleasant smell that annoys many people.

There is also the question of the Chessie's personality. No one ever claimed the dog to be a happy-go-lucky roustabout. At best he's comfortably friendly and can be downright aloof—until he sees a gun or a duck boat. If he is brought up in a household around children, he is kindly and protective. It's generally when he's made a kennel dog, as he has been for generations, that he becomes aloof and serves only one master. He tends to be all business, not too eager to please, hence not too tractable. From this comes the accusation that the dog is hardheaded, which is not always a justified claim. Take the best example—Mrs. Eloise Heller's FTC, AFTC, Can. FTC Nelgard's Baron, CD, highest-scoring Chesapeake of all time. Mrs. Heller bought the dog as a seven-year-old, being honestly told in advance that he was as tough a Chesapeake as ever lived. The dog had been beaten, shot and generally mistreated during his training to break him. She made a house pet of him and within a month he was working his heart out for her. She had only to scold him when he disobeyed her and he would drop to the ground in dejection. She praised him when he did well, shamed him when he did poorly, and he gave his best in response. In one year they won three all-breed open all-age firsts and he made his field-trial championship. Which only shows what a certain type of handling can accomplish with a certain type of dog. Had she started off with the dog, he would have matured entirely differently, and no one can ever say whether he would have been more or less effective. The good dog that has been knocked around and treated coldly in his early years will often perform spectacularly for the kind handler.

Through the years some of the great Chesapeakes which have appeared among the field-trial ranks besides Nelgard's Baron are FTC Skipper Bob, the first retriever champion of any breed ever crowned in the United States; FTC Dilwyne Montauk Pilot, winner of the coveted *Field and Stream* trophy in 1936 as the outstanding retriever of the year; FTC Shagwong Gypsy; FTC Chesacroft Bob; FTC Tiger of Clipper City; AFTC Gypsy; FTC Montgomery's Sal; FTC, AFTC Deerwood Trigger; FTC, AFTC Nelgard's King Tut; FTC, AFTC Raindrop of Deerwood, Dual Ch.; AFTC Mount Joy's Mallard; FTC, AFTC Star King of Mount Joy; FTC, AFTC Atom Bob; AFTC Chesonoma's Louis; FTC, AFTC Meg's Patti O'Rourke, who was the 1958 National Derby Champion; and FTC, AFTC Mount Joy's Louistoo.

The next statement will shake up a lot of people, especially after they have read the above long list of names and titles, but Chesapeakes are not outstanding field-trial dogs. The list proves there have been some great ones and Chessies have won their percentage of wins when their number of entries is considered. Nevertheless the fact remains that no Chessie has ever won the National Championship, and their field-trial growth since 1947 has been nil, even slightly on the decline, while the Labrador and Golden have shown amazing growth every year. Most of the successful field-trial Chessies are amateur-handled, which would indicate that they tend to work better for their masters than for professional trainers.

Another thing, he is not as competent at hunting upland game to the gun as are the Labrador and especially the Golden. This has hurt his growth because the 200-ducks-in-a-day period is forever gone. The retriever in our time has become a dual-purpose dog, proficient in water retrieving and working upland game to the gun. The Chessie can do it but this isn't his forte.

The problem with the Chessie is that he is a peerless duck and goose dog but that's all. He hasn't changed or been changed to suit our times.

If the above seems like remorseless criticism, it isn't meant to be. I love the dog. He is one of the greatest specialists, if not the greatest, ever developed in America and I don't want to see him die out.

The Labrador has come to his dominant position because he is a great dual-purpose dog, has an excellent field and family disposition, possesses a practical coat that doesn't burr up or require maintenance or emit any odor. He is equally effective on land or water and, above all, he responds to almost any type of training whether it be forceful or easygoing.

The Chesapeake Bay Retriever—America's contribution to the duck dogs.

Generally the Chessie requires a heavy hand and the Golden a light hand. The Lab, because of what he is, composes almost 90 per cent of the field-trial entries and wins that much too.

The Golden has been able to make vast inroads into the retriever ranks because it is a most beautiful dog and has a particularly joyful personality, both elements making it attractive to show people and families. It's an excellent dual-purpose field dog, trains easily for the easygoing person, and when you get a really good Golden, he's great.

The Chessie, as we have explained, does not offer these widespread advantages, and unless he is improved there are signs that he may fade from the ranks of the retrievers within another generation. I say all this with misgivings because such a great dog deserves to continue, not just at the survival level among die-hards but as a real standout dog contributing to the American hunting scene as the Chesapeake has for over 150 years now.

What has to be done?

First and foremost, he must be bred for a tractable disposition—that is, to quote the standard, "bright and happy" and hence appealing to the general public. Breeders should work away from the dogs with very oily coats. The other retrievers get by without it; so can the Chessie. He's got the guts to carry him where few other dogs will go. Those in the breed which show the ability to work upland game well should receive preference in breeding programs. Above all, Chessie people should run their dogs in field trials and really try to mow down the opposition.

To quote the standard again: "Courage, willingness to work, alertness, nose, intelligence, love of water, general quality, and, most of all, disposition should be given primary consideration in the selection and breeding of the Chesapeake Bay dog." If this were accomplished, the dog would come roaring back to its former glory.

Recently while chatting with a white-haired, weatherbeaten duck guide who had retired to a little shack along Maryland's Eastern Shore, I mentioned the Chessie to him and saw memories tug at his heart. Memories composed of one of the greatest hunting sports on earth and the dog that was once king of it.

"Let the young fellows have their Labs and Goldens and field trials," he said ardently. "The man who really hunts ducks uses a Chesapeake— along the windy tip of Montauk or around the rugged coast of Cape Hatteras where the waves have no mercy, on the icy lakes of Manitoba or along rivers like the Missouri where wicked currents will drag a weaker dog clean out of sight, if not to the bottom. This is Chessie country"—he shook a gnarled fist at me—"it will always be Chessie country."

I hope so. I hope so.

The Irish Water Spaniel

This, the largest and oldest member of the spaniel family, is often called a clown because of his amusing shaggy-dog looks, but he's far from a clown when it comes to hunting. For centuries he's been fetching ducks and geese from water in his homeland of Ireland, in England and here in America. That he is classified as a retriever despite his spaniel name is due to his size and the fact that this is his primary occupation.

Earliest-known mention of the dog—in fact, of the word "spaniel"—is in the Irish Laws of 17 A.D., by which water spaniels were given as tribute to the king.

The breed as we know it today was developed in Ireland well over a century ago. Prior to 1850 two strains, the South Country Water Spaniel and the North Country Water Spaniel, existed in Ireland. The North Country dog was similar to the now extinct English Water Spaniel, parti-colored and of medium size. The South Country dog, used around the bogs of the River Shannon, was larger in size, curly-coated and of solid dark colors, brown and black, and was called the Shannon or Rat Tail Spaniel. It is from this breed that the modern Irish Water Spaniel evolved.

An Irishman named Justin McCarthy is given credit for the pioneering which perfected the modern Irish Water Spaniel. We know he was breeding them in their present form around 1850 and started at least a decade or two before that. Boatswain was his most famous dog and his descendants won both field and bench titles to a degree that established the breed in early retriever days.

Justin McCarthy would never reveal one scrap of information as to the crosses he made to create the modern Irish Water Spaniel other than to say that the South Country dog (Shannon or Rat Tail Spaniel) was the base. But this was rather obvious. Since that time authorities have persistently linked the Irish Water Spaniel with the French Poodle because, except for the Irisher's smooth face, topknot and rat tail, they are almost identical. McCarthy said himself that the Irish Water Spaniel could not stand a retriever or setter outcross and maintain its basic characteristics. Some allude to the Tweed Spaniel which helped establish the Golden Retriever, but the coat, color and conformation are too far afield. The Poodle had for centuries been used for water work in retrieving wild fowl, thus his ability and intelligence would have helped the Irisher while not destroying his looks.

The only other dog that might have served McCarthy's purposes, in fact the nearest thing to both the Irish Water Spaniel and the Poodle, is the Portuguese Water Dog called the *Cão d'Agua*, an old, old breed which may have had a part in producing the original South Country dog and the Poodle. For centuries this dog has helped fishermen along the entire Portuguese coast. He comes in two varieties, one shaggy-coated, the other with a dense, curly coat and topknot just as the Irisher has. This latter dog might have been the ancestor of the Shannon or Rat Tail Spaniel, for we know the Irish carried on extensive trade with the Iberian Peninsula and possibly obtained early water-dog blood from the Portuguese. Or perhaps McCarthy used this dog as an outcross at a later date.

Whatever the case, the Irish Water Spaniel was one of the first retrievers to come to this country. Old books indicate the breed was widely used by duck hunters in the 1860s, so he must have arrived well before that. The first volume of the National American Kennel Club's Stud Book, published in 1878, contained an Irish Water Spaniel male owned by Richard Tuttle of Chicago. Later, several hundred were registered.

The early Irish Water Spaniels, many of McCarthy bloodlines, were almost identical with what we see today, except that they were a little smaller in size. The East and West Coast hunters increased his size for the rough coastal-water work he was required to do. The dog is always liver in color, stands 22 to 24 inches and weighs 55 to 65 pounds; bitches 21 to 23 inches, 45 to 58 pounds.

Three characteristics distinguished the dog: its rat tail, its bare face (the Poodle has a long-haired face which is clipped), and its topknot, which is a clot of long loose curls growing into a peak above the eyes on the dome. The dog has essentially a Poodle head, possesses gay, quick movements

There's no more willing retriever than the Irish Water Spaniel.

and a coat that is dense with tight, crisp ringlets of hair without woolliness. In personality he's friendly with those he knows but inclined to be aloof among strangers.

In the early days the Irish Water Spaniel was the best water retriever we had—bold, fearless and a great swimmer. No doubt he contributed strongly to the Chesapeake Bay Retriever which overtook him in popularity after 1900, though as late as 1922 the Field Dog Stud Book registered more Irish Water Spaniels than any other retriever breed. The dog also was fundamental in the formation of the American Water Spaniel, a smaller native dog popular in the Middle West.

The Irisher came into first use as a river dog for duck hunters in the Midwest. Soon he spread to gunners and market hunters in Long Island, Cape Cod and along the New Jersey coastline. A little later, Californians began using him. The dog is very intelligent, probably inheriting this from his Poodle ancestry. He's easy to train, catches on quickly to a situation,

The Irish Water Spaniel closely resembles the Standard Poodle, but has shorthaired face and rat tail.

works well from a short blind, a duck boat or from rocks. He's a powerful swimmer of almost inexhaustible energy, which makes him a great dog on cripples. He treads water until a diving duck surfaces, then he plunges for it, sometimes diving underwater to grab it.

On land he's also a standout retriever and can spring game with the best of any of his brother breeds. He takes to heavy cover readily, but where burrs are thick they quickly clog up his coat.

Among the early supporters of the breed was the Reverend Thomas Moore-Smith who moved from Ireland to Scotch Plains, New Jersey, in 1904 and brought with him a kennel of great Irish Water Spaniels which produced many outstanding dogs, including several bench champions. During and after World War I Dr. Herbert E. Rodley and Mr. Percy K. Swan, both of Checo, California, went to great lengths to breed and promote the dog, as did Dr. C. H. Searle of Franklin, Illinois. In more recent times Mr. Thomas C. Marshall of Fairfield, Connecticut, and Mr. Russell G. Lindsay of Milwaukee have been staunch supporters of the Irish Water Spaniel. Mr. Marshall's Ch. Blackwater Bog was the first dog to win his CDX award in this country in 1937, the year in which Irishers led all other sporting breeds in Obedience awards. Mr. Lindsay's Ch. Handsome Mahoney was one of the great bench dogs and sires of recent years.

In 1937 the Irish Water Spaniel Club of America was founded, soon boasted fifty members and ten bench champions in its first four years of existence. In its first year a field trial for the breed was held, and from time to time several Irishers have competed in open retriever trials throughout the country. Though they have scored some worth-while wins, their owners too often have not finished their dogs to the fine polish necessary for real success. The breed appears quite frequently on the show bench where he has had many outstanding triumphs. In the field these days he is used as a duck dog like the Chesapeake.

Faithful are the hunting followers of the Irish Water Spaniel because they know his merit, but they become fewer and fewer as time passes.

The Labrador is a fine upland game dog.

The Labrador Retriever

The Labrador is king of the retrievers.

As much as the opposition may object to this, the facts are undeniable. Ever since his rise in England around 1905 the Lab has dominated the retriever scene there. Ever since his entry into this country in the 1920s the Lab has dominated the retriever scene here. Over the last five years he has won nearly 90 per cent of all the placements in open all-breed field trials in the United States.

Yes, cry the opposition, but he composes almost 90 per cent of the entries so why shouldn't he win so much? He's everywhere, swarming all over you.

This argument crumbles before the deeper truth that the reason he composes and wins almost 90 per cent of field-trial competition is because he's that much better a dog on the average. If this were not so, the percentages would be different. You may have to breed five Goldens to come up with one good field-trialer, maybe ten Chessies, but possibly three out of five Labs of field blood will be good enough to win.

The Labrador is to the retrievers what the Pointer is to the pointing breeds, what the Yankees are to baseball. Over the long haul you just can't beat 'em.

What makes the Lab what he is?

First, he is a man's dog—virile, stouthearted but possessed of a wonderful disposition. He never cringes before a whip in training or a mountain-sized wave to fetch a duck, neither is he bullheaded. He's strong, animated, stylish, always puts on a good show no matter what he does. Besides, he's intelligent enough to learn his business, whether a soft-handed amateur or a school-of-hard-knocks professional is teaching him; in other words he will train with or without affection. He is as tough and hardy as the Chesapeake, better on upland game and generally equal to the Golden in this, the latter's forte. He's better than the Golden in water, has the ideal coat—heavy enough for protection in any kind of weather, not long enough to require any upkeep, not oily enough to be smelly. He's gentle and affectionate to a fault, but when a gun, duck or retrieving dummy appears, he comes roaring to life. His over-all ability in water and land retrieving, flushing upland game, raises him head and shoulders above the rest of the retriever breeds.

The Labrador is popular because he most nearly combines the elements needed and wanted in a modern retriever. He is an all-purpose dog; he is a handsome and ideal house dog for the active young man of suburbia who likes to hunt; he is superior at field-trial work under any kind of control and condition.

All the above is a lot of praise, but the Labrador Retriever has earned it. At the same time, don't gain the impression that every Lab is perfect. There are hardheaded ones, stupid ones, mean ones the same as in any other breed of dog, but these are not his characteristics.

One criticism that old-time duck hunters raise is his black color. They claim that, sitting beside a blind or in the light grass one finds in the Middle West, the dog is easily seen and ducks will flare away from him. This argument, though it sounds logical, doesn't stand up under hunting conditions. For some reason ducks are *not* frightened by his crouching black figure. At least, hunters report this over and over. But for those who refuse to accept it, there is the Yellow Labrador who blends in neatly in lighter environments, also the chocolate Lab which comes along occasionally and perhaps throws back to the same line of St. John's Newfoundland from which the dingy-red dog Sailor, progenitor of the Chesapeake, originated.

We don't know the exact history of the Labrador. We know he is a direct descendant of the St. John's Newfoundland, which reached its peak in England around 1850 and tapered off around 1865. Earlier, the 2nd Earl of Malmesbury and Colonel Hawker, each of whom obtained excellent specimens off the Newfoundland fishing boats at Poole in southeast England in the early 1800s, both referred to the St. John's dog as the Labrador,

National Retriever Ch. Del-Tone Colvin.

possibly to avoid confusion between it and the larger Newfoundland. The original St. John's retriever was probably very similar to the Labrador today, only a shade smaller and the tail a bit more otterlike—thicker and parted down the underside.

As the St. John's dog became more and more difficult to obtain, because of English quarantine and Newfoundland's dog tax and sheep laws, the kennels, which had kept the dog relatively pure, began to outcross to retrievers like the Curly-Coat and the Flat-Coat. Some claimed that

Pointers and Setters were used, but we have no confirmation of it. Possibly smaller members of the massive Newfoundland breed were employed. In any case the St. John's dog's characteristics of color, water ability, coat, and general conformation prevailed in the larger Labrador which we have today.

In the 1880s the 3rd Earl of Malmesbury, continuing in his father's footsteps, the Duke of Buccleuch, and the Earl of Holme gave the modern Labrador great impetus through their kennels. Malmesbury Tramp and Netherby Boatswain were two foundation sires of that era, while Ned, Avon, Neth and Kielder were great working dogs from which the breed gained momentum through the 1890s.

The first Labrador to run in a field trial was Munden Single, owned by the Hon. A. Holland-Hibbert. The dog ran in the International Gun Dog Trials at Sherbourne in 1904 and earned a Certificate of Merit. Up to that point Flat-Coats had dominated retriever field-trial competition but that soon came to an end. In 1906 Major Maurice Portal's Flapper placed second in two trials and won first in the Kennel Club's trials in 1907. By 1910, in a short space of six years, the Labrador has assumed a supremacy which has never been surrendered.

Major Porter's Flapper and Captain A. C. Butter's Peter of Faskally, whelped in 1908, were both great early field-trial dogs. Peter of Faskally and Ilderston Ben, a bench champion, are the two main sources from which the modern field Labrador rose. Other early English champions include Hindson Zulu 1906, Patron of Faskally and Peter of Whitmore, both whelped in 1911 and sons of Peter of Faskally, Tag of Whitmore 1915 and a son of Patron of Faskally, Titus of Whitmore 1912 and son of Ilderton Ben, and the famous Dual Ch. Banchory Bolo 1915 and grandson of Peter of Faskally. From these field champions practically all the Labs winning in the United States today are descended in part or many times over.

During the middle and late 1920s the Labrador began to come to our shores. In those days the Chessie was king, ruling over Curly-Coats, Flat-Coats and Irish Water Spaniels. He was a great dog, first in water, first on land, first in the hearts of all duck hunters. But in a matter of a decade the Labbie overtook and passed the mighty Chessie. He did it via the field-trial route, a most infallible way of settling any argument about the ability of hunting dogs.

Retriever trials were just beginning in this country then. The first licensed one for Labradors was held in 1931 at Glenmere, Chester, Orange County, New York, with sixteen dogs in the Open All-Age stake. The winner was Mrs. Marshall Field's Carl of Boghurst.

The first all-breed retriever trial took place at Strongs Neck, East Setauket, Long Island, on December 29, 1934. Labradors finished first, second and third. A Chesapeake was fourth. From then on the Chessie began to sink, although the first Field Trial Champion Retriever in America was Skipper Bob, a Chessie, in 1935. The first Labrador Field Champion was W. Averell Harriman's Blind of Arden later that same year.

As the Labrador began to dominate field-trial competition, the hunting public realized the dog must possess qualities equally effective for shooting. Soon gunners began using him in all climates and under all conditions, and in a few years he spread across the length and breadth of the United States, even into Canada. He was just as good in the hot swamps of Florida and Louisiana as he was along the New England coast, the wheat flats of Kansas or the rivers of Colorado and Oregon.

He had an outstanding nose for finding crippled ducks in a marsh or trailing a wounded pheasant half a mile to fetch it. His short coat shed burrs in upland game work and was no drag in water. He loved the water, hit it with a great splash that was a joy to see, was a fast and powerful swimmer, perhaps not quite as rugged as the Chesapeake but more than adequate for any duck or goose hunt in our time. Above all, he loved his

A Yellow Lab works a pheasant.

work. He was a retriever to the core and it showed in every eager, joyful movement he made.

Thus he overtook the Chessie and today dominates in all working phases of the retriever world. Almost 60 per cent of the retrievers registered annually are Labs. As we said earlier, they compose nearly 90 per cent of retriever-trial entries and win nearly 90 per cent of the prizes. They are used the country over for all types of waterfowl hunting and retrieving as well as upland game hunting.

The Labrador Retriever Club, Inc., was formed in 1932 to promote interest in the breed, though this proved hardly necessary. Dr. Samuel Milbank of New York was the first president. The club has grown to be a powerful organization.

Many women have taken avidly to the sport of retriever field trialing and a considerable number compete with Labradors, in open stakes against the top professionals, in amateur stakes against men, even in the National Retriever Championship. The first woman to compete in the National was Mrs. Mahlon B. Wallace. Some of the other ladies have been Mrs. A. A. Jones and Mrs. Marian McPhail, each three times, Miss Frances Griscom, twice, Mrs. Alan Williams, Mrs. Clifford Brokaw, Jr. and Mrs. Milton D. Orowitz.

Three other women, Mrs. Carl Erickson, Mrs. J. Gould Remick and Mrs. Frances Garlock have at various times been judges for the National Retriever Championship, the highest honor a retriever follower can be paid.

Through the years many outstanding Labradors have appeared both as competitors and as producers. More than 400 retrievers of all breeds have earned the title of Field Champion. Of these about 80 per cent have been Labradors. But that doesn't tell the whole story. To earn such a title a dog must amass a total of 10 points in open all-age stakes or 15 points in amateur stakes for an amateur field-trial championship. He must win first place in one all-age stake of 5-point value (sixteen or more participants); the rest he can pick up with second-, third- or fourth-place wins. Thus it's possible to win a field title in two trials, but this very seldom happens because any good stake is crammed full of already crowned champs gathering more points or trying to qualify for the National, which must be done each year. More than half the Labrador champions have scored enough points for two or more titles, some enough for half a dozen, even ten or twelve open championships. The all-time high-point retrievers are all Labradors and every one was a black one.

Labs are great water dogs, fearless swimmers.

Labradors have always been popular show dogs, especially in England, though we have had many bench champions here in America. Mr. Franklin B. Lord's Boli of Blake in 1933 was the first to win his bench championship in this country. But about the most outstanding show record of all Labs was put together by Earlsmore Moor of Arden, owned by Dr. Samuel Milbank. He entered the show ring 42 times and won 40 best of breed, 12 winner of sporting group, 27 times placed in the sporting group and 5 best in shows.

There have been 21 or 22 dual-champion Labradors, a point which has always made followers of the breed proud. It meant that the dog bred very true to type and even the handsome ones had excellent field qualities, because a field championship is much more difficult to come by than a bench-show title. In recent years, however, the style has changed to the extent that the large-size Labrador that Americans prefer for water and field work no longer wins in the show ring. At the moment, show judges want the small English Lab that is pretty but doesn't have the power to win field trials or take heavy water work. Thus the Labrador seems to be heading the way of most sporting breeds and unfortunately dividing into show strains and field strains.

Dual champions are becoming more and more scarce, but there have been some great ones in the past. Mr. and Mrs. Paul Bakewell III have owned two immortal ones, Dual Ch. and Triple Nat. Ch. Shed of Arden and Dual Ch. Little Pierre of Deer Creek. Both these dogs were among the great Lab field-trial dogs of all time, and like the top field dogs of any breed their conformation was good enough to finish on the bench. Mr. Blakewell, who is an amateur, trained and handled them to their victories as he did with the immortal Golden, FTC Rip.

Labradors are vigorous dogs whose characteristics are very dominant, yet not infrequently two black Labs will throw yellow pups. Because the color is striking, several people have tried unsuccessfully to found strains of Yellow Labs both in this country and in England. But it is a recessive color, hence their efforts for the most part have been in vain. Besides, all the outstanding Labs have been black.

Many have been the great producing Labradors. Some of the immortal sires are Drinkstone Pons of Wingan; FTC Freehaven Jay; FTC Glenairlie Rover; FTC Hiwood Mike; Hiwood Risk; FTC, Dual Ch. Little Pierre of Deer Creek; 1949 Nat. Ch., FTC, AFTC Marvadel Black Gum; Mint of Barrington; Odds On; Raffles of Earlsmoor; Triple Nat. Ch., Dual Ch. Shed of Arden; FTC, AFTC The Spider of Kingswere; FTC Timber Town Clansman; and Dual Ch. Treveilyr Swift.

Some of the immortal Labrador bitches are Bracken of Timber Town; FTC Decoy of Arden; Marvadel Cinders; Peggy of Shipton; FTC Tar of

Mission accomplished.

Arden; FTC Gilmore's Peggy; FTC Keith's Black Magic; FTC Truly Yours of Garfield; FTC Zipper of Sugar Valley, 1962 Nat. Ch.; FTC Bigstone Hope, 1945 Nat. Ch.; FTC Black Magic of Audlon; and 1960 Nat. Am. Ch. FTC, AFTC Queenie of Redding.

In appearance the Labrador is short-coupled and strongly built, a very active dog but with a lot of composure. He has a good wide skull, only a slight stop and long, powerful jaws free from snippiness. Eyes can be brown, black or yellow; the last is the least preferred. The dog has good bone structure and plenty of muscle, giving him a look of substance. His tail is a distinctive feature, very thick at the base and tapering off, free of feathering, with a rounded appearance which is the "otter" tail. It is usually carried gaily but should not curl over the back. The coat is short, very dense and without wave; it should feel rather hard and have great sheen.

In color, the Black Lab may have a small white spot on the chest. Yellows may vary from fox-red to light cream. Nose should be black or dark brown, although "fading" to pink in winter is not serious. A "Dudley" nose (pink without pigmentation) is penalized in the show ring. Chocolates range from light sedge to chocolate brown. Eyes may be light brown or clear yellow. Noses the same as with the Yellow Labbie. Dogs weigh approximately 60 to 75 pounds in working condition and stand 22½ to

24½ inches; bitches 55 to 70 pounds and 21½ to 23½ inches in height.

The Lab's beauty is in his latent power, his black coat, his extreme alertness, his proud bearing, his sizzling run, and tail cracking gaily as he streaks off to retrieve. Looking at him, you know he's no ornament, yet he has charm and great amiability at all times and under all conditions. His long heritage of working for man, especially around water, has given him a natural intelligence so he understands quickly what is wanted. When it involves anything to pick up and bring to his master, he is overjoyed.

To gain a little attention when the boss of the house comes home at night, a Lab will soon develop the habit of fetching something for him—a slipper, the evening paper, a child's toy—just to say, "Hi-ya, boss. When are we going to get to work?"

If you're looking for the combination land and water dog, maybe a little field trialing, along with a house pet and watchdog, the Labrador is nearly impossible to beat. He is kindly, obedient, handsome, loyal, and under all this he is a whale of a lot of dog, one who has earned his title—King of the Retrievers.

Here you are! Training the young Poodle.

The Poodle

Outdoorsmen raise an eyebrow and most retriever folk shudder when the Poodle is mentioned as a hunting dog. They fail to realize, for one thing, that the Poodle is the oldest-known retriever in the world; for another, that more and more people are using him as a working field dog here in the United States as they have been for centuries in England and Europe; for another, that he may someday run in field trials across America against the big-time retrievers—Labradors, Goldens, Chesapeakes, etc. For these reasons we discuss him here.

First off, let it be clearly understood that we're talking not about the Miniature or Toy but the Standard Poodle, which stands 23 to 25 inches high and weighs 50 to 65 pounds. He possesses a superb double coat ideal for water work, is a strong, rugged dog full of life and bounce, full of intelligence too. It is this last fact that has probably cost him his birthright in this country. Because he has appeared in circuses and dog acts for so long and been a stylish bauble for milady's world of high fashion (particularly the miniature and toy models), he has been classified in the United States as one of the do-nothing breeds of the non-sporting group— which he definitely is not!

He's a retriever and we can trace him as such well back into history. With relatively little change in looks, even down to a lion's clip, he appears carved in Roman bas-reliefs of the first century. During the Middle Ages the dog spread to most parts of Europe. In fifteenth- and sixteenth-century Germany drawings by Albrecht Dürer portray the dog almost as we know him today. The breed gained its name from the German word *Pudel* or *Pudelin,* meaning to splash in water. In France the dog (a shade smaller in size than our Standard) is called the *Caniche,* from the French words *canard* and *cane* meaning duck, while the *Barbet,* one of the Poodle's illustrious French ancestors, gained its name from a species of bearded duck common in France in early times. Through the paintings of Goya and other seventeenth- and eighteenth-century Spanish artists the Poodle is connected to the Iberian Peninsula, also through his close relative, the Portuguese Water Dog, which even today bears him a close resemblence.

We are fairly certain that the Poodle came to the United States in colonial times, because a man named W. R. Furness wrote glowingly about him nearly 100 years ago. In his *American Book of the Dog* he mentioned that the Poodle has "extraordinary power in the water" and "excels all his race in that element, at least, being able to distance the strongest water spaniel and swim round and round a Newfoundland."

The painstaking haircuts we see on Poodles today and regard as frivolity —the Continental, Royal Dutch, English Saddle and other clips—were developed centuries ago so the dog's weight would be lessened in water and his joints and vital organs remain protected while he retrieved. If he weren't clipped, he'd be little more than a conglomerate mass of woolly hair and would bog down terribly when swimming through water.

All the above is elaborated to convince unbelievers that the Poodle has had a long and proud heritage as a retriever.

About ten years ago a group of Poodle owners living along the shores of Maryland (of all places!), cognizant of this heritage, formed the Greenspring Poodle Club to experiment with the use of Poodles as duck dogs. Under the guidance of Mr. Charles LeBoutillier, Jr., of Towson, Maryland, and Mrs. Gordon Fisher, Jr., of Easton, a program was started to determine whether the Poodle still had any "retrievability" left in him. They soon discovered not only did he have plenty left but he also excelled in certain phases of the work—marking, memory, spectacular nose, an exuberant desire to hunt, very tender retrieving mouth.

The club grew to nearly thirty active members, all with standard Poodles of household and bench-show backgrounds, all in training for non-slip retriever work on land and in water. Even a "Poodle retriever clip" was worked out—an all-over clip that leaves the dog looking like a Curly-Coat but with a pompon tail.

For many centuries the Poodle has been an excellent retriever, highly intelligent and very tender-mouthed.

The first Poodle field trial was held in 1957 at Mrs. Fisher's Wye Town Farm, a most successful event. Later, many dogs were used for duck shooting in and around the Chesapeake Bay area while the outstanding dogs like Mr. LeBoutillier's Show Champion Stonewood Gold Standard struck out for retriever field trials. At first retriever people were stunned to see a Poodle run in sanctioned trials on this, the hallowed ground of the Chesapeake Bay Retriever. Because the Poodle was not listed as a retriever it couldn't compete for placements, but judges scored it along with the other entries and afterward gave owners an idea of where they stood— usually well up in the stake.

Beyond the standout qualities mentioned before, the Poodle showed exceptional swimming ability even under icy conditions, exceptional ability for jumping over obstacles in the path of a retrieve, exceptional response to whistle and hand signals. The Poodle's intelligence is clearly indicated in field-trial work—to his advantage and disadvantage. He was not as brash or bulldozing as our modern retrievers, but tended to think of the easiest way to do the job. Judges like to see a big Labrador or Chesapeake crash through a thicket or swim a straight line to a mark. A Poodle would more often than not skirt the thicket or skip around the shoreline to make a retrieve—and usually in quicker time.

As a result of all this, Poodle field-trial fanciers discovered that certain bloodlines were more satisfactory than others, and breeding programs were set up to produce dogs of greater field ability. It was found that the lighter-colored Poodles made the best retrievers—the whites, creams, apricots. The darker-colored dogs didn't always have the endless determination so necessary in any retriever.

From the retrieving program came a revitalized interest in the Standard Poodle not only in the immediate area but in various parts of the country. The publicity which the club received brought a response from many other Standard Poodle owners who wanted to train their dogs or were already using them for retrieving work, even flushing upland game to the gun and fetching it *à la* spaniel style.

Several owners joined the Maryland and Talbot County Retriever clubs, trained their Poodles with the cream of retrieverdom and gained the respect and cooperation of old-time ducking members.

The hope is that, in the words of Mr. LeBoutillier, "eventually a national interest in Poodles as retrievers can be generated and when that happy day comes we will be able to draw up a set of rules and a standard, and work for the recognition of our breed in field-trial competition by holding qualifying matches and conducting licensed trials. The fascination of the sport is sure to catch on and the pleasure of owning a Poodle as a companion as well as having him a contestant in a challenging activity can be an absorbing pastime."

To date this has not happened, mainly because of the lack of an organization through which it can be accomplished, but perhaps someday we shall see it come about. And why not? Some of the leading kennels in England are breeding whole litters of Poodle gun dogs. In France and elsewhere on the Continent the Poodle is used extensively as a duck dog. So don't be surprised next fall if you see a cream-colored Poodle bounce out of a duck blind, hit the water and retrieve a mallard in jig time. They've had what it takes through history and they still have it.

Chapter 5

The Scent-Hunting Hounds

Once upon a time a family lived in a cave, and one howling, stormy night as the father, mother and three children sat crowded around their sparkling fire, a mangy wolf or dumb jackal or a just plain dog crawled in out of the rain. The bearded man grabbed a club, but his wife restrained him. They waited and watched the animal drag itself weakly over to the fire and lie down. The next morning the children gave it a bird's head and it wagged its tail. That night and each night thereafter it slept at the mouth of the cave and kept everything and everyone out. By day it took to following the bearded man whenever he went hunting, fishing or gossiping. And in those secret moments when the bearded man sat down on a boulder and waxed eloquent about his dreams of success or mumbled of his failures, the dog listened sympathetically. If the man spoke heatedly of his wife and shouted to the heavens, "Don't you think I'm right?", the dog would wag his tail. Soon the bearded man became so odd that if anyone as much as laughed at his pet animal he was ready to bust his head open with a club. You could tell him his wife was a poor cave keeper, that his children were stupid, but God help you if you mentioned anything wrong about his dog.

As a result of this companionship several millenniums ago, we now have a canine population in the United States of 27,000,000.

During the interim, *canis familiaris* did more than lend sympathy to his pal, mankind. He earned his keep by hunting. He had two methods: using his eyes to sight-hunt, which meant chasing a quarry at great speed as it crossed an open field or plain, overtaking it and catching it; or using his nose to scent-hunt, which meant smelling the trail left by an animal and following it over hill and dale until the animal, by one way or another, came within the hunter's reach.

In time the nose-hunting dogs came to be called tracking hounds and today they can trail a particular scent, weak or strong, through a thousand others. It may lead across roads, through drainpipes, over water, into mountains, over city streets, but through innate perseverance the hound will follow it to its conclusion. That may mean treeing a raccoon or squirrel, boxing in a bear, catching a fox, bringing a rabbit around for the hunter to shoot, cornering a criminal or finding a lost baby.

The family of tracking hounds is the largest in all dogdom. Its members come in all sizes, shapes and colors, are coated with smooth hair, wire hair and long hair. They range from the snub-legged Dachshund, which toddles along patiently following a rabbit trail, to the long-legged Coonhound that flies through the woods like a cannonball. Some are identical except for size—the large Foxhound, the medium-sized Harrier and the small Beagle.

With all their variations, tracking hounds have a lot in common—except for three breeds. But let's take the majority first. Hounds, since the earliest of times, have been heavy-boned and muscular for endurance. Their principal colors are black, tan, red and sometimes white. They have big, well-domed heads that smack of brains, and good solid snouts for smelling. They are usually loose-skinned, some more so than others, but nearly all have dewlaps at the neck and loose skin around the head and face, and all have long, limp, soft ears. In fact the rule seems to be the longer the ear, the better the hound's scenting power. They usually have high sickle tails, often with white tips, that flash as they bounce across the countryside.

The three hounds which are different from the general order of hounddom are the Basenji, diminutive Egyptian "barkless" dog; the Norwegian Elkhound, built on the Spitz lines with a tightly curled tail and small, prick ears; and the Rhodesian Ridgeback, an African lion dog altogether different from anything else. But no matter, at least all the hounds hunt and they do a good job of it, sometimes an incredibly good job of it.

Another thing about the hound world is the verbiage. If you listened in on a hot discussion by fox hunters or coon hunters or beaglers, the parlance would soon drift over your head and you'd swear they were either mad or talking a strange dialect. Below is some of the basic vocabulary necessary to talk hounds. It could extend into a dictionary, but this list will have to suffice:

Babbler: a hound that barks on any kind of scent, or no scent at all but just out of general excitement.

Bawl and chop: a good Coonhound has a bawl voice on the trail and chop voice (quick yip-yip-yip) at the tree, thus a hunter can tell exactly when his hound has treed a raccoon.

Cast: hounds searching for a lost trail are said to be casting.

Couple: a pair of hounds. Foxhounds, Beagles, Bassets are counted in couples when packed; thus 5½ couples would be 11 hounds.

Drawing: hounds searching for a new trail are said to be drawing.

Hound jog: the tireless working gait of slower hounds like the Bloodhound.

Hound-marked: tricolored, black, tan and white.

Line: the scent path of a fox to the fox hunter; the trail of a rabbit to a beagler or Basset man. Coon hunters, lion, bear and wild-boar hunters use the word "trail" to mean the same thing.

Riot: same as Trash or Junk (below) but used by fox hunters.

Saddle: black marking on back, often shaped like a saddle.

Speak, give tongue, open: to bark or bay on the line or trail.

Stallion hound: a male Foxhound that has sired puppies.

Strike: When a hound hits a trail for the first time and opens strongly. For example, a fox hunter's report may read: "Hounds struck at 11:05 near Trimble's Hollow and moved northward over Turner's farm . . ."

Trail: see "Line" above.

Trash or Junk: undesirable scent-giving animals like deer, squirrels, moles, field mice, house cats, etc.; said particularly of Coonhounds which should be trashproof or junkproof, hence will not trail anything but raccoon.

Voice: the tone and quality of a hound's bark. Every hound man can identify each of his hounds by voice, tell exactly what animal is being run and how hot or cold the trail is, all by the voice of his hounds.

Weedy: said of hounds that lack bone and substance.

For nearly two centuries American hounds, though they have forged tradition, even social prestige, by their ability, have never been registered because they were considered strains rather than breeds. Men bred more for voice and competence rather than looks. The result was so wide a variation of Coonhound strains, even Foxhound strains, that no standard could reconcile the differences.

Though there were no registries, accurate records were kept at the great hound kennels in this country by such men as John W. Walker and "Uncle Wash" Maupin, Colonel Haiden C. Trigg, George F. Birdsong and Dr. Thomas Y. Henry, the Plott family and G. P. Ferguson. The result is that in recent years registries have sprung up for all kinds of American hounds from the Walker and the Trigg to the Plott and Mountain Cur. Coon trials have become almost a national craze, with prize money at major events often totaling $30,000 or more and upwards to 10,000 people in attendance. It is nothing for a good Coonhound to sell for $300 to $500, and often they bring $1000 or better.

But money isn't what attracts people from all walks of life to follow the hounds. The quality that has endeared the hound to man's heart through the ages is his ability to "sing," "make music," "talk up a storm," and all the other expressions which describe his baying voice when trailing.

Hounds can be hunted singly or in pairs, but they are best in packs where their voices form a chorus that sets the countryside to ringing and stirs the marrow in the hunter's bones.

The pack in full cry!

The roaring chase!

It flutters the fox hunter's heart, makes him urge his galloping thoroughbred faster over stone walls and fences.

It holds the coon hunter hypnotized on a hilltop in the moonlight, listening to the faint, bawling chorus reach to the black horizon, bend, then turn back and finally chop at a tree.

It grabs the lion hunter's stomach as the pack suddenly shatters the silence of a pine forest floor, roars up a rocky canyon, finally setting up a barrage of noise that means "At bay!"

It holds a boy immobile on a path, shotgun ready, as he waits for his singing Beagle or cur-hound to bring the cottontail around.

To a hound man the greatest music on earth is not opera or jazz or a slinky gal singing blues under a spotlight. It's a pack of Walkers or Redbones or Beagles bawling on the line. And when he dies he expects to be piped to heaven by their music for he knows the old pack will be waiting for him and they'll go on hunting for ever and ever.

Ch. Windy Brow of Panther Ledge, owned by Mrs. R. H. Inslee of Newton, N.J.

The Bloodhound

Though he may not be alphabetically first, the Bloodhound must start off any discussion of scent-hunting hounds. He is not only the venerable founder of the tribe of tracking hounds but has contributed so much to other hunting breeds that to place him otherwise would be unfair.

Since earliest record Old Wrinkle-Puss has been famous for his fantastic ability to sort out a trail, hot or cold, and stay with it until he reached its source. Writers throughout history have mentioned this, though no one has been able to pinpoint the dog's origin, so far back does he trace. It's rather certain that the Greeks around Byzantium (ancient Constantinople or to-day's Istanbul) raised and used him for hunting around 200 B.C. or earlier. The original blood may have been found by Alexander the Great as he marched about, conquering the Middle East, around 330 B.C. The Greeks were always great lovers of hounds. Xenophon wrote a masterful discourse on the use of hounds in hunting hares in 400 B.C. and chances are they were some early sort of Bloodhound.

The belief is that the Bloodhound spread from Byzantium to Greece to Rome, then fanned out from there. The Roman, Claudius Aelianus, wrote glowingly of him in his famous *Historia Animalium* in the third century

A.D. From Italy he probably tagged along with Roman legions to all parts of Europe.

There seem to have been two strains, black and white, both of which, in the eighth century, were taken under the wing of the abbots of St. Hubert, who kept them relatively pure for several hundred years. Almost every monastery maintained a kennel and pack of hounds with such pride and care that these dogs became referred to as "blooded," meaning pure and of the highest order. Hence the name Bloodhound is a contraction of the expression "blooded hound" and does not originate from anything to do with gore or a desire for blood.

During the Crusades, returning armies brought back more hounds and eventually, when crossed with the St. Hubert's Hound, there developed the French Bloodhound, the English Bloodhound (from the black variety) the *Schweisshund* or Swiss Hound, which was red in color, as well as the later German pointing breeds.

But to the monks of St. Hubert must go our unending gratitude for guarding the purity of this greatest of all medieval tracking hounds in a time when the indiscriminate crossing of dogs was the order of the day. Without their efforts we would have little more than a hodgepodge in many of our breeds today.

To the English belongs the credit of perfecting our Bloodhound to the type and quality we know today. In the early 1600s the Bloodhound, similar to his present form, hunted deer. Though not a swift worker, he was relentless in his pursuit and thus archers had a relatively slow-moving deer as a target to shoot at, rather than one flying at full speed; but soon sport came into it and faster-running hounds were developed. But Old Wrinkle-Puss took on another chore, that of tracking bandits and thieves who made a living by holding up travelers and hiding out in the forests of North England and Scotland. For this he gained enduring fame and was dubbed the sleuthhound.

The Bloodhound came to the American colonies in their early days, and here too he gained fame, but a rather ignominious kind, as a tracker of slaves trying to escape the South before the Civil War. In more recent times he has redeemed himself by tracking down criminals. For this work he has gained a fantastic reputation, brought about thousands of convictions, trailing his quarry sometimes more than fifty miles.

Contrary to what one might think of a dog doing this type of work, the Bloodhound is one of the most docile and lovable of all dogs. He will, after having been given a scent of the wanted person, trail slowly, methodically, relentlessly, until he has found the criminal, then wag his tail at him. Many too have been his rescues of small children who have wandered off and become lost or fallen in holes from which they cannot escape. The

Bloodhound almost unfailingly finds their scent and tracks them down.

If only from Thurber cartoons, most everyone knows the Bloodhound look of loose, sagging skin. It hangs in great folds about the head and neck, giving an expression of lugubrious wisdom. The dog has a very high crown or dome to his skull; eyes deeply sunk in diamond-shaped orbits; ears thin and soft, hanging very long and curling in graceful folds; deep-hanging flews and a dangling dewlap at the neck.

Although slow of gait, the Bloodhound is a powerful dog. He has an easy, swinging hound jog that moves him along for hours at a time. His chest and back are built strongly, his legs have plenty of bone and muscle, his stern (tail) is long and carried high with a moderate amount of gaiety. Dogs stand 25 to 27 inches at the withers and weigh 90 to 110 pounds, while bitches stand 23 to 25 inches and weigh 80 to 100 pounds, with specimens on the larger side preferred. The standard expresses his temperament perfectly when it says, "he is extremely affectionate, neither quarrelsome with companions nor with other dogs. His nature is somewhat shy, and equally sensitive to kindness or correction by his master."

Though the Bloodhound is a celebrated dog, he remains rather rare here in the United States, and in England during the last century he came close to extinction several times. His lack of popularity as a working dog stems from his slow and relentless, consequently unglamorous, manner of hunting. Other hound breeds to which he has contributed his tracking genius hunt with a wild abandon that is considered more sporty and exciting. Yet some hunters, particularly in crowded New England, still use him for shooting foxes. He is particularly good at this trade because he moves slowly, and the fox is more amused than frightened by his pursuer, consequently doesn't roam over such a vast area. A fox worked by a Bloodhound will often stay within a 100-acre area, and a wily hunter who knows the country can generally station himself on a run and shoot his quarry. Whereas a rip-roaring Walker or Trigg drives a fox so fast and furiously that Old Brush-tail will run clean out of the country and perhaps cover a thousand or more acres before turning back. Thus one of the best ways to shoot a fox in a semirural area is with a Bloodhound.

This age-old hound is also used occasionally for coon, possum and rabbit hunting as well as human tracking and is, of course, seen frequently as a show dog. Wherever he goes, he's a most kindly, lovable gentleman, nothing like what his name implies.

Perhaps Old Wrinkle-Puss is not the most resplendent name for him but it certainly fits the look of the dog. I'm sure that if he overheard someone call him that, he'd smile back good-naturedly and say in his deep, melodious voice, "At least there's no one else quite like me."

That's true in many wonderful ways.

The Beagle

The Beagle—merry, stouthearted little fellow with the Foxhound profile —is America's most popular dog. Some estimate his ranks to be 4,000,000 in the United States alone. East and west, north and south, he is used for one great purpose, the pursuit of all forms of rabbits—jacks, snowshoes, English hares, and especially the cottontail.

The registered Beagle is seen in the show ring, in the field trial, in beagling packs, as an apartment-house dweller, family pet in suburbia, hunting pal of farm boys across the country. The unregistered Beagle is all of this too, only in far greater numbers. Comes the fall, when dog thieves prowl about stealing hunting dogs, the Beagle is the most prized target.

What has made this big little fellow all that he is?

He's a handy dog, easy to keep—no fuss, no bother. He lives easily in a small kennel, doghouse and chain, a box in the corner behind the stove, even under the back porch. He's playful and friendly, but always in the back of his head is the thought of that luscious rabbit scent which makes him an eager, tireless hunter. There's not much to training a Beagle. Just run him with an older one and he learns the trade in a jiffy. And when three or four of his kind pack up and hit a line, their joyous and excited baying is thrilling music to all who listen.

The Beagle is more than just a rabbit dog, too. He's a master at trailing and flushing pheasants, working all types of upland game for that matter. Some have taught him to run the fox, knowing that whatever the situation the Beagle will work it with stout determination. His keen nose will follow a cold trail, rout out a quarry and stick to the trail or line until it has gone to earth, taken flight, been shot or he catches it himself. He'll work any kind of country, from rough, rocky hills to easy flatland; he'll dive through briars; he'll swim brooks, climb into drains, hollow trees, gullies, go anywhere that a trail leads or where there might be game.

Like most hounds, he's not particularly sensitive but he likes attention and always responds to kindness and affection. He learns quickly the ways of hunting, and the more he can work for his master afield, the better dog he becomes in all respects.

The Beagle is a cocky little devil. Whether in his swaggering trot with tail flying high, ears and eyes alerted for action, or plunging all-out in hot pursuit of game, he grabs your attention. And when he sits beside you, tail wagging, he is friendliness to the core.

All this has endeared him more than any other dog to Americans. Not only Americans but Englishmen too, for he comes originally from that country, where for centuries he has been the warmer of hearts of kings and commoners alike.

His name first appears in a book called *Esquire of Low Degree* published in 1475. It reads:

> With theyr beagles in that place
> And seven score raches at his rechase.

Origin of the word may trace to the Old French *begeule* meaning open throat, or to the Old English *begel*, the Celtic *beag* or the French *beigh*, all meaning small.

The English king Edward III (1312–77) was reported to have carried sixty couples of hare hounds, probably Beagles, as he went to the wars in France. Queen Elizabeth (1533–1603) loved this little breed enough to have one painted with her in a portrait. King George IV (1762–1830), an ardent beagler, did the same with his famous pack of dwarf Beagles.

From 1550 to 1800 Beagles came in several coats, smooth-haired to rough-haired like the Otter Hound, and ranged in height from five inches up. Nine- to eleven-inch size was the favorite. The miniatures were, as one writer put it, admirably suited to be "enjoyed by ladies of the greatest timidity as well as gentlemen laboring under infirmities." So small were some of these little fellows that a whole pack could be taken to the field in two panniers, the deep wicker baskets that fitted one to each side of a horse.

Before the early 1800s everyone who could had a pack of Beagles. After that time, sport demanded a faster chase and faster hounds, thus the rise of fox hunting, swifter in all departments. Many of the Beagle packs broke up, particularly the smaller-sized ones, under 10 inches. Still some great packs remained, among them that of Mr. Hames Crane of Dorchester and that of the Reverend Philip Honeywood, of whom the famous engraving "The Merry Beaglers" is known by sportsmen everywhere.

In America about the earliest mention of the Beagle is in 1642 in the Town Records of Ipswich, Massachusetts. It reads: ". . . for the better destroying or fraying away wolves from the town it is ordered that . . . every householder whose estate is rated 500 pounds and upward, shall

Beagles and boys go together, as every game warden knows.

keep a sufficient mastiff dog; or 100 to 500 pounds, shall provide a sufficient hound or beagle, to the intent that they be in readiness to hunt and be employed for the ends aforesaid."

American colonists certainly brought Beagles with them for hunting. They would have been a most practical dog. From the scanty records we have prior to the Civil War these Beagles were snippy-nosed, crooked-legged dogs more on the Dachshund or Basset order.

The first modern Beagles arrived in the United States about 1868 when General Richard Rowett imported Sam, Warrior, Pilot and Dolly. Warrior was bred to Rosy (Sam-Dolly) and produced Dodge's Rattler, pillar of the famous Rowett strain which contributed so heavily to our Beagle today.

Mr. Norman Gilmore of Granby, Connecticut, imported some early Beagles that crossed particularly well with the Rowett blood. Later, in 1880, a Mr. Arnold imported a pack from Northern England, as did Mr. James L. Kernochan in 1896. After that the Beagle's popularity grew by leaps and bounds, and great strains like the Blue Cap, developed by Hiram Card of Canada, began to appear.

In 1884 the American English Beagle Club was formed, a standard drawn up, and seven years later this group merged with the National Beagle Club which is today the parent organization of the many clubs around the country. All are associated with American Kennel Club, which does the registering.

The first Beagle field trial was held at Hyannis, Massachusetts, November 4, 1890, but because of paucity of rabbits and the fact that scrub oaks and underbrush made judging impossible, the trial was immediately moved to Salem Depot, New Hampshire. It was a great success, and the sport grew steadily until 1940, fifty years later, when fifty-three trials were licensed by AKC. Since that time the figures have sprawled phenomenally. In 1960 there were 57,322 starters in 399 licensed trials and an untold number more in some 2000 sanctioned or fun trials which were run in every state across the country.

Today three types of Beagle field trials are held: Plan A Sanction (two days); Plan B Sanction (one day), and Licensed, which is the big-time, important trial lasting four to five days, attracting sometimes as many as 200 entries and giving points in All-Age classes toward field championships. One point is awarded to the winner of first place for each Beagle started; one-half point for second; one-third for third and one-quarter for fourth. Thus if thirty-six hounds were entered, the first-place win would be worth 36 points; second, 18; third, 12; fourth, 9. To gain the title of Field Champion a total of 120 points must be amassed, including three first-place wins. Sanction trials do not carry points and are held for fun, training and getting the group together.

Beagles are divided very accurately into two groups for both showing and field-trial work: 13-inch class and 15-inch class. In the former, hounds must measure 13 inches or less; in the latter, they must measure over 13 inches but not over 15. Any over 15 inches are ineligible to compete in the show ring or at field trials.

All trials are held by local Beagle clubs who usually own or lease grounds which are kept well stocked with rabbits. During heavy winters, feeding stations are set up, providing pellets, old apples, alfalfa and other feed, and members have access to the grounds for working and training their dogs during the legal season.

In the regular, licensed trials, dogs are run in braces. The judges call back those they like best for a second series. Winners can be announced at this point, but each dog placed must have beaten the dog beneath him in direct competition.

To begin a brace, the two handlers move to the starting point where "brushers" or "beaters" (usually other handlers) are spread out in a line. After the two judges have identified the dogs, they are cast off by handlers

Taking a check at full speed.

and drawn (hunted) through a designated area in the hope of starting a rabbit. More often it's a beater who jumps one, whereupon comes the age-old cry, "Tallyho!"

Handlers call in their hounds, pick them up bodily and carry them to the point where the rabbit was flushed. If handler has difficulty catching his hound, this counts against him.

Dogs are put down together on the line and theoretically they should take off at a racing gallop and in full cry, but most of the time the startled rabbit leaves almost no scent for the first fifty feet or so, and often the hounds begin to babble out of sheer excitement. The judges are usually lenient for the first hundred feet, then the dogs had better straighten out and get down to business. If one of the dogs starts his own rabbit the bracemate is harked in and both are immediately under judgment. In either case the beaters gather up and wait for the next brace.

Once the dogs begin to work the line (scent trail), the handlers must stay behind the judges, who run after the brace to see how each comports himself. Dogs are judged on ability to carry a line, whether they have a

There's the rabbit just ahead!

good clean voice or are babblers, or too quiet. Some dogs lie back and let the lead hound do the work while they just babble along comfortably, and out of sight you'd think they were great. Some dogs weave back and forth across the line of scent as they run and are constantly losing it.

Invariably the rabbit, after running straight for a while, will dart sharply to right or left, and the dogs flying down the line will overrun it and lose it momentarily. Such a point is called a check, for the hounds must go back, check the scent and pick up the new direction quickly. Some make a huge circle, some mill around waiting for the other dog to do the work. Losing a line at a check is not a fault. It's bound to happen. The question is how fast and effectively the hound picks up the line again and moves on. Some hounds are intensely jealous and at checks will find the line, then move out silently to get the jump on the bracemate before giving tongue. This is called stealing the line and is a fault.

Speed is essential, but some hounds run so fast that they can't stay on the line, thereby have too many checks, in which case speed is a fault. Pottering anywhere is a major fault, as is backtracking, which is running the wrong direction on a track. Sometimes a rabbit will cleverly double back on his own trail, then take a bound to the left or right and move on. The hounds go flying to the end of the scent and find nothing. This is where the experienced hound knows enough to backtrack (permissible in this case) and make a circle to pick up the trail again. The judges and gallery must hold back so the line is not trampled or fouled by human scent.

The good hound must have ability in all departments, for, as the old saying goes, "Any fool can drive a rabbit but it takes a Beagle to bring him back." The ideal has been described as one who "runs all of his line; picks checks, if any, promptly; tongues always and only when making headway on a true line; and goes like hell." The one thing that this type of trial does not test is stamina. If a Beagle had to run for two or three hours, it might be a different story.

At a Beagle trial the judges' jobs are the most difficult of all. Depending upon the terrain, they will ride horses or work from foot. If they're on foot, they must run after the hounds continually for eight to ten hours a day, sometimes for two or three days. To a big trial will come competitors from several states, ex-ballplayers, housewives, politicians, prize fighters, bartenders, doctors, all with their cocky little Beagles trained to the last degree and ready for the big one.

The vast majority of beagling centers around the cottontail, but hare trials, in which hounds are run in packs, form another interesting and challenging type of competition. These events are run in the northern latitudes of the United States and Canada, where the larger snowshoe hare or varying hare is found. This 4-to-6-pound bounder is considered the gamiest and most elusive of all quarries for the Beagle because of his swiftness, cleverness in laying a trail and the fact that he almost never goes to earth (holes up) though pursued all day.

The first licensed hare trial was held in 1916 at North Creek, New York, deep in the Adirondacks by the Northern Hare Beagle Club, which still holds one of the best hare trials in the country each October. In all, there are between thirty and forty clubs across the northern part of the United States and Canada which hold hare trials annually.

A hare trial is a pack stake. As you enter your hound, a number is painted on his side to identify him at a distance. When his time to run arrives, he is put in with a pack of other hounds and assigned a handler. The owner goes back and sits in the gallery, which must stay at the starting

Can we go hunting again tomorrow, boss?

point and not wander around. This is a three-hour stake, no half-hour breezes like the cottontail trials. Judges are mounted on horses and they have to do a lot of hard riding to see what's going on. Once a hare is started and the hounds pick up the line, the judges follow the pack, making notes as to what number hound is leading, pottering, picks the checks first, shows jealousy by leaving the pack and trying to cut ahead to the hare. If a hound goes back to his owner in the gallery, he is given fifteen minutes to return to the pack before being counted out.

Actually the judges see little more than one tenth of the work, but they can tell quite accurately what's going on, and not as much luck is involved as you might think. After the first hour the eager-beaver young hounds who have been leading persistently begin to let up a little. During the second hour the stronger dogs come on and the lazy ones begin to stand around at checks waiting for the better dogs to pick up the scent again. The third hour usually decides the winners. The hounds that keep up the pace, pick the checks persistently, work with the pack yet lead it, are what the judges look for. Hare stakes offer the finest of all competition to real dyed-in-the-hound beaglers.

Another facet of the vast and burgeoning Beagle world centers around organized Beagle packs, long an English tradition and very similar to fox hunting afoot if you can imagine this. The sport is 98 per cent pleasure, no shooting of game, no judging, no competition, just hounds for hounds' sake and they are by far the most thoroughly trained of any group. There is all the color, action, ritual, and formality of dress among the huntsmen that accompanies a fox hunt, everything but the jumping horses and riders, for here you get out and walk.

Packs are registered as such by the National Beagle Club, and every year since 1888 a pack trial has been held—nowadays at Aldie, Virginia. Classes include two-, four-, and eight-couple events as well as individual stakes similar to hare trials.

But far and away the glory and appeal of a registered Beagle pack lies in its weekly outings, usually on Sunday afternoons from October through March over property of landowners who permit it because they enjoy the cry of the hounds as much as do those who follow.

Each pack has a Master (MBH—Master of Beagle Hounds) who is usually the Huntsman, and at least three Whippers-in or Whips, each with a whip about four feet long. All are dressed in the traditional hunt livery— green coats with the registered hunt colors on the collar, white trousers and black-velvet caps for men, white skirts for women. The Huntsman carries a silver horn by which he controls the pack. The gallery, numbering from fifty to a hundred followers of the general public, gathers behind the pack which stays close to the Huntsman. The Whips flank the pack to the

The Tanheath Hunt Club Beagles, Uxbridge, Mass., Mr. William A. Albin, Master, are often worked from horseback.

sides, snapping their whips if a hound begins to stray. Between five and fifteen couples are used, ten being a comfortable number.

If, as they move out to begin the hunt, the hounds cross a deer trail or other "riot" scent and show signs of following, the Whips crack and the Huntsman sounds a series of sharp notes on his horn. This raises the heads of the pack, gets their noses off the scent, and at the command "Pack together!" they move back into a tight group.

The Huntsman decides what areas are to be drawn (hunted). The hounds are cast out and the gallery also spreads to the flanks to help start game. In northern areas the snowshoe and European hares are preferred because they give excellent chase and do not go to earth, but Ye Olde Cottontail suffices generally. Often the gallery starts the game, in which case "Tallyho!" is called and the hounds harked into the area to pick up the line. Soon they are off and flying, the Huntsman running behind them, the Whippers-in far to the sides in the event that the hounds cross a road and traffic must be stopped. The gallery jogs along behind, pauses at hilltops to watch and listen to the music of the singing pack, take in fresh air and gain a glimpse of the lovely countryside.

If the quarry is a cottontail and he goes to earth, the pack is gathered and moved out for another strike. The gallery—at least those who have any breath left in them—comes up, fans out and again lends its assistance to the start.

Thus the afternoon passes, the spectators outdoors in usually glorious surroundings, following the Beagles afoot, gaining exercise, relaxation and above all enjoying the melodious cries of the pack in this, its purest form of hunting.

Beagle packs in this country are either supported by subscription or owned privately by people who genuinely love the age-old challenge of putting together a great pack of Beagles and watching them work. To assemble a superior pack requires great effort, time and breeding. Hounds must first off have the ability to work together. The overzealous leader is sold, no matter how good he may be as an individual, as are the babbler, the skirter, the cheater, the mute. The ideal is to have the pack even or "level" all phases of ability and looks. For example, when the hounds carry a line, they should move so closely and evenly that a blanket would cover the pack. After this point, the Master begins to weed by color.

To establish and maintain a great Beagle pack is an endless and sometimes near-exhausting task, but there are approximately twenty of them in the United States today and one in Canada. They range by states from Massachusetts, New York, New Jersey, Delaware, Maryland and Virginia to Pennsylvania, Ohio and Michigan. The one Canadian pack is maintained and hunted by the Royal Canadian School of Infantry, the equivalent of our West Point. In England, several schools and organizations maintain packs for the enjoyment of members, employees and the general public.

Beagling combines true sport with outdoor activity and the thrilling music of the chase. The public is always welcome to join the gallery, and I urge everyone to take in a bright Sunday afternoon's beagling and enjoy a taste of "the good life" in a traditional way.

Despite all the activity mentioned, the Beagle sees by far the most use as a practical hunter, working for Mr. Average Hunter who wants good rabbit shooting or dropping his limit of pheasants. Here is the backbone of Beagle work across the country and here he will always remain strong, for he can drive a pheasant out of a swamp where the best Pointer or Setter, even spaniel, will fail. And a hunter soon learns to know exactly the type of game his Beagle is working by the tone and regularity of his cry.

The size of the Beagle, the dual 13- and 15-inch groups, has already been mentioned. His weight is immaterial, being governed by his height. Generally it's around 25 to 30 pounds. He can sport any true hound color, explains the standard, which goes on to say that the most important aspect of him is his general appearance. In this regard it says he should be "A miniature Foxhound, solid and big for his inches, with the wear-and-tear look of a hound that can last in the chase and follow his quarry to the death."

This is truly the Beagle, a lot of ruggedness in a small, friendly package, and all of it lovable.

The Basset Hound

One of the oldest and most distinguished of the hound breeds is the Basset, low-slung and husky, slow but persistent, favorite of those who wish to follow hounds leisurely and enjoy a melodious voice to its fullest.

At first glance, the Basset looks like a combination of several other hounds, but he isn't. He simply derives from a similar origin, hence has many hound likenesses. His head has the loose-skin, soulful look of the Bloodhound. His long-drawn-out conformation resembles that of an over-sized Dachshund. His tricolor markings match those of the Beagle and Foxhound.

Bassets had their origin in northern France and Belgium. Some drifted into Russia, and England obtained her first ones just after the middle of the nineteenth century. The word *Basset* is the Old French diminutive for *bas*, meaning low, hence Basset means lowest. The name was probably applied to the lowest-sized hounds that appeared in the old St. Hubert line and were found very useful for hunting in heavy and overhanging cover. In early days, 1700s and before, Bassets were probably not as short as now, for they ran the roe deer, wild boar, badgers, rabbits and foxes successfully. Because they worked slower than large hounds, they never lost the trail, and the animal being pursued was not frightened into running at great speed, hence was easier to shoot.

We do not know the outcross used to shorten the Basset's legs, perhaps some toy dog that was also an ancestor of the Dachshund, or even the Daxie himself, a very old breed. Several Basset varieties were produced in France—smooth- and rough-coated, and three types of front legs: full-crooked (a very slow mover); half-crooked (slow); and straight (agile and fairly swift).

In 1866 a pair of Bassets was sent by the French Comte de Tournow

Beyond being a lovable pet, the Basset is a fine hunter.

to England's Lord Galway. Later their offspring were sold to Lord Onslow who began a pack of Bassets by importing more from Compte Couteulx de Canteleu, who is considered the father of the modern Basset in France.

The breed caught on in England mainly through the efforts of Lord Onslow, Mr. George Krehl and Sir Everett Millais. This last gentleman used a Bloodhound cross to produce the bulky English type of Basset while others crossed in the old Southern Hound—heavy, deep-tongued, dew-lapped—of Lancashire. French Bassets were always rather light and the English wanted a heavier dog.

The first European Bassets were brought to the United States in 1883 from England, one for Mr. Lawrence Timpson of New York and a brace for Lord Aylesford, who used them for rabbit shooting on his Texas ranch. Previously some Bassets had been imported from Russia and these were crossed with the heavy English Basset to produce the American type, which is in between the heavy English and the lighter French. In 1884 the Westminster Kennel Club held a class for the breed, the entries probably being of the early American straight-legged kind. Our Southern Beagles at that time were much closer in conformation to the Basset than to their small Foxhound appearance of today, and it is reasonable to assume that they, too, played a part in early Basset formation here.

It has taken a long time for the Basset to catch on in this country. For one thing, he has always been overshadowed by the more fleet-of-foot Beagle, who hunts exactly the same game—rabbits and pheasants. Because the Basset is slow, he cannot be hunted effectively with any but his own kind. The fact that there have been several types of Bassets has also confused the issue. The public image of the Basset Hound is that of the ponderous English type, nearly impossible to hunt in any but the flattest country. Actually the field-type Basset in the United States is the medium-sized, leggy dog that can move along almost as briskly as the Beagle. He doesn't have much of the Bloodhound head or the ponderous body but is a practical and most effective hunting dog. He has a beautiful voice and a great nose that, along with his slowness, seldom allows him to lose a trail.

The hunting Basset is such a different dog from the show Basset that they are almost two different breeds. The show standard says that the Basset head "is most perfect when it closest resembles the head of a Bloodhound, with heavy flews and forehead wrinkled to the eyes. The expression when sitting or when still should be very sad, full of reposeful dignity. The whole of the head should be covered with loose skin, so loose in fact, that when the hound brings its nose to the ground the skin over the head and cheeks should fall forward and wrinkle perceptibly."

This may be all right for the show ring, but it is senseless for a field dog and is one of the very reasons why the Bloodhound is no longer a field dog. Our modern-day working hounds—Coon, Fox, Beagles, Bassets, whatever—do not have tight-skinned faces, but neither do they drip with useless skin.

Because of all this disagreement the Basset has had a struggle gaining acceptance in the field with hunters, but he is getting there now. In Pennsylvania, Ohio, Indiana, Illinois, Kentucky, Michigan, Wisconsin, the Basset has found roots and gained an ever widening following in recent years. Field trials, sanctioned and/or licensed by AKC, are run every weekend through the fall and winter season, and field champions are being constantly crowned on the same system as explained in the last chapter on Beagles.

As a hunter, the Basset's value lies in his ability to work rabbits and pheasants. Some claim he can work raccoon, fox and the like. No doubt he can, but other hounds are so far superior to him that he should stick to what he can do best. In working a cottontail, America's number-one game species, the Basset has only the Beagle as a rival. A strong one he is, but the Basset has a lot to offer—that deep, resonant voice that sends a thrill through you every time he opens up, a nose that is second to none, thoroughness as opposed to speed. On pheasants the Basset also excels. When he puts his nose to the trail of a wily ringneck and starts to sing, it's not long before Mr. Pheasant takes to the air.

Packs of Basset Hounds are also finding backers in the eastern part of the United States. The three original ones, the Kilsyth Bassets of Long Island, the Bijou Bassets at Old Chatham, New York, and the Starridge Bassets of Brewster, New York, have all been dismantled but in their places have grown new ones. At the moment they number eight and include the Bridlespur and Somerset packs, the Tewksbury Foot Bassets, also the Poona and Ashland packs.

Each is thoroughly trained, has a Master (MBH, which signifies Master of Basset Hounds) and is maintained privately or by subscription of members, who take to the woods on foot at least once a week during the season and follow the pack as it runs rabbits. Basset packs are registered the same as Beagle packs and have the same colorful procedures described in the preceding chapter. They are usually entered in the National Beagle and Basset Club trials at Aldie and in the Bryn Mawr, Pennsylvania, trials.

In size the Basset ranges from 11 to 15 inches, and weighs 25 to 50 pounds, with some show dogs sometimes going as high as 60 pounds. For the field Basset, 12–13 inches in height is best, and 30 to 40 pounds in weight. The field dog has a good hound head, broad skull, long ears, but not the vast amount of hanging, loose skin of the Bloodhound face. He has a muscular neck and shoulders, powerful and relatively straight fore-legs of heavy bone, with massive paws. He is deep-chested and strong-backed, and there's some light under his belly—not much, but it doesn't drag on the ground. His hindquarters are muscular and "round as an apple" as they say. Stern is carried gay and high in traditional hound fashion. Any Foxhound color is acceptable, which means tricolor—white, black and tan—or any two of the three colors. They tend to have a little more black on them than Beagles or Foxhounds.

Now that the Basset has received the opportunity to prove his long-vaunted hunting ability, he is doing so with a soundness in keeping with his great past. In the United States his heartland will probably always be the Midwest where the land is relatively even and flat. The Basset is not suited for extremely rough, stony or hilly terrain, but where the country is rolling to flat, he'll give the Beagle a run for his hide—and the cotton-tail too.

The Somerset Bassets, owned by Mrs. James N. Andrews, Jr., are shown packed and moving out to hunt the Virginia countryside.

The Dachshund

This short-legged, long-bodied little guy has probably borne the brunt of more jokes and cartoons than any other breed, but he takes it good-naturedly, as he does most everything.

The Dachshund is a lot of little dog and until you're around him for a while to see his courage and strength you wonder how he was ever a badger dog. The badger is a tough, well-clawed, 25-pound animal who builds his home underground, and the Daxie was developed to slither his way down the hole and get him. It is also said they were used effectively against foxes in the hole, also European hare and ermine.

The Dachshund's history is German, his name meaning literally badger dog. Tapestries and book illustrations from the fifteenth, sixteenth and seventeenth centuries show him or a dog similar to him at work at his badger trade. It is impossible to say how the Germans bred the remarkably small but strong front legs on this dog, that is, what cross was used. Through the years three coats evolved, smooth, longhaired and wirehaired, also three sizes, heavy, medium and miniature.

The Daxie came to this country in the 1870s, probably in the arms of German emigrants. Eleven appeared in the second volume of the American

Kennel Club Registry of 1885. The Dachshund Club of America was organized in 1895 and the breed grew steadily until World War I when this country's tide of nationalism and anti-German feelings caused it to decline sharply. The breed quickly recovered in the 1920s, however, and has since flourished, creeping into the hearts and homes of people across the country, particularly city residents. In recent years it has been consistently within the top five most popular breeds registered by American Kennel Club.

The Daxie's unusually short legs and its most pleasing disposition make it an ideal city dog. Though quiet and always friendly, it can be taught to bark when someone comes to the door, making it a watchdog. It is small, neat and clean, and because of its short legs, most easily exercised. One turn around a city block is the equivalent of a half-mile jog for a bigger dog.

Everyone knows the shape of the Dachshund. In his various sizes he stands anywhere up to 9 or 10 inches high and weighs over or under 9

The Dachshund, originally a badger dog, comes in three varieties of coats, long-haired, wirehaired, and smooth or shorthaired.

pounds. He comes in just about all colors but most frequently in red, black-and-tan, chocolate or dapple.

Primarily a pet, the Daxie is seldom used as a field dog though its hunting instincts remain deeply imbued. However, in 1935 the National Club decided to sponsor an annual field trial in an effort to maintain the Dachshund's ability in this, the area for which he was created. Each year a trial is held in New Jersey and of the hundreds of thousands of Daxies in the country, only fifteen to twenty-five entries show up. The event is run on rabbits, which the Daxies work in Beagle and Basset fashion. Some Daxies are very effective and through the years since 1935 about a dozen field champions have been crowned. In this type of work the Daxie's sharp voice rings out crisply and he is a slow, meticulous trailer with a good nose.

Undoubtedly more people use the dog for hunting during the season than is known, for on opening day of rabbit and pheasant season in any state, one sees an unbelievable assortment of house pets nosing through the bushes. Certainly the Dachshund, small though he is, would be more effective than most, for his hunting heritage in "the Old Country" has not left him.

The misty-morn beginning of a fox hunt.

The American Foxhound

According to my experience there are four major and incurable maladies which afflict hunters the nation over.

The first is the pursuit of quail, known throughout the South as bird hunting, for which cause I have often walked twenty-five miles a day behind a brace of Pointers or Setters just to level off and shoot at a covey as it exploded in front of me and whizzed out of sight.

The second is duck hunting whose followers, to me, appeared mentally deranged to rise at 3 A.M., drag a bunch of tangled decoys and a lurching dog to some cold, wet blind in which they sat all day shooting at ducks that passed by almost out of range. One rainy day I tried it, and succumbed.

The third malady is that nutty nocturnal adventure called coon hunting, to be described later in gory detail.

Fox hunting is the fourth malady, herewith discussed, and admittedly the most insidious because it carries the prestige of time and tradition as well as quality and quantity of followers. As every Defender of the Faith tells his tearful wife each time he deserts her for the hounds, "The Father of our Country spent the happiest years of his life fox hunting." To which she replies, "Well, he must have been as crazy as the rest of you."

Be that as it may, the fox-hunting fraternity is a true fraternity dedicated to the pursuit of the gray ghost and the red raider. Members will argue among themselves, to the point of fighting, over the merits of a certain hound or strain of hound, but let the outsider condemn the scrawniest cur that runs a fox and they will pounce upon him with verbal oaths, knives and guns.

They will be justified, for no breed of dog has had a more colorful past, is today more truly American or, above all, more dog from nose to stern, from crown to pads, than the American Foxhound.

Put together over a period of more than three centuries by a host of little breeders, the American Foxhound consists of families or strains dating back to the earliest colonial times. We know by diary that the Spanish explorer DeSoto had hounds with him when he discovered the Mississippi River in 1541, but the first pack of consequence to be brought to America arrived here from England in 1650, the property of Robert Brooke—friend of Lord Baltimore—who settled in the province of Maryland. Brooke died after only five years in the colonies but is recognized as the first Master of Foxhounds in America. His pack lived on in his family, reached a height of popularity around 1825 and the blood was still being bred a hundred years later. Brooke's black-and-tan variety eventually covered Virginia and became the foundation for the Black-and-Tan Coonhound of today.

In the first half of the 1700s Thomas, Lord Fairfax and Thomas Walker, both distinguished Virginians, imported English Foxhounds, as did George Washington in 1770. With Thomas Jefferson, Alexander Hamilton and Thomas Marshall among the ranks of early American fox hunters, the sport got off to an auspicious start. In 1785 Lafayette sent Washington some French Stag Hounds which didn't adapt to fox hunting too well, but they were crossed in and proved their worth by increasing the size of our early Foxhounds. In the 1830s more French Hounds and some Irish Hounds were imported, the Irish blood being particularly fast though lacking in melodious voice. From these three sources—England, France and Ireland —came the blood that has formed the American Foxhound.

Maryland and Virginia were the early focal points of fox hunting. Here first began the practice of following the hounds from horseback in the pattern of the English chase. Fox hunting with its color and formality fitted neatly into the sporting life and traditions of the Old South.

But all the people who hunted the fox did not pursue the pack on horse. Some waited on a fox run, shot him as he whizzed by and thus obtained a pelt and cut down on what they considered vermin.

The vast majority of fox hunters ran their hounds for sport as they do today. They let the hounds run the fox until the end—that is, until the hounds caught him, ran him to ground or lost him through sheer exhaustion. As the country expanded westward and became more settled, this type of fox hunting grew by leaps and bounds in Kentucky, Tennessee, Ohio, later in Illinois, Missouri, Arkansas. As a city person might cherish a great painting or attend a concert, so a country person cherished his pack of Foxhounds. They were his form of amusement, competition, pride and joy, and he went to great lengths ever to improve his pack.

When General G. W. Maupin, John W. Walker, and several friends chipped in and imported a male and female Foxhound from England in the 1850s, the whole town of Richmond, Kentucky, turned out to greet their arrival by stage. Excitement ran so high, with everyone wanting to see what "them ferrin hounds" could do, that Mr. Maupin took the male,

Foxhounds are alert dogs.

Rifler, out of his crate after two weeks' confinement and they went fox hunting that first night. Foxhound men have always tested their dogs by do-or-die methods, which is greatly responsible for what the Foxhound is today. Although a three-hour chase was unfair to Rifler, it tested him and he "did"—to the satisfaction of all. This hound, when crossed into the offspring of Tennessee Lead, helped produce the famous Walker strain of Foxhound.

One of the profound events which changed the course of breeding Foxhounds here in America was the importation of the English red fox. His first recorded release is in Talbot County, Maryland, in 1738, but he was probably brought here before then and released in Virginia. Earlier, the much slower gray fox provided all the activity for the hounds and it didn't take a very fleet hound more than a two- or three-hour chase to run him to earth or catch him. The red proved a different story. He could be chased all night, seldom went to earth and it took a mighty lot of hound to catch one. So nimble and swift was the red fox that it soon turned the old Virginia Black-and-Tan into a Coonhound, and as this clever newcomer spread westward into Kentucky and Tennessee, fox hunters had to improve their packs and breed swifter hounds to deal with him.

The American Foxhound has always thrived more among the ardent foot hunters than among those who rode formally to the chase. The latter were justifiedly more concerned with their mounts. As long as the pack was well trained and could provide a chase, that was enough. The former were the purists who experimented with crosses of all kinds to Bloodhounds, Pointers, Greyhounds, all without success. They bought, sold, traded, always with the idea of producing a better Foxhound. From them grew the great strains we have today, which are now passing slowly but surely into breeds. Few of those men kept records but they hunted and knew what a good hound was. Often a man loaded his pack into the back of a wagon or put them on a train and hauled them to the next county or state for a run with another fox hunter. In this way they got to know the great hounds, exchanged blood, and the element of competition inevitably involved formed the basis for field trials.

The first Foxhound field trial was held in November, 1889, at Albany Hills, Maine, by the Brunswick Foxhound Club. The hounds were judged on hunting ability, trailing, speed and driving ability, endurance and tonguing, a pattern which was followed more or less as other trials were held. Today hounds are painted with numbers on their sides and cast off in a pack, while judges on horseback gallop here and there, rating them by the glimpses they catch of the pack and what it is doing. A big trial will last three or four days or more, during which time hounds

Foxhounds know no barriers.

are rated, the better performers called back, the poorer ones scratched (dropped) for loafing, not packing, skirting, babbling and other faults. Fewer and fewer hounds keep being called back until the judges have sorted the best and placed those. Field trials currently form a great part of the interest in Foxhounds and many champions are crowned annually.

Dealers and traders have long been a colorful part of the Foxhound scene. The story is told of one who bought hundreds of hounds, always at the conclusion of big field trials when losing owners were disgruntled or needed money. He would sit on a camp chair and as the hound was led up to him say, "Four dollars." If he happened to like the dog's looks he might say six, but never above seven. If the seller didn't accept, he was waved aside for the next man in line. A helper loaded the hounds on a big truck as fast as they were bought, and they were carted away and sold elsewhere for $10, $12, $15.

For all the odd aspects of the Foxhound world, good individuals have constantly arisen and general improvement taken place, but quality hounds most often result from careful breeding and rigorous selection, and the great ones are an Act of God.

Nevertheless the American Foxhound anywhere is an amazing animal, possessing more versatile qualities, and the corresponding intelligence, than almost any other domestic animal used for sport. If he is to catch the fox he chases, he must have more speed and endurance—enough of the latter to last for six, eight, even twelve hours at a time. He must have an exceptional nose to keep him on the line as he flies along. He must have the agility to negotiate any terrain, whether water, heavy cover, rugged hills or wide-open flats. He must know how to start a fox and match his cleverness with determination. He must run with the pack, not be jealous but hark to the others when they open a fresh trail. He must have a good voice so he is pleasing to hear, because this is one of the great joys to his master. He must work hour after hour, seldom if ever seeing the fox he is chasing, following only its scent. He must not run deer, raccoon, rabbits, inviting though the scent may be. And he must have that strange intuitive quality which leads him home after the hunt is over or he is lost. He may end up two counties away, but a good Foxhound manages his way back home.

What is he supposed to look like? What is his standard?

In the early days it was anything that could do the job. Gradually a type emerged. It is still loose today, which is why we have so many strains being registered as breeds. Generally he stands between 22 and 25 inches and weighs 45 to 60 pounds. He has a clean look, solid but not heavy bone, lean muscle, not hulking. He is built to run and shows it. His front legs are long and straight, lots of light under him, and the tail he sports is a good high flag that is white or white-tipped and slightly brushed. His head is broad, full, with a moderate stop and wide-set eyes that contain a gentle, pleading expression. He comes in all hound colors, but principally in the traditional tricolor of white, black and tan. Long-legged, speedy American Foxhounds should never be weedy. The good ones have plenty of substance and that thing called "class."

English Foxhounds, on the other hand, are a little shorter and much more stocky than their American cousins. The English strain has a similar head but his ears are shorter from being rounded—that is, the bottoms are cut off about 1½ inches so they don't fly so much when they run. He's a heavy-boned and muscular hound, more thick than his American counterpart though the similarity is immediately apparent.

This is a good place to discuss the English Foxhound since he does not have a section of his own in this book, yet has contributed the major portion of the blood that makes up our American packs.

The first packs recorded in England for fox hunting were in the late 1600s. Before that, the larger Stag Hounds had the support of the English hunting aristocracy, but as the stag grew scarce, the pursuit of the fox with hounds and horse became the rage. The original Foxhound blood had long been in England, in various forms like the Southern Hound, the black St. Hubert's Hound, the white Stag Hound, the Dun Hound, all of which were used or blended at one time or other to produce the final result. Much of this early blood was brought to England by the Norman invasion of William the Conqueror in 1066.

As packs were developed, the English Foxhound was bred more to standard than merely for ability as was the case in America. The English Foxhound Stud Book began in 1880. The Brocklesby pack of the Earl of Yarborough and the Belvoir pack of the Duke of Rutland were among the early standouts.

English Foxhounds are still imported to this country and used with particular success for crossing. The Green Spring Valley pack of superb Foxhounds is an example of this.

Irish hounds are occasionally imported but not as frequently as in the early days. They did their part by adding to the American Foxhound the speed so needed to deal with the swift red raider.

Early American Foxhound strains were usually named after the owners of great packs. Some of these were the Goodmans, the Birchfields of New England, Trumbo, Birdsong, Sugar Loaf, Robertson, the Wild Goose strain of Tennessee, the Cooks, the Byrons and the Arkansas Travelers. Three more great strains have survived to this day and we now discuss them.

The Walker

The Walker Hound is the most popular strain of Foxhound in America today. It also has a great following among coon hunters, who call them Treeing Walkers.

The foundation for the Walker strain was laid by General George Washington Maupin of Kentucky, close friend of John W. Walker, from whom the name derives. Both men were avid fox hunters during the twenty-year period prior to the Civil War. Both had kennels of hounds descended from early Maryland and Virginia blood and were always on the lookout for new and better blood. Maupin was presented a hound by a livestock-dealer friend who had stolen it in the hills of Tennessee. Named Tennessee Lead, the dog was medium-sized, black with a tan spot over each eye, and rat-tailed. He was such a fine Foxhound of over-all high class that he soon became the talk of that section of Kentucky and Maupin sent his two sons back to trace him and buy more, but they were unsuccessful. Tennessee Lead was bred to the best Foxhounds in Maupin's and Walker's kennels, and the improvement immediately become apparent. Later Rifler, the English import previously mentioned, was added.

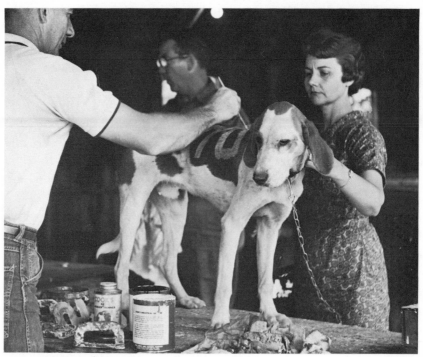

Preparing for a field trial.

When Maupin and Walker, Sr., died, both kennels were taken over by Walker's sons, W. S. and E. H. From time to time they imported an English hound to outcross and sent their blood to all parts of the United States where it gained fame as a good packer and a strong, rugged, tireless hound that could run every night of the week.

Most all the Walkers today trace back to Top, a standout around 1870. Later greats were Canle and his son, Big Stride, around 1915–20, and Cork, who appeared a little later. Through the years Walkers have been consistent winners in field trials and on the bench. They are handsome hounds, generally white, black and tan, often with a black saddle, and can trail just about anything if trained for it.

The Trigg

Still alive and running strong after more than a hundred years is this master of speed and endurance named after Colonel Haiden C. Trigg of Glasgow, Kentucky.

Colonel Trigg in 1845 hunted the gray fox with a pack of old Virginia Black-and-Tans, long-eared, musical in voice, but his hounds could not cope with the red demon when it came along. As a consequence he began a breeding program after the Civil War to develop a new and swifter breed of hound.

In 1866 Colonel Trigg obtained five hounds from George Birdsong of Thomaston, Georgia, for $400, a large price in those days, but the Birdsong strain of hounds was famous, having come from two Maryland hounds, Mountain and Muse, of Irish blood through the kennel of Dr. T. Y. Henry, grandson of Patrick Henry. Two years later Trigg bought two more from Birdsong for $500, this time the blood being line-bred to July, a famous hound which started its own strain, and which Mr. Birdsong owned at that time.

Earlier Colonel Trigg had obtained stock from Maupin and Walker, and thus by skillfully combining this Birdsong-Walker-July blood, he produced one of the outstanding packs of the country, popular to this day in the pursuit of the fox.

Trigg never used English blood, nor did he breed for color or markings —ability only was his motto. His original stock included all hound colors from black-and-tan to fawn and tricolor and red with white points. Today the Trigg Hound most often appears in solid black or red with white ringneck and white points, and breeders seem to be heading more and more toward standardizing these colors for the strain.

The Trigg is a ruggedly handsome hound, strong and rangy but not gaunt, weighs either side of 50 pounds. He's a real worker with a good nose and has a reputation for speed and endurance.

The July

This hound has long been popular in the South, where his burning speed and determination have made him a favorite. The strain dates back to about 1860 when Miles G. Harris, a wealthy plantation owner and fox hunter in Georgia, made the acquaintance of Ben Robinson who, in his time, probably knew more about "fox dogs" and strains and the men who imported, bred and hunted them than anyone else in the country.

After Mr. Robinson and Mr. Harris became friends, they made a trip to Maryland together to visit fox hunters. Mr. Harris, on Mr. Robinson's advice, bought two puppies of fast Irish Hound stock from Nimrod Gosnell. They were descended from the same old Mountain and Muse blood that founded Dr. Henry's kennel, which later became Mr. Birdsong's kennel. Back home in Georgia, Harris named them June and July. The July Hound became the sensation of the area, many stories claiming he could catch a red fox unaided, which was a real feat.

Later Mr. Birdsong obtained the dog and crossed him into his stock which traced back to the same Irish Hound origin, but with several outcrosses. In time July Hounds spread to Mississippi, Louisiana, Missouri and most of the Southern states. Today the blood is not as widely found as it once was because many July owners don't sell their stock, only give away an occasional hound rather than breed on a commercial basis.

In 1918 the American Foxhound Breeders Stud Book was established and from that point on, record keeping made possible the wider application of science and genetics to the breeding of Foxhounds. Though the great Foxhounds may be just as few and far between as they were a hundred or two hundred years ago, the general average is of higher quality. The prices, too! A superior Foxhound sells for anywhere from $500 to $1000 today, and a real real good one for $2500 or higher.

But I have the feeling that if Old George came back today he'd be pleased with what he saw. He'd soon put a pack together and be running them day or night, whenever the opportunity came along, and he'd be right in the thick of those four-day trials whenever and wherever they were held. And Martha would shake her head sadly and say, "I can't understand it. I just can't understand it."

Full Cry!

The Harrier

An old, old breed is the Harrier, master at hunting the hare. In color and conformation he is indistinguishable from the English Foxhound and the Beagle. In size he stands between the two, males being 19 to 21 inches in height and weighing about 45 pounds, females 18 to 20 inches and 38 pounds. They are tricolor—white, black and tan.

Every discussion of the Harrier seems to start with Xenophon, Greek general and historian who wrote in 400 B.C. about hare hounds. Certainly there is little or no connection between the hound of that time and the English Harrier as developed in the Middle Ages, although Xenophon loved the sport and knew of what he wrote.

The Harrier appears to have originated from a cross between the Beagle and the old Southern Hound of England or perhaps the St. Hubert's Hound. It may even have come from France, the name possibly deriving from the Norman word *harier*, meaning hound. Confusing is the fact that many varieties of English hounds were referred to as Harriers—Stag-Harriers, Fox-Harriers, etc.—as late as the 1700s.

Hare hunting in England predates fox hunting and has always been popular because the Harriers could be followed from foot or horse. Even to this day many packs are kept in England, and these form the chief source of new blood in this country.

When we speak of hares we do not refer to cottontails and other small varieties of rabbit, but to the large continental hare of the English and German varieties, also to the varying hare or snowshoe of North America. These long-legged, speedy members of the rabbit family provide great sport for a pack of lively hounds and almost never hole up.

In the United States the Harrier has never seen widespread use, principally because there aren't enough hares here to provide the excellent sport possible in England and Europe. Harriers do not work well on cottontails. They run them so fast that they soon take to a hole to escape. On fox the Harrier is not as effective as the Foxhound developed for this purpose.

The first pack of Harriers was brought to this country by the late Oakleigh Thorne of Millbrook, New York, in 1910. A year later Robert P. Huntington of Staatsburg, New York, brought over a pack. During the 1920s and 1930s packs were maintained and hunted by E. S. Reynal of

The Harrier.

Millbrook, S. Prentice Porter of Virginia, Windsor T. White of Ohio and a few others.

During World War II the Harrier packs in this country fell apart and today there appears to be only one remaining, that of Mr. Armory L. Haskell, president of the Monmouth Park Jockey Club. This thirty-couple pack is maintained at Red Bank, New Jersey, by Mr. Albert H. Smith, who came from England with a Harrier pack in the 1920s and is one of the last surviving Harrier men in this country. The pack is hunted from horseback during the regular season. Huntsmen and Master wear green coats instead of the crimson of fox hunters.

The future of Harriers would appear to be very limited in the United States. Several scattered importations from England have been made in recent years, though no new packs have been formed and none is likely to be. However, a few have appeared at bench shows recently and Mr. Smith reports that he is besieged weekly with inquiries about obtaining Harriers for hunting the varying hare or snowshoe in our northern climates. Perhaps the Harrier's future lies in this direction. Certainly he can give the snowshoe a real run and provide the gunner with outstanding sport as well as hunting.

The Coonhound

As I stated two sections ago, coon hunting is one of the major maladies of the American hunter. Prevalent since the days of the pioneer, it has become more and more widespread in our time. Basically it consists of staggering through the woods in total darkness, or maybe with a miner's light on your forehead, cracking your shins on fallen trees, entangling your neck in hanging vines, falling into unseen brooks, holes, pits, et cetera, all for the sake of a bunch of dogs that have a ring-tailed animal up a tree and are telling the world about it.

I swore I would never indulge in such nonsense, but one of my friends kept hounding me until I finally went a few years ago. The above perfectly describes our hunt, only we found three coon that night so we repeated it three times instead of once. The coon were good-sized, about 20 pounds each, which by 3 A.M. meant 60 pounds in the gunny sack. We alternated lugging the bag six miles back to the car, but the one who wasn't carrying had to maneuver three hounds on leads through brush and bushes, which was worse.

"How'd you like it?" my friend asked as we staggered the last fifty yards.

"All right," I answered in a tone that could have been taken for weariness or disapproval.

"Moonlight nights are better," he said.

I went home, slept three hours and got up bleary-eyed and cussing my bruises. At work I tried to concentrate but through my brain kept floating that rolling bawl of the Black-and-Tan, the high bugle and chop of the little Walker gyp and the deep foghorn of the brindle Plott, who must have weighed 80 pounds. I remembered how they started their plaintive bawling along a stream, infrequent at first, faster and with a chop or two as the trail got hotter, then the really excited music as they drove the coon, finally the yak-yak-yak chop which meant treed. When I went home that night I looked at the calendar to see when the next moonlight night was due. I had the fever all right. But before I tell you what happened, let's look at the slightly mad but wonderful Coonhound world.

Mr. Raccoon is an amazing animal. He inhabits just about every state in the nation, thereby providing hounds and hunters with a most worthy and clever quarry. He does not wash his food, as is generally thought, but hunts creeks for frogs and fish, and when treed, hides his face in his paws so a hunter's light won't reveal his beady eyes. With rare aptitude he adapts himself to local conditions. In Maine and Canada, where it's cold, his pelt grows thicker, but in Florida he will have a light coat suited to hot temperatures.

With all of man's advancing civilization the coon does not withdraw or die out. When his forests are cut down and brooks destroyed for housing projects, he takes to living in drains and eating from garbage pails. Not only has he survived man's upheaval of the earth but he has actually grown in numbers. Hail to the ringtail! Without him we'd lose a world of pleasure hunting.

The Coonhound, which tracks him by scent, has been around since colonial and pioneer days. A valuable dog he was for the settler moving westward with the frontier, for the raccoon provided not only a source of income from his pelt (two bits apiece), but was meat on the table. Coon hunting also provided the backwoodsman with much of his pleasure and entertainment. For this work he wanted a good open-mouthed hound that could work a cold trail and stay with it to the end, which meant either treeing the coon or, once in a while, catching it on the ground.

To build his dog the coon hunter took hounds that the fox hunter had discarded as being too slow or not packing. These he taught to tree by squirrel hunting and then produced his Coonhound by selective breeding. Even today it is almost impossible to take a Foxhound and make a Coonhound of him because he lacks treeing instinct. He'll trail the coon until he trees him, bark a few times, then take off to hunt another one. The

Coonhound must have an innate desire to stay at the tree, a whole day if need be, but at least until his master comes and ends the hunt by dispatching the treed animal whether it be a raccoon, bobcat, mountain lion or bear. This is a basic difference.

Beyond having a desire to tree, a Coonhound must be a good water dog. This seemingly minor detail appears in almost every coon hunt, for old ringtail is found around swamps, along creeks. When pursued and cornered he will take to water if it's available, for he's a great swimmer. The hound must be an equally good swimmer and be fearless about attacking him in deep water. Many a good Coonhound has been done in by a clever old coon who climbed up on his back, clung to the top of the dog's neck, pushing his head under water until he drowned. The hound should either do battle in water or drive the coon fearlessly to the shore, where he can finish him quickly.

Which brings us to the next of the Coonhound virtues. He should have a great desire to catch and kill coon. If he is afraid of them he is next to useless because when the moment of truth arrives, he won't attack but will let the coon escape, and he will be terrified of entering water in pursuit. There is the occasional exception where the hound, seriously roughed up by a big coon when young, will run and tree well when worked with two or three other hounds, but will never be worth a nickel alone.

A Coonhound must also have a good nose. Most all can smell scent, but they have different types of noses that affect their methods of hunting. A cold-nosed hound is highly effective on cold trails and loves to unravel them, but often he loses interest when the trail gets hot, preferring to go off and find another cold one. The hot-nosed hound is great on a fresh trail, but is inclined to ignore a cold one, and since most of the trails are cold he doesn't run as much game as he should. The good-nosed Coonhound is a happy medium, always working the cold trail because he knows sooner or later it will lead to his quarry.

Perseverance and endurance are two other qualities all good Coonhounds must have. They must love their work so much that they carry a cold trail wherever it leads, over rock ledges, across creeks, through swamps and briars, under fences. And to continue on for hours at a time, often all night, a hound must have endurance which is both an inherited quality and a matter of health and conditioning. Coonhounds do not move as fast as Foxhounds but they must have the same stamina.

The last great quality needed in a Coonhound is a good voice. This is somewhat aesthetic, especially when one considers the number of silent trailers that are hunted. But most men hunt to hear their hound cry melodiously as he trails through forests and fields. Or, if two or three hounds are running, to hear their ringing tones, each with a different

Treed!

quality, each more excited as the trail warms. The voice should be pleasant and strong. Sometimes it must carry two miles or more back to the hunter who listens and finds their location only when they chop "He's treed! Come! Come! Come!"

As was stated earlier, the Coonhound's history derives for the most part from that of the Foxhound, although his rise has been effected by various crosses such as Bloodhound, Pointer, Setter, Airedale. Most of these proved ineffective though the Airedale is still used occasionally with grade hounds (unregistered). Today many are crossing the Greyhound into the Coonhound to obtain a speed demon for field-trial competition. He has little practical ability for night hunting on wild coon though he serves his purpose for what is wanted, but more of that later.

For two hundred years or more, coon hunting was a very practical vocation for many while also being a sport. Coonhounds sort of sprang up from a lot of sources, none of which ever claimed or made fame as did the Foxhound kennels which produced great strains. With time and persistent breeding, and especially with the rise of Coonhound clubs and registries in the last twenty years, the old-fashioned "coon dog" has become the modern Coonhound and the old strains are fast becoming breeds. We are right in the middle of this changeover. The grade hound still outnumbers the registered hound, but the latter, because of his newly acquired status and "papers," is commanding a higher price, much higher. A good Coonhound these days goes for $300 to $500, with the superior ones as high as $1000 or more.

The early coon hunter built his Coonhound by crossing the best dogs together, regardless of type, color, background or anything else. The result was such conglomerations as a Bluetick with Black-and-Tan conformation, but such oddities made no difference as long as the hound was an effective worker. Despite the myriad of crossings, the basic blood persisted, and in the last twenty-five years breeders began the task of reclaiming the original strains so breeds could be formed. Standards were written and a registry started under the guidance of the United Kennel Club of St. Louis, Missouri.

As more effort was expended in this direction, the blood became stronger. For example, if two Blueticks produced a litter of five Blueticks and two Black-and-Tan pups, the latter had to be destroyed and could not be used for either Bluetick or Black-and-Tan breeding. As this was done more thoroughly by breeders, especially with registration processes in effect, the strains gradually stabilized until they are now called breeds. At this point not all of them consistently produce offspring like themselves, but in another twenty-five years they undoubtedly will.

Let's look at the newly emerging breeds and see how they compare.

Their histories are so conflicting that I shall avoid them except where definite information can be proved. Most Coonhounds are now registered by the United Kennel Club and its standards are used for the following descriptions.

The Black-and-Tan

This is a beautiful old hound, dating back possibly to the Black-and-Tan Foxhound pack brought to Maryland by Robert Brooke in 1650 and later spread across Virginia. Some claim it descends from the Talbot Hound of William the Conqueror in 1066. How anyone can trace a Coonhound back beyond nine generations, let alone nine centuries, is beyond me, but the Black-and-Tan remains a lot of hound and that's all that matters. He's a close relative to the Bloodhound and has even bigger—or rather, longer—ears. He has a gleaming black coat with tan markings on front legs, sometimes under belly, throat and muzzle, and always two little tan pumpkin seeds over the eyes.

He has a strong, heavy head, plenty of bone in his frame, and his black whip tail is carried proudly over his back as he works. He stands 23 to 25 inches, weighs 50 to 60 pounds, has an ear spread of 23 to 25 inches. His fine deep bugle-and-bawl voice has long been a favorite with hunters, as has his great trailing ability and treeing instinct. He's a friendly, good-natured dog, a little more so than the average hound, and has plenty of courage in all situations.

The Black-and-Tan is registered by both the AKC and UKC. The show

Black-and-Tan, owned by Fred B. Way, Orangeburg, S.C.

dogs of the former are large, massive fellows reaching up to 27 inches at withers and with an ear spread approaching 30 inches. The UKC registered hounds are more the working blood, this group claiming that such long ears are ridiculous on a Coonhound that works at night in thick places. Not only do they become slashed but they impair his scenting by being considerably longer than his muzzle, which means that when he drops his nose to ground-scent, his ears drag 4 or 5 inches or more.

There is a small version of the Black-and-Tan which is popular among field-trial people because the hound is a real sprinter. It does not have the characteristics of the long-eared, leggy, larger size, but is short-eared and on the Treeing Walker type.

Not only is the Black-and-Tan a good cooner and a good-looker, but he's a music maker all the way.

The Plott

This is one breed that didn't come from the Foxhound but was brought from Germany as a boar hound by Jonathan Plott. Emigrating to the United States in 1750, Plott settled a little west of Asheville, North Carolina, and used his hounds for bear hunting. They quickly gained a reputation throughout the Great Smoky Mountains of North Carolina and Tennessee, and to this day the Plott family has carefully kept the breed as pure as possible. In fact, the only admitted outcross was a Georgia bear

Plott Hound—Ch. Nite Ch. Brandenberger's Drum, owned by Dale Brandenberger, Millstadt, Ill.

hunter's dog more than 150 years ago. How true this is cannot be said because there are different types of Plott Hounds and many a brindle coon dog has been peddled as a Plott.

The Plott Hound is a powerful animal with a good solid head for tackling big game, is generally brindle in color, often with a black saddle, occasionally solid black. White on chest is permitted. His voice is a powerful, rolling bawl with a chop. In size, the Plott varies considerably. The standard calls for 22 to 25 inches for males and weight between 50 and 60 pounds, but some run smaller than this and many run larger, up to 80 and 90 pounds.

The Plotts are good fast hounds, vicious fighters on game, and usually have a super treeing instinct. They take readily to water and have excellent endurance. In recent years the Plott has developed a reputation as a wild-boar dog. He has always been a big-game hound and seen widespread use on wildcat, mountain lion and bear.

The Redbone

Old Reliable of the coon hunters is the Redbone. He's been around for a long time and spread to just about all the places where men hunt coon. He reproduces about as true to type as any of the new breeds and is a nicely balanced hound with plenty of brains and speed. On a trail he very

Redbone with raccoon at bay.

seldom potters but follows with determination. His voice has a short bawl that is extremely pleasing and a loud, steady chop at the tree.

There are a few large Redbones around these days, but for the most part he stands 22 to 26 inches and weighs 45 to 60 pounds. In color he's red, with a small amount of white on the blanket or feet not objectionable. His dark-brown or hazel eyes have a pleading expression that is a breed characteristic, as are its high-set ears.

Originally the Redbone is said to have come from the Birdsong Foxhound crossed to Bloodhound stock with some Irish Hounds used afterward. The breed used to be called "Saddlebacks," for the early dogs had black saddles but this has been bred out of them.

The Redbone has great determination on trail and is a particularly strong treeing hound. Redbones have been known to remain at a tree for hours at a time. Beyond being a coon expert, the Redbone enjoys a reputation as a big-game hound.

The Bluetick

There are probably more Bluetick Hounds in the world than any other type and they probably vary more in size and shape. I have seen Bluetick rabbit dogs that looked like Bassets and also the giant Bluetick Coonhound of 100 pounds, built like a pile driver. Obviously ticking is only a color, hence the wide variation in conformation, but as the Coonhound strains have striven to become breeds so has the Bluetick tried to collect itself and is succeeding.

The standard calls for the male to be 23 to 26 inches at the shoulder, and weigh 55 to 80 pounds. Colorwise, he is ticked all over but usually has a black saddle and head with tan pumpkin seeds over the eyes and often tan on the front.

A close relative of the Bluetick is the English, who resembles the Foxhound considerably, is often found in the same litter as the Bluetick (less now than before) and is another good worker. Obviously, with Foxhounds playing such an important role in forming the Coonhound, there were bound to be cases where the tricolor and conformation came out almost as the original. In addition, the English appears in red ticking. Males weigh 50 to 70 pounds and stand 22 to 25 inches at shoulders. The body doesn't have the roached back of the American Foxhound but resembles more the English Foxhound. He has a good hound bawl and is a diligent worker.

Bluetick.

The Treeing Walker

This hound resembles his cousin, the Walker Foxhound, more than he does the mental image one has of a Coonhound, but his work can't be condemned. He really knows his business, is one of the fastest Coonhounds in the woods today, and wins field trials left and right.

The Treeing Walker carries his head high. Muzzle is medium square rather than long, with no dewlap at the neck. He has a racy, streamlined appearance, gracefully arched, rather short back, and straight front legs that are plenty long. Tail is saberlike, strong at root and without flag. In color, he is basically white with black and tan spots, the white always predominating. Males stand 23 to 26 inches and weigh 50 to 75 pounds. Voice is a clear, ringing bugle on cold trail, changing to chop or turkey mouth on running trail, and deep throaty loud chop at the tree.

The Treeing Walker is a graceful, speedy hound, bold and able to run anything. His widespread growth among coon hunters and big game hunters speaks for itself.

Through the years many outstanding "coon dogs," a polite term for mongrel or cur, have appeared on the coon hunting scene. Some were handsome, and many old-timers still think that a hound crossed with a Springer Spaniel or Collie or Airedale makes a better than average dog. But some qualities are always lost. The voice becomes yappy, maybe even silent on trail. The hound looks fade into a nondescript conformation. And when a superior individual appears, his offspring invariably lose his quality in recessive characteristics.

One of the amazing phenomena of the Coonhound world is its field trials and the extent to which they have spread in the past few years. Trials fall into three types—night hunts which are run on live wild coon, drag races, and water races. The first is what you would imagine a Coonhound field trial to be. The dogs are turned loose in the woods to hunt and find coon. They are judged for their skill in this work and earn titles of Night Champions.

The second two—drag races and water races—are really coon dogs running at a race track. In a drag hunt either a live coon or a scent stick is dragged over a course of a minimum of half a mile, and the entering hounds are turned loose in packs of six. First across the finish line wins that heat, some money and advances to the heat winners. There may be a hundred dogs or more in the event, and the winners of the quarter-finals, semifinals, the finals, win money each time they cross the finish line first or bark at the tree first. Water racing is the same idea only dogs have to swim across water to win. Here the best swimmers get the dough.

These trials are great fun, provide entertainment for thousands of people and considerable money to the winners. At the Kenton National in Kenton, Ohio, in 1962, there were 1355 entries, $40,000 in purse money and $5200 to the finalist winners. At the World's Championship Water Races in Anderson, South Carolina, in 1963 more than 15,000 people attended. The first-to-the-tree final winner received $1000. Five doped dogs were

Treeing Walker—owned by Carl T. Johnson, Cadillac, Mich.

World's Championship Coonhound Water Races at Anderson, S.C. The caged raccoon on a float is dragged ahead of the dogs, luring them on. First hound to white circle on the shore wins.

pulled; one man was sent to jail and another fined. Betting at these events is widespread, to the extent that the drag and water trials usually held near Poughkeepsie, New York, were recently barred by the district attorney.

Certainly in a few years Coonhound field trials have become big business and we may one day see them organized under license and parimutual betting. Certainly this is the most sensible direction in which they could head. It is in this phase of Coonhound trialing that the Greyhound-Coonhound cross has been utilized. Not that the resultant speedster is good for anything but coon trial racing, but he is sure okay at that.

Which brings us back to the story that began this section. The very next moonlight night I called up my friend and he took me hunting. Soon afterward, I became a coon hunter, who, by definition, is a bleary-eyed worker by day and a hip-booted follower of the hounds by night. I don't own a Coonhound yet, but I go to every field trial and look around, just waiting for some nice-looking Redbone or Plott to have a bad day, and while the owner is still steaming I ease over and ask him how much for his dog. I know one of these days I'll make a fast deal. They say that's the only way to get rid of the fever.

Ch. Ameliett of Coptokin, owned by Mrs. Gwendolyn Stanich of Polo, Ill.

The Basenji

Small, silent, swift and agile—this is the Basenji, native hunting dog from the Congo and one of the oldest and relatively unchanged breeds known to man. In ancient Egypt the Pharaohs received the Basenji as a highly prized gift from Central Africa. 'Way back then he was somewhat longer-legged and probably served as a coursing hound.

Today Congo natives use him as a tracking hound to stalk and drive small game into nets or to turn game into the path of other natives with spears. The dog trails silently, hence they often outfit him with wooden rattles to follow his quick movements in tall grass.

So relatively mute and silent is the dog that he has been billed here and in England as "barkless." He does emit slight noises, however, nothing like a yip or baying sound but more of a gurgling chortle of happiness.

Beyond his relative silence, the Basenji possesses many other qualities that have endeared him to many people since his arrival in this country in 1937. He's a classy little fellow with the springy grace of a deer. His short, silky coat of chestnut red glistens like polished copper, and his large prick ears reach upward from his chunky fox head like two antennas scooping the air for sound. A high degree of intelligence reflects in his alert eyes and the peculiarly wrinkled brow.

One nice thing apartment people like about the dog is its habit of cleaning itself with the regularity and precision of a cat. It's also a wonderfully friendly animal, full of play around children and adults, and a real ham at heart.

The Basenji male stands around 17 inches high and weighs approximately 24 pounds; the bitch, 16 inches high and 22 pounds. Considering its size, the dog has excellent bone quality and strength. Its white-tipped tail curls over its back and tucks neatly to either side. In color he can be chestnut red (the deeper the better) or pure black, or black and tan, all with white feet, chest, and tail tip. Whether he has white legs, white blaze on head, and white collar is optional.

Though the Basenji has not been part of any organized hunting group or trial in the United States, some startling examples have been recorded which show what the dog can do if given the chance and a little training. There are proven instances of the Basenji outmaneuvering and outdistancing Greyhounds in broken-field running to bring jackrabbits to earth in the Southwest. Basenjis have also treed and held large mountain lions in the West, taken on and killed the Louisiana swamp boar, one of the most vicious animals found in the United States. And when used on raccoon, they don't tree as the Coonhound does but, because they trail so silently and stealthily, run the coon to earth and kill it before it can reach a tree.

Breeders and owners of Basenjis are constantly amazed by what these little fellows do. They are all muscle to begin with, and their speed is little short of astounding. As witness their extraordinary agility, one owner reported that her Basenji bitch was lying in the yard, prone, taking a sunbath. Within an instant, she went from this relaxed position straight up in the air and came down with a bird in her mouth. There were no trees or bushes within a distance of 25 feet from where she lay resting, so the bird must have been caught in mid-flight, a feat almost no other breed would be capable of.

The Basenji, though he has found a niche in the United States as a playful, bright, silent family pet and show dog, has all the potential of a terrific field worker. With time he will undoubtedly prove more than his worth in this, his original purpose.

The Norwegian Elkhound

The first dog I ever had in my life was a Norwegian Elkhound. He was a tremendously alert little guy, about 21 inches tall, compactly built from his short prick ears to his chunky body and tightly curled tail. No matter where he ran, his brindle coat with its black points always glistened like glass and, winter or summer, snow or heat, he was a bouncing ball of energy. King was his name, and I guess that in my youth I never realized the depth of his loyalty.

Nor did I know about his proud Viking heritage, that his was the oldest pure breed of dog in Europe, buried along with weapons beside Viking masters as far back as 4000–5000 B.C. And I didn't know his ancestors had long been hunters of elk in his native land, herders of sheep, defenders against bear and wolves, even sled dogs. I only knew my King was the best squirrel dog that ever lived. I shot him just one squirrel and after that he was a squirrel dog.

In the fall when the leaves began to turn, King would wait for me to come home from school—he always did anyway—and if I so much as leaned toward my .410 he'd go into his bouncing act. Until we reached the woods, that is—then he'd be all business. I'd sneak toward the big oaks and chestnut trees and he'd cakewalk 40 to 50 feet ahead of me, looking this way and that, sniffing the air, ears pricked, listening. Before I could see or hear anything he'd take off like a shot and I'd glimpse a gray tail spinning up a tree. He had a great pair of eyes and he'd bounce from tree to tree on the ground as the squirrel darted high across the branches above him.

King was a smart dog. He knew he couldn't get a squirrel without my shooting it and he soon learned that if he cut up a commotion on one side of the tree, old brushtail slid around to the other side. So he developed the habit of treeing quickly and barking wildly on the far side of the tree from me, and sure enough, the squirrel would come sliding around so I had a good clean shot at it.

If I knocked one down and it hit the ground very much alive, thrashing, biting and scratching, King pounced on it fearlessly. He was fearless in everything he did; honest, too. When King treed, even though it was two hundred yards away and he had to move another hundred yards under thirty or forty different trees, you could be sure there was a squirrel somewhere up in the one he finally yipped under. Never in four years did he make a mistake, though it sometimes took me half an hour of squinting and going round and round to find it.

I knew a man and his wife who loved squirrel stew, and I gave them so many squirrels that they finally thanked me for my trouble and bashfully explained that they were getting tired of it. So King and I went after a more varied bag. He had a great nose, and he soon learned to run anything he could smell, rabbits, pheasants, possum. Late one afternoon we ran into a flight of woodcock. Neither one of us knew what we were doing. He'd sniff around and soon that tightly curled tail would jiggle a little, then he'd dive in and flush Mr. Longbill. I made my first double on them and came home with five.

When I went away to college, we had to get rid of the dog. I hated to do it but we gave him to a man who owned a farm out in the country. We thought King would be happy but the man never hunted squirrels or anything, and when I spoke with him a couple of years later he said King had died. He couldn't figure it out because the dog was only six. But I knew. That Viking loyalty had broken his heart.

The Norwegian Elkhound has become a very popular dog since its arrival in the United States in the early 1930s. He stands 20 to 21 inches at the withers, weighs around 50 pounds, and every inch of him is alive and bristling with energy. Though a fervent watchdog, he is excellent around children and loyal beyond belief. Conditioned to the rugged winters and mountains of Scandinavia, he thrives on cold weather and snow.

Here in this country the Norwegian Elkhound Club of America has promoted him primarily as a show dog and family pet. Still, he has seen considerable field use hunting bear, mountain lion, bobcats, and makes a superior squirrel and rabbit dog though he doesn't have a typical hound voice. Possessed of one of the finest scenting abilities in all dogdom, he hunts silently until the quarry is treed or brought to bay. His superior intelligence allows him to adapt easily to almost any hunting situation, though basically he is a big-game dog.

When you see a man in the woods hunting with a Norwegian Elkhound, you can be sure he'll bring home something.

Norwegian Elkhound.

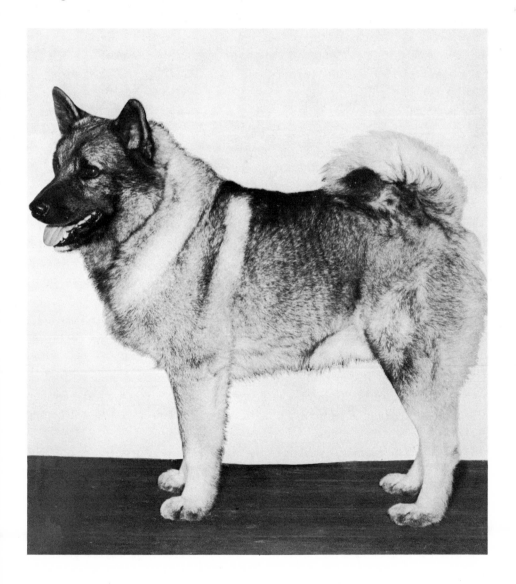

The Otter Hound

Certainly the best of all hounds in and around water is this rare old English breed, the Otter Hound. His crisp, shaggy coat is oily enough to permit almost any amount of immersion and his webbed feet make him a great swimmer. Since the fourteenth century he has been used to hunt the otter that devastate English fishing streams by catching the plumpest trout and salmon.

The dog trailed his prey melodiously on land, attacked him with fury and courage in water. The otter is a strong, savage 20–25-pound member of the mink family, and more at home in water than on land when it comes to fighting.

Otter hunting reached its peak in the nineteenth century, but even then no more than twenty packs were hunting in England. The usual practice was for the owner and his pack to be called by the landlord of an estate to come and catch the otters which were destroying his trout. The finest pack ever assembled belonged to Squire Lomax of Clitheroe, who spent the bulk of his life breeding and training these dogs, only to have most of them die in one year of a contagious disease around 1870. He never rebuilt his pack because the dogs were never numerous enough to obtain easily, as were Foxhounds or Beagles.

The Otter Hound looks like a longhaired Bloodhound and undoubtedly carries quite a bit of this breed, also some Terrier and Water Spaniel blood as well as a little Foxhound. He stands some 24 to 26 inches in height and weighs up to 70 pounds. His color is grizzle or sandy, with black and tan in quite clearly defined patches.

We don't know just when the Otter Hound first came to the United

Ch. Ranter of Dumfries, owned by Mrs. Carolyn Babson, Batavia, Illinois.

States, some authorities say not before 1900, but certainly there is repetitious mention of an Otter Hound of sorts in the early 1800s, even before. Otters were numerous in those days and their pelts of great value as they are now, so a dog or pack of dogs that could catch them would easily have earned its keep. We know Otter Hounds existed and though they might have been a handy local cross, they would not have served the purpose nearly as well as the English specialist which was bred and trained for the work.

All this is brought out because early American dog writers speak of an Otter Hound in the Chesapeake Bay area, and local legend has long connected him with the formation of the Chesapeake Bay Retriever. If this old English water hound gave his aquatic ability, his great courage and determination, and his oily, almost waterproof coat to the Chessie, then his contribution to America has been a great one.

Though a kindly and devoted animal, the Otter Hound is today a rare breed. He is seen only at the largest shows, and the people who love and appreciate him enough to perpetuate him are becoming too few and far between. He still sees a little action on possum and coon hunts, particularly in wet, marshy areas where a lot of hounds refuse to go. And he still has the courage and strength, the tracking ability and melodious voice that endeared him to the heart of Squire Lomax.

The ridge of hair on the Ridgeback begins at the withers with two crowns and runs to the rump.

The Rhodesian Ridgeback

This, the newest of all hounds in the United States, came across the water from Africa in the late 1940s, and the growth of its popularity in the intervening years has been little short of sensational.

Several sound reasons account for this.

The Rhodesian Ridgeback is a handsome, shorthaired dog capable of standing heat or cold. The reverse streak of hair up his back makes his appearance unique in all dogdom. He has size and masculinity, yet remains even tempered around the home or apartment, loves children and is calm, never noisy or quarrelsome. He's also a good watchdog, fearless in any situation.

This, the only breed of dog we have from southern Africa, had its origin half from European dogs, half from a semiwild African dog. It seems that the Hottentots, a race of small black people living in the Transvaal, had a rather small hunting dog which hung around their villages. He was a peculiar-looking animal in that he had a ridge of hair running in the wrong

direction up the middle of his back. Through the years he had become accustomed to the broiling daytime heat, the cold nights, ticks, flies and other hardships that go to make up life on the African veld.

When the Dutch, Germans, and French Huguenots emigrated to South Africa in the 1500s and 1600s, they brought with them dogs of all descriptions, from mastiffs and hounds to terriers. In 1836 these people, the Boers, began a great migration into the Transvaal. They came upon the Hottentots' dog, strange-looking but practical because it could hunt and was acclimated to Africa's rigors. They crossed the largest of their own dogs with this ridgebacked one, and the result was a strong dog of greater size which could be used for hunting all types of game, for flushing partridges or taking an antelope. The dog was also a bold and fearless guardian of the home against marauding night animals.

In the late 1870s a pair of the Boers' ridgebacked dogs reached Rhodesia where they fell into the hands of big-game hunters who began using them most successfully for hunting lions from horseback. More were brought in, some were bred, all were enthusiastically absorbed by hunters and farmers in their new country and soon became known as Rhodesian Ridgebacks. Breeders organized themselves in 1922 and drew up a standard which helped solidify the breed. Before that time the Ridgeback had appeared in a wide variety of sizes, shapes and colors, because all kinds of Boer dogs were crossed to the Hottentots' with more thought given to obtaining a practical dog than producing a new breed.

Ridgebacks went to England in 1928, and photos from that period show a rather different animal from the one we have today. The early specimens had a large amount of white on legs, chest, even neck and face, and had a Mastiff-Foxhound air to them. Although the Ridgeback does not have the typical hound look, it was classified as one because of the work it did in Africa. Probably larger breeds like the Mastiff and Dane did more to form the European side of the dog than did the hound. The Ridgeback is hunted in packs, doesn't open on a trail like the ordinary hound, but has a chop (quick yip-yip-yip) when it gains sight of or corners its quarry. Essentially the breed is a scent-hunting hound, but Ridgebacks are so alert that they often work their game by sight when the opportunity presents itself.

The Rhodesian Ridgeback is a powerful dog of great endurance and a fair amount of speed. His head is rather flat in skull, broad between the ears, free from wrinkles. The muzzle is long and deep for attacking and holding on. Ears are set high and shaped like a Mastiff's, not pendulous like a hound's. His chest is deep rather than wide and never barreled. Forelegs are straight as posts and just as solid. His hindquarters are strong, and he has a full-length tail, thick at the root and tapering, with a slight upward curve, on the order of a Great Dane's but proportionally shorter.

The ridge up his back—his hallmark—is a little less than two inches wide and tapers symmetrically from shoulder blades to top of hips. It should contain two crowns opposite each other.

The Ridgeback has a beautiful glossy coat that is short and dense. Its color ranges from light wheaten to red wheaten, though most of the dogs I've seen were golden "wheaten." A little white on the chest and toes is permitted, but it should not be excessive, and white any other place is undesirable. The dog is good-sized, standing 25 to 27 inches and weighing around 75 pounds; bitches 24 to 26 inches and about 65 pounds.

To date the Rhodesian Ridgeback has found his way in the United States as a graceful and intelligent family dog of unique appearance. He is also receiving wider and wider support in the show ring. Judges often come from Africa to handle big classes at the major shows. In recent years as many or more of the breed have been imported from the Union of South Africa as from Rhodesia.

As a working dog, the Rhodesian Ridgeback has been used successfully in the Rocky Mountain region and for wild-boar hunting in the hills of Tennessee. With his success already assured as a companion dog, this newest of the hounds will undoubtedly find wider use as a hunter as the years go by.

The Rhodesian Ridgeback is a strong, well-conformed dog.

Chapter 6

The Coursing Hounds

Unlike his brother, the tracking hound, who works by scent, the coursing hound works by sight. He moves about at high speed, generally in pairs or threes, never more than half a dozen, over a vast open area like a plain or desert where visibility is unimpaired. His effectiveness is limited to the distance he can see, hence in high brush or dense woods he cannot function.

Coursing hounds have probably been man's oldest hunting companion because they chased and actually caught the game. He didn't have to stone it, shoot it or anything else. The hounds were simply unleashed within sight of the game and away they went, at great speed. The hunters followed either on galloping horses or running as fast as they could on foot.

Because the game was nearly always a sizable quarry like deer, gazelle, wolves, elk or the like, the coursing hounds had to be equally large and especially swift to overtake their prey and kill it. For this, one of the dogs usually grabbed a hind leg of the fleeing animal, throwing it, then the other dogs pounced on it, seized its throat and held on until the animal died or the hunters arrived. For all this the dogs had to have courage, powerful jaws and plenty of agility.

Thus the coursing hounds, whether short- or long-haired and no matter what part of the world they come from, have a similar look. They're extraordinarily tall dogs with long, sinewy limbs that provide tremendous speed when they jackknife to full length. Many have been clocked by car in the Midwest at between 35 and 40 miles an hour. For endurance they have deep chests which house strong lungs and a mighty heart. In repose they are not too beautiful, being often roach-backed, even camel-backed, but when they unlimber and pour on their burning speed, their bodies undulate with power and grace. Their backs become giant springs, coiling and uncoiling as their lean legs propel their gaunt bodies forward in leaping, ground-devouring strides. The long heads and snake tails act as counterbalances for the rhythmic sweep of the body. They make a fantastic sight as they race across a barren plain in hot pursuit of game.

The coursing family of hounds is centuries old, originating in the Middle East in the cradle of human civilization. Most people think of the Saluki or

Irish Wolfhound as a remnant of a bygone era, no longer serving any useful purpose in the world, especially in the United States. But they're wrong. In the Plains states of Nebraska, Kansas, Iowa, Missouri, Oklahoma, north Texas, hunting with coursing hounds has become a very popular and practical sport in recent years. Ranchers and stockmen own packs of giant-sized hounds trained for sight-hunting predators like coyotes or nuisance animals like jackrabbits.

Sight-hunting hounds coursing for coyotes are shown in action here by a dramatic series of photos of a hunt in the sand hills of Nebraska. After the coyote is spotted the hounds are released from the rear of the truck and charge after the quarry.

Coursing hounds roar across the Great Plains in hot pursuit of a coyote.

The coyote is boxed in by these huge, rugged hounds.

The kill!

The coyote is the principal target because he destroys cattle and sheep. Despite the fact that there has been a bounty on his head for many years (currently $2 in most states) he is more plentiful today than in the days of the frontier. He is too wily and clever for the Foxhound, can throw him any time he choses, but the big coursing hound, roaring down on him across an open plain, is his equal.

In this sport hunters never carry guns. The general procedure is to load the hounds into cages on the back ends of pickup trucks and take off across the flats. It's important that the hounds be able to see what's going on, so the cages usually have slots or a gap in the rear through which they can stick their heads and see everything that happens behind the truck. As a stockman drives across the plain, his front-seat or rooftop partner scans ahead and to the sides with binoculars. Once a coyote is spotted, the driver chases it full speed until he passes it, at which point the coyote turns and runs in the opposite direction and the hounds, looking out the rear, catch sight of it. The driver slams to a halt, drops the tail gate and the hounds pour out in hot pursuit. Chases last up to half a mile and fifty per cent of the time the coyote escapes.

The hounds do not run the coyote until it gives out, then catch it. They overtake it with a phenomenal burst of speed shortly after leaving the truck. They can't keep up their torrid pace very long, which is why the coyote often gets away and what makes it great sport.

These coursing hounds are big, rough dogs. Their origin is an interesting one. Farmers of the Great Plains area found the ever increasing number of coyotes raising havoc with sheep and calves while the rapidly multiplying jackrabbits often ate crops to the ground. Trapping, poison, shooting, even annual roundups were tried. Then some of the farmers in the Kansas area where Greyhounds are raised and trained for the track were given castoffs which couldn't make the grade. Gradually, coursing for jackrabbits with these dogs became a practical sport which spread across the Great Plains states.

But Greyhounds have light snouts, tend to snap and nip rather than come boring in and grab a bone-crushing hold as the Irish Wolfhound does, for example. They proved excellent on jackrabbits but didn't have the striking power necessary to attack and kill coyotes. Farmers and ranchers could not pay the high prices of purebred coursing hounds, so they took their Greyhound track castoffs and crossed them in any way they could for improvement. They bred for stamina, speed, courage, more fight, tougher feet. They wanted relatively shorthaired dogs that required no combing of coat. And they allowed only the best to survive and reproduce because the dogs are so big and eat so much that they couldn't afford keeping a poor one. In recent years just about all the major breeds of sight hounds have been crossed into the basic Greyhound blood—Irish Wolfhounds, Scottish Deerhounds, Salukis, etc.

Some of the hounds that have been produced are beautiful dogs, dynamite in a large package, and they are serving their purpose admirably. At this moment they come in all colors and their conformation varies as to the crosses which have been made. The best description of them would be to say they are big, exceedingly alert and built on coursing-hound lines. In time they will breed more true to type and as this happens we shall see the rise of a new breed of dog which might best be called The American Coursing Hound. This may take twenty-five or fifty years, but the groundwork has been set and we are seeing the building right now.

To most purebred-dog fanciers, the crossing of one breed with another is a sacrilege and I find from my own personal experience that they look upon these coursing hounds as mongrels and curs, which in a way is true. But they fail to realize that the American-bred field Pointer, or the American Pointer as I prefer to call him, is a magnificent mongrel, a cross between the pottering English Pointer and Foxhound, that the American-bred English field Setter is a superbly successful cross between the Llewellin Setters of England and the early American grade Setters which included a hodgepodge of what was available, that the American Foxhound is a brilliant blend of God-knows-what. On and on it goes.

America has always produced what was needed to meet a situation, whether it was hunting dogs, beef cattle or jet engines. If breeders of pure-bred Salukis, Borzois, Irish Wolfhounds, etc. had given stock to farmers and ranches originally, I am sure they would have been more than glad to keep it pure provided it met their needs. But such was not the case, so the farmers and ranchers bred their own the best way they knew how. As far as I'm concerned, they are succeeding admirably. Their dogs love coursing, quickly learn to watch from the rear of the truck. They go crazy with excitement when the coyote appears, charge after him with spine-tingling speed, strike fearlessly with great power. To my way of thinking, these are magnificent dogs.

A superb specimen of the coursing hound being bred and hunted in the Great Plains area of the United States today. Note the fine alertness of eyes and face, the tremendous neck, the powerful shoulders and hindquarters, deep chest, the splendid over-all conformation that contains strength in every line. These rugged dogs whose blood is composed of an assortment of coursing hounds, mostly Greyhound, may someday become a breed known as the American Coursing Hound.

Coursing is an ever growing sport in the United States. It is necessarily limited to those open areas like the Great Plains states and the Southwest. Each year the National Coursing Association holds a spring trial in Kansas. On the average, 400 to 600 coursing hounds show up and compete for eight days for some eight to ten thousand dollars in prize money, not including side bets, which run hot and heavy. The dogs run jackrabbits and are judged on speed and several points of agility, including proficiency of kill.

With all this activity it's not impossible to imagine the age-old breeds of coursing hounds coming back into service once more, perhaps not in their original use of dropping antelope or wolves or deer but at least as coyote chasers and jackrabbit grabbers in sport and in field trials.

Ch. Ahmed Farouk of Pine Paddocks, owned by Mrs. Esther Bliss Knapp of Valley City, Ohio.

The Saluki

Among the earliest recordings of civilized man—in the 3000–7000 B.C. empire of Sumer (today's central Iraq)—the Saluki appeared in stone carvings. Sacred dog of the Pharaohs, he has been found mummified in Egyptian tombs of 2100 B.C. When Alexander the Great invaded Mesopotamia and Persia in 329 B.C. he met this elegant and effective coursing hound. Some people even claim that the word "dog" in the Bible refers specifically to the Saluki.

That may be going a little far but it's safe to say that the Saluki is one of the oldest, if not the oldest, pure breed of dog in the world.

His specific purpose has long been as a hound for sight-hunting rabbits and especially the gazelle, small swift desert antelope of the Middle East. Both are highly prized additions to the Bedouin diet, hence the Saluki has been guarded with care and jealousy for centuries by nomadic tribes which spread from the mountains of northern Iran, Iraq and Syria to the hot Sahara, Egypt and North Africa.

Two of the most prized possessions of a sheik are his Arabian horses and his Salukis. Both are magnificent animals, graceful, aristocratic, superbly adapted to their environment through centuries of careful breeding and survival of the fittest. Isolation has kept them pure, so has their fantastic ability, so has the Moslem religion. An Arab thinks it a sin to cross his beautiful desert horse to any other type; the same with his Saluki. Moslems consider all dogs unclean except the Saluki, which is "the noble gift of Allah" and is permitted to lie on the carpet of the sheiks' tents.

The dog has lines similar to the Greyhound, long, bony legs, lots of light under the body. His coat is soft and silky with slight feathering on legs and tail and long, silky hair on the pendulous ears. He varies considerably, depending upon what area of the Middle East he comes from. In the mountainous regions of the north he will have a longer coat and more featherings and will be larger in size; in the arid and desert regions of the south his coat will be lighter and his size smaller. Generally he stands 23 to 28 inches and weighs 55 to 75 pounds, although the bitches are often considerably smaller and lighter. In color the Saluki is most often seen in cream or fawn but also comes in white, golden, red, grizzle, tan, white-and-chestnut, tricolor (black, white and tan), black-and-tan, and solid black.

The Saluki's head is lean and sensitive but not weak. It rests on a long, thin neck which flows into a rangy body of sinews and bone balanced by a long tail which curves naturally. Like his running mate, the Arabian horse, he is the product of survival in heat and cold, hence is inherently durable and healthy. In disposition the Saluki is usually politely aloof from all but his own master and household. He is not an aggressive watchdog but is a reliable one.

The breed became established in England around 1900, crossed the ocean to our shores shortly after World War I but in very limited numbers. The Saluki Club of America was formed in 1927 and a moderately steady increase in his numbers has followed since that time. He is seen frequently in dog shows and has earned a sound reputation in this area by gaining many championships.

In hunting, the Saluki has remarkable eyesight and great endurance. He is not as fast as the Greyhound, but the thick hair which grows between his toes protects his feet so he can race over the roughest terrain. In his native Middle East the Saluki tends to wear down his prey rather than overtake it with tremendous speed. Often Salukis work in pairs or threes, two driving a gazelle into the reach of the third. Often falcons are used to distract the gazelle, thus enabling the Saluki to move in and strike.

Generally Salukis are such one-man dogs that they don't accept, or work effectively as hunters for, another master. This plus the facts that they cannot survive harsh treatment and do not have great speed have made them of little use in this country as coursing hounds. They have been tried as purebreds and as crosses, but without success, thus their contribution to the Great Plains coursing hound is very limited.

The Borzoi

This magnificently elegant dog was kept for centuries by the nobility of Czarist Russia as a symbol of grandeur and also for the sport of hunting wolves which infested the country in early times. In fact the Borzoi was called the Russian Wolfhound until 1936.

Exact origin of the dog is indefinite, but one old record mentions a Russian Duke who imported a number of Arabian Greyhounds, possibly Salukis, to hunt wolves. He soon found that their coats were too thin to survive the fierce Russian winters so he crossed them into a heavy-coated Russian breed similar to the Collie but with longer legs and more refined body, also a type of coursing hound. The result was the Borzoi, a tall, thin dog built on Greyhound lines but with a beautiful silky coat of curls that provided warmth in winter.

Because the dog has a long coat and a clean face, his narrow, elegant head with almost no stop is dramatically displayed. His snubby ears lie flat on his long hairy neck, and the lines of his long body and legs flow from one gentle curve to the next, ending in the low, graceful sweep of the lengthy tail. A big dog, the Borzoi stands from 28 to 31 inches at the withers, even higher occasionally, and weighs 75 to 105 pounds. Generally the bitches are quite a bit smaller and lighter.

Though the Borzoi is built for speed, he is so beautiful that he was long the darling of aristocrats, both for hunting and as a graceful palace pet. This made him a hated dog among the Russian peasants, consequently the Borzois of the Czar's great kennel were destroyed during the Revolution in 1917, as well as those throughout the country. But long before that aristocrats elsewhere in the world had acquired him, and as early as 1889 a Borzoi was imported to Pennsylvania. Around 1900 several Americans imported Borzois from Russia and Germany and the dog became a popular showpiece of the "Roaring Twenties." Today he is seen on a less limited scale but nevertheless remains an active show dog, always dramatic in appearance, serene in temperament and of great poise.

Like all coursing hounds, the Borzoi has an extremely deep chest and, because of his height, gives the impression of being narrow in width of body. In color he is white with markings of lemon, tan, brindle, gray or black. Occasionally he appears in solid colors.

Because the Borzoi needed speed and good strong jaws to attack wolves, he has proved useful in the United States as a coyote coursing hound. However, his heavy coat does not help him in our country because the Great Plains area where most of the coursing takes place is relatively hot. Also, too many years of being bred for beauty have robbed him of the fierce, hard-charging determination of the coursing hound to overtake and catch his quarry, but he has been employed as a cross from time to time.

Ch. Czarina H.H.F. of Gwejon, Am. & Can. CDX, owned by Mrs. John M. Pinette of Claremont, N.H.

The Afghan

One of the most exotic members of all dogdom is the Afghan Hound.
With his long silky hair falling like Spanish moss from his ears, neck, shoulders, legs, stomach, tail, and his smooth dark face with its triangular eyes bursting forth from under a topknot, this amusing-looking fellow is often called "monkey-face" or "the baboon dog."

Though we have a papyrus writing in which the Egyptians mentioned him more than 4000 years ago in exactly the same terms, there is little doubt that his home is and has always been the mountains and plains of Afghanistan. Here he chases leopards and gazelles, mountain deer and hares with a lightning speed that is nothing short of phenomenal. Without question, old as the dog is, he was developed specifically for hunting in this wild, rugged country. His extremely long, loose coat insulates against the freezing winters and torrid summers as well as flies and insects that might drive a shorthaired dog insane. His unusual hipbones, set wide apart on his strong hindquarters, provide him with a swiveling maneuverability and springing power possessed by no other dog. In his swift, long-striding run

Ch. Spartan of Grandeur, hunting jackrabbits in Texas.

he can bound over an eight-foot-high rock or fallen tree as though it didn't exist.

At first impression the Afghan seems material for a cartoonist's dream, but the more you look at him the more you sense his dignity—in his proudly erect carriage, gay tail with its hooked tip, in his refined face and dark, reflective eyes. Though his legs are so heavily furred with silky coat that they jiggle like loose trousers as he pads along, you know this dog can really exert himself if given the opportunity. Down his back he sports a saddle of short hair which, along with the topknot, is a trade-mark of the breed. The Afghan grows very uniform in size. The standard calls for dogs to be 27 inches high at the withers, plus or minus an inch, with weight around 60 pounds, bitches 25 inches, give or take one, and about 50 pounds. Any color is permissible, but combinations should be pleasing to the eye and white markings, especially on the head, are undesirable. In temperament the dog is aloof and dignified but gay.

The Afghan was brought to England after World War I by British Army officers returning from the Middle East, and a few years later, in the mid 1920s, he reached American shores, though he didn't catch on at first. Once the Afghan Club of America was founded and the breed accepted for registration by the American Kennel Club, the dog acquired a following and has grown increasingly popular in passing years. He has had considerable success in the show ring because he's a proud dog that comes to full animation easily and catches the eye immediately by his unique looks and way of moving.

The Afghan as a coursing hound in this country has not seen wide use. Though extremely agile, he is not quite as swift as some of the other breeds, and in hunting the coyote, speed is a most essential ingredient. Another thing is his coat which, though beautiful, requires a lot of upkeep that Midwest farmers and ranchers just can't be bothered with. There is no doubt that the Afghan could be used to advantage on jackrabbits because of his high maneuverability, but that day hasn't arrived yet. When it does, we may even see the Afghan take to the dog track like the Greyhound. A pack of galloping Afghans would be a sight to please any dog-track devotee and would probably light the parimutuels up like a Christmas tree.

The Greyhound

Greyhound—swiftest of all dogs, symbol of speed itself!

Far and wide across the earth his name and fame have spread from the earliest days to our present time. Today the Greyhound, because of racing, is one of the most popular dogs in the United States, supports a near half-billion-dollar industry that mushrooms wider each year, provides entertainment for millions of Americans, north, east, south and west. But more about this later.

His origin?

Dog of the Pharaohs, who, 3000 to 4000 years ago, cherished him so dearly they had him mummified and taken into tombs to rest beside themselves so he might accompany them to the next world. The Greeks and Romans loved the dog, not only for sight hunting but for his wonderful disposition and beauty. He spread through Europe at an early date, is illustrated in a ninth-century English manuscript, mentioned in Danish law, woven into French tapestries, painted by Spanish artists, discussed over and over in the writings of all countries.

Long a favorite of royalty, he has been raised in luxury and pampered beyond belief at times, yet he's always been able to get out and sprint after game when given the opportunity. Deer, hart, foxes, hare have been his traditional quarry, but anything that ran in the open he'd try to catch.

The Greyhound is a beautifully symmetrical dog, powerful too, particularly our American racing variety. Because of his short coat you can see the superb muscle structure, the tight, lithe grace. Everything about him is streamlined—the long, narrow nose that widens back to the racy skull that flows into the long muscular neck that stretches gradually into the lean, sinewy shoulders. The deep-chested body narrows off to lengthy hindquarters and long legs and fine, tapering tail. Nothing coarse, not a line wasted, no brute muscle, just long, thin graceful strength and speed, speed, speed, right down to the small, finely textured ears folded tightly against the neck.

Great spirit and intelligence lie in the keen dark eyes which pop half out of the lean skull. Disposition: lovable, kind. Height: 28–30 inches. Weight: 65 to 70 pounds. Coat: short, smooth. Color: immaterial. Any color will do so long as he runs, and if he's a Greyhound he'll do that automatically.

The ancient sport of coursing with Greyhounds was organized competitively in England in the 1700s and in 1836 began the now famous Waterloo Cup event, a track meet for Greyhounds, held almost every year since. Here in the United States, coursing came early to the colonies. This type of hunting was popular in Virginia and in 1886 the first Greyhound registry was established. Early coursing events along with Whippet racing in the mill towns of Massachusetts set the stage for the Greyhound to take to the track in 1925.

The National Coursing Association of Abilene, Kansas, started in 1906, registers all racing members of the Greyhound breed, some 10,000 annually. Not all of these make the grade as racing dogs, but the majority do.

There are some 35,000 active racing Greyhounds in the country today. They race until they are 4 to 4½ years old. Dogs attain speeds up 38 miles per hour and run at 5/16 and ⅜ of a mile distances. Each year outstanding ones are declared champions.

A good racing puppy sells for $200 and up, with a litter from champions or a previously successful niche bringing as high as $750 each. Yearling dogs are worth $400 to $1000, depending upon their potential, while the occasional outstanding racing dog that may come up for sale—through death of owner or other unusual circumstances—may bring up to $10,000, even more.

Among the thirty-four tracks located in the country there are three in Massachusetts, two in South Dakota, three in Colorado, one in Portland, Oregon, four in Arizona as well as several in Florida, Texas, Kansas and elsewhere.

Kansas and the other Great Plains states comprise the heartland of the Greyhound. Here he is bred more extensively than anywhere else because he must be taught to sight-run rabbits. The jackrabbits of Kansas and adjoining states are ideal for such training. In short order the slow dogs

Two racing Greyhounds, Dody O Do and Heart o' Dixie, owned by George Fuller, Mobile, Alabama.

are weeded out while the good prospects continue their growth, training and conditioning for the day when they'll be coursing the mechanical rabbit at a track. The whole process is not unlike horse racing. They are given the best possible food and care, conditioned to the point where they're nothing but bone and sinew.

Some of the large racing kennels make a profession of raising, training and racing Greyhounds. There may be 100 to 125 dogs in one such operation. For many, though, it's a one-litter-a-year hobby, and they go at it with the same zest and determination to win as the big fellow.

In the Great Plains area the sport of coursing Greyhounds has a wide following too. Here hunters run them on coyotes for protection of sheep

A Greyhound coursing coyotes. He is also used for jackrabbit hunting.

and cattle as well as for the sport. Also, the National Coursing Association sponsors two field trials in Kansas and two in Texas each year. At these, 400 to 600 registered Greyhounds participate, as mentioned at the beginning of this chapter.

The Greyhound is also used on a much more limited scale as a show dog. These slim, slinky beauties, registered by American Kennel Club, are generally pets when not being shown. Though they don't have the sensational sprinting ability of their racing brothers, they can step out and fly whenever they're given the opportunity.

For that matter, the Greyhound remains today as he was 4000 years ago when the Pharaohs prized him so highly, the swiftest of all dogs, the king of speed.

Scottish Deerhound.

The Scottish Deerhound

Royal dog of Scotland is the Deerhound, hunter of the stag and ransom for noblemen's lives since medieval times. It's hard to say whether this great shaggy-coated animal was at some point in the past the same dog as the Irish Wolfhound, then grew to his present form as a result of crosses to the Greyhound, or whether he springs from a completely different past. Certainly he bears close resemblance to the Irish Wolfhound in size and coat, and to the Greyhound in conformation. In fact, if you clipped him closely he might pass as an extra large Greyhound.

So far as being good ransom is concerned, the Scottish Deerhound was so valued during the Middle Ages for his hunting ability and guard-dog loyalty to a master that a nobleman condemned to death often gained reprieve by giving a leash of these hounds (three) to the king. At various times they have been called the Scotch Greyhound, Highland Deerhound and Rough Greyhound, but have been a definite breed since the sixteenth century.

As big game grew scarce in the British Isles, the smaller, more delicate Greyhound became the popular coursing dog, but the Scottish Deerhound still held sway in the highlands of Scotland, hunting large stags weighing up to 250 pounds in their last stronghold. After 1750, however, the big dog faded almost from the scene, and only through the efforts of Archibald and Cundan McNeill was the breed successfully restored in the 1830s.

Many famous people have loved the Scottish Deerhound, among them Queen Elizabeth. Sir Walter Scott called his Maida "The most perfect creature of heaven." Because the Deerhound was, since earliest times, the companion and guard dog of Scottish Chieftains, he possesses in his nature a deep desire for human closeness. He isn't happy in a kennel but must live around people and follow his master, to whom he is utterly devoted in his quietly dignified way.

In conformation the dog resembles a rough-haired Greyhound, but he does not stoop when coursing, as the Greyhound does. His coat is harsh and wiry, about 3 or 4 inches long, the ideal one being thick, loose-lying and ragged, also crisp to the touch. The dog has a slight mane of hair down the back of his neck, also a good mustache and beard on his face. His body has Greyhound lines but is larger in size and bone structure. His long tail extends to within an inch and a half of the ground. He comes in all colors, dark and light grays and brindles, yellow and sandy red with black ears and muzzle, but dark blue-gray is most preferred. White is not at all desirable, but a slight white tip appears on the hindquarters of some of the best strains.

The Deerhound stands 30 to 32 inches, but can be higher if he maintains symmetry and does not become coarse; he weighs from 85 to 110 pounds. Bitches often come as large as the dogs, weigh 75 to 95 pounds.

Though never highly popular in the United States because it takes space to keep him, the Scottish Deerhound has been an estate dog and several champions have been crowned in the show ring. Though the taking of deer by hound is illegal in this country, he's been used most effectively to hunt wolves, coyote and jackrabbits in the Midwest. He has keen scenting ability, and this trait is most useful under certain conditions such as woodland hunting or in those areas where scrub pine, mesquite and the like make straight sight hunting difficult. For breeding, he has been used in much the same way as the Irish Wolfhound, though not quite to the same extent.

The Irish Wolfhound

Largest of all coursing hounds, the giant Irish Wolfhound is bone-crushing power combined with galloping speed. Though he undoubtedly carries Greyhound blood in his veins, he doesn't have the same graceful symmetry or loveliness. With his long, ragged coat and intense yellow eyes peering out from beneath a shaggy brow, he looks fierce and far more commanding. Consequently for centuries he was the favorite of mighty kings who found the Greyhound too soft and effeminate for their tastes.

According to Irish history this huge dog was developed to hunt wolves and the giant Irish Elk, which was said to have stood six feet at the shoulder. The Greeks claimed the dog accompanied the Celts of northwest Europe when they sacked Delphi in 273 B.C. The Romans knew him well, for he performed in the bloody arena of the Circus Maximus. Throughout the Middle Ages, writings clearly describe his hunting prowess as well as the fact that he was a highly prized gift to kings and noblemen of other lands.

By the early 1800s the huge dog was fast disappearing. His quarry, the wolf and the elk, had been totally destroyed in Ireland and, though

The Irish Wolfhound is a huge and powerful animal.

possessed of a wonderful disposition, the dog was too large to keep as a pet. Had it not been for a Scotsman named Captain G. A. Graham, the Irish Wolfhound would have died out. In 1862 he collected a few remnants of the breed and worked for twenty years to bring it back, crossing to both the Great Dane and Scottish Deerhound to accomplish his task. Some authorities claim he never obtained any of the original Irish Wolfhound but simply used this cross to replace a breed which had become completely extinct. In any case the Irish Wolfhound of today looks as though he just stepped out of the Middle Ages and fits the ancient descriptions of him.

The standard calls for the dog to be "of great size and commanding appearance . . . remarkable in combining power and swiftness with keen sight." His head is long, skull not too wide, muzzle long and moderately pointed. His ears are small and carried tight to his neck in coursing-hound fashion. His body is deep-chested and sweeps back to powerful hindquarters. Beyond his size, his distinction is his coat, rough and wiry from nose to tail, especially over the eyes and under the jaw.

Minimum height of the Irish Wolfhound is 32 inches at the withers; if he goes to 34 or above, so much the better. He weighs 120 pounds or more. Bitches are smaller, 30 inches in height and around 105 pounds.

As a sight-hunting hound the Irish Wolfhound is used on a limited scale throughout the world. In Europe he hunts wild boar and deer with an occasional turn at a fox. In Kenya and other parts of South Africa he is used on all types of medium-sized game up to and including lions. Australia runs him on timber wolves.

In our own United States he is being used more widely as a hunter. Though not as nimble or agile as the Afghan or Greyhound or Saluki, he has the speed and tremendous striking power so strongly needed in a coursing hound. He has been valuable to coyote hunters as a purebred coursing hound as well as a cross to other breeds. He blends particularly well with the Greyhound. Such puppies have great substance, heavier bone, more strength, tougher coat and hide, more striking power than the purebred Greyhound, and more agility than the purebred Irish Wolfhound.

In the Plains states of the Midwest we are seeing the beginnings of a new hound which may someday be called the American Coyote Hound or the American Coursing Hound. In time, when he becomes a breed, one of his key founders will have been the age-old huge, fearless hunter, the Irish Wolfhound.

The Ibizan Hound

The newest breed of field dog to come to America is the Ibizan Hound, pronounced E-beeth'-an. He hails from the Balearic Islands off Spain—Majorca, Minorca and Ibiza, drawing his name from the last islet, which he especially frequents.

This ancient breed is descended from the Egyptian ring-tailed hound carved in stone in the tomb of Amten, the Fourth Dynasty, 3500–4000 B.C. Phoenicians brought the original stock to Ibiza around the eighth century B.C. and their likeness is stamped on the earliest coins of the island. Thus he is one of the oldest breeds of dogs we have, surviving on Ibiza today because of its relative isolation and because the dog is a great rabbit hound, used by most of the island's farmers for sport and filling the pot.

In appearance the Ibizan has that leggy, streamlined gracefulness and farseeing facial expression of the coursing hound, which he is basically, although he has excellent scenting powers and usually augments his hunting by this means. Standing 22 to 26 inches at the withers and weighing up to 50 pounds, he is red in color with patches of white markings confined generally to chest, neck, face and legs. His head, animated by pricked ears, rests on a long powerful neck and he has a strong set of jaws. The body, like all coursing hounds, is on the lean side and deep-chested, set on long legs of excellent bone, so there is plenty of daylight under him. He's a gay dog in movement, gentle and highly intelligent in personality. Possessed of ample speed, he is particularly agile and a good jumper, hence very effective in rough country.

Followers of the Ibizan claim him to be an ancestor of the English Foxhound and English Greyhound. The dog certainly possesses some features similar to both these breeds, his tail being brushy in the manner of a Foxhound's flag, while his long powerful body shows some Greyhound lines, so there may be justification to their claim though we have no specific record to prove it. Dr. Johannes Caius in the sixteenth century mentions a hound that fits the description of the Ibizan quite closely.

The hunting habits of Ibizan Hounds are not entirely coursing nor entirely scenting but a combination of both. Thus they work effectively in bushy country, even in woods. On their native island farmers generally hunt them in small packs and the hounds are fast and agile enough to often catch the rabbit before it can be shot. The males tend to give voice more than the females although they do not open nearly as much as a Beagle. Their voice is more crisp than throaty.

The Ibizan was first brought to this country in the early 1950s, major importations being made by Colonel and Mrs. Seoane of Rhode Island and Mr. and Mrs. William L. Prescott of Tuxedo Park, New York. A national club has been formed and there are more than 100 of the breed here in America at the present time. As the dog grows more numerous, recognition will come and registry will begin.

The future of the Ibizan as a working hound can be an interesting one. He is a good dog of exceptional ability and his method of hunting could provide an exciting variation to the rabbit-hunting world.

The Ibizan Hound is a rabbit hunter in his native Balearic Islands.

The Whippet

An elegant miniature of the Greyhound in appearance, personality, and ability to run, ball of fire on the race track yet quiet and dignified in the home—this is the Whippet. At first glance the little fellow looks so frail that you'd think a good gust of wind would bowl him over. But he needs no special pampering and is a lot tougher than he looks.

The breed was created in the 1850s by crossing small Greyhounds with different types of terriers, the Manchester, Bedlington and the like. Later the Italian Greyhound, tiny beauty of a dog, was used for greater refinement.

The purpose for making the dog seems to have been for "snap-dog coursing." In this gambling sport, Whippets chased loose rabbits within an enclosure and the one that caught the most won. Later the dog was trained for line racing and because he was small, hence easily and cheaply kept, coal miners of Lancashire and Yorkshire dubbed him "the poor man's race horse."

Whippet races were a sight to see. A slipper (assistant handler) held the dog at the starting line while the handler ran down the 200-yard straightaway behind the finish line waving a towel. At the crack of the pistol, the slipper jetted the dog by the collar and tail down the runway, whereupon the dog bolted to his towel-waving handler. This is still being done today, and these pint-sized demons often reach speeds of 35 miles an hour, almost as fast as their cousins, the Greyhounds.

In America, Whippet racing became popular in the mill towns of Lowell and Lawrence, Massachusetts, later in Baltimore. The sport in this country evolved from towel waving to circular tracks over which the Whippet chases a mechanical rabbit. In recent years, though, many of the Whippet tracks have been taken over by the bigger, more striking Greyhounds to please the crowds.

In looks, the Whippet is an extremely alert dog that moves with no lost motion. He has a long, lean face and head, and a racy, streamlined body that is deep-chested just like the Greyhound. He has the same small ears folded against the long neck, semipricked when attentive, never gaily erect. His large eyes should be hazel, not yellow in color, and round, not oblique. His back has a high arch over the loins, giving him considerable tuck-up. It is this highly arched back, which coils and uncoils like a whip as he runs, that gives him his amazing speed—pound for pound, the

The Whippet is a slender, smaller version of the Greyhound. This is Ch. Great Circle Mad Hatter, owned by Mrs. Robert B. Henderson of Hillsborough, Calif.

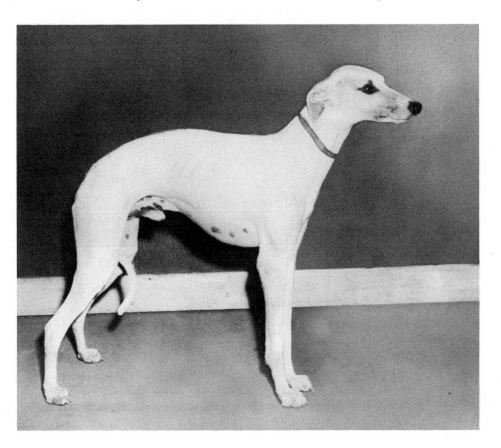

fastest in the entire dog world. Actually he doesn't gain his name from this source but for being quick and smart as a whip. In size, he stands 19 to 22 inches at the shoulder and weighs a little either side of 20 pounds.

The Whippet makes an excellent house pet, better than the other coursing breeds because he is small enough to fit easily into an apartment. Though he's a very keen little dog, he's not bouncy and barky like a terrier, but gentle and calm and uniquely classic in his looks and grace. For all this he has become very popular with the general public in recent years and is seen in the show ring on a considerable scale these days.

As a coursing hound he was used quite frequently by farmers and ranchers in the 1930s and 1940s for killing rabbits that began to infest the Midwest and destroy crops. Some Whippets are still used for this work and are very effective.

SECTION II

Introduction

Now that the great variety of field dogs has been examined, let's turn to the practical aspect of their care, management and training. No field dog will work satisfactorily unless he is well conditioned and in good health. Good health means good care. So it's of vital importance to know how to house a dog effectively, what and when to feed him, even how to buy him.

Caring for one's dog can cover a lot of ground, and books have been written just on various phases of it. Nevertheless certain over-all rules and principles can be applied which will keep the dog in good health so he can be enjoyed to the fullest. Nothing is more pathetic than a sick animal. You can see that he's sick but you can't communicate with him to ask what's wrong. A sick dog is not only pathetic but useless in the field, and prolonged treatment can become expensive. In 75 per cent of the cases better care and some foresight would have avoided the situation.

A proper diet is most essential, especially when a dog is being hunted hard. You can figure on your dog covering five to ten times as much ground as you do, depending upon how active he is. If you walk ten miles, he will have run fifty to one hundred miles. The drain on his body at times like this is tremendous and it must be replaced if the dog is to hold up. When I hunt all day I rest an hour or so at noon, and when I eat, my dog eats, usually a can of dog food that I have brought along. Many a time I've seen a wise old quail hunter shoot and skin a rabbit, then feed it, bones and meat, to his dogs at noon. I can feel the anti-bone people quivering now, but it never hurt them and I think that without it they might not have gotten through the day.

A good diet is most essential for puppies, of course. They must be fed several times each day during their period of fast growth, as is the case with brood bitches in whelp. Fortunately great strides have been made, not only in the nutritional content of dog food but in the way it can be fed.

In the area of training, the basic methods have not radically changed, but new devices like the electronic collar, which shocks the dog at a key moment, have been devised and effectively used to break bad habits. A dog can be prevented from chasing cars, chasing a farmer's chickens, fighting, bolting and a multitude of other major and minor sins.

Vast improvements have been made in canine medicines, particularly in the intestinal-parasite area. Today there are most effective shots for hookworms and whipworms, both difficult to control up to this point. In fact these two parasites, along with roundworms and heartworms, have probably killed more dogs in the past than any other type of disease.

A word or two about the veterinarian. He plays many important roles in the life of your dog. Not only does he keep the general health level of your dog high by means of immunization shots and medical treatment when necessary, but in case of emergency like a severe cut, accident or poisoning, he can probably save the dog's life. At times of whelping puppies he will give valuable advice and come immediately if the bitch runs into any difficulty in delivering her puppies. He should also inspect a dog and give it a clean bill of health before it is purchased.

Today the veterinarian, with his modern equipment, can perform some amazing operations that parallel those in human surgery. For his convenience you should keep a health record on every dog you have. This will include when it was born, the shots it has had, the injuries and illnesses. In the event that you move, this information can be presented to the new vet so he knows clearly the history of the dog.

When you arrive at a new location, one of the first things to do is to find a veterinarian. Ask neighbors or look in the telephone book for one and make his acquaintance for the time when you will need him. Most vets are competent and conscientious people. Some specialize in field dogs or have a particular interest and experience in them. Such people are worth seeking out.

The fees they charge are generally moderate, five dollars or less for an office call. Many have health programs for dogs. I know of one such arrangement which costs twenty dollars a year. It includes office calls at half price, free treatment and medicine, free laboratory tests such as stool checks, blood count, heartworms, etc., a worth-while proposition. In any case, if you see your dog is ailing and needs professional attention, seek out a vet before complications set in and either take the life of your dog or make his cure lengthy and difficult.

In caring for and maintaining a field dog, let me point out that there are usually several ways of doing a certain phase or job. If your hunting pal comes along with an idea, make sure he has tried it before you do. The methods and suggestions which follow have been proved to work.

Chapter 7

Buying a Dog or Puppy

Many people wonder how to go about buying a dog. It's quite simple, but if you want a field dog, make sure you get one of field blood. A neighboring kennel man can often put you in touch with someone who handles the breed you're interested in. Local and Sunday papers always carry pet ads, but generally this is show blood or pet-shop stock. One sound way to obtain field blood is to subscribe to a breed magazine or field-dog magazine and wait for a good ad to appear. Usually someone who hunts or runs in field trials can lend you a few back copies or tell you how and where to begin.

One of the best plans for the beginner is to go to a professional trainer of field dogs. All of them have hunting dogs for sale from time to time. There you can usually see two or three of varying prices and abilities. A choice becomes easier and more distinct then.

But before you actually buy, there are several questions to consider. First is what age dog should you buy. There are three possibilities: the mature, fully trained dog, the young dog under two years of age, or the puppy.

If this is your first hunting dog and you are at all green, I would recommend buying a mature one that has been trained. This way you can use and enjoy him immediately, also learn considerably from him. The young dog will be inconsistent and inclined to take advantage of his handler upon occasion, whereas a mature dog knows what should be done and will go about doing it even though he may not be handled correctly at all times.

The difficulties of buying a mature dog are twofold: a good one will not be easy to come by, and he will not be cheap—$200 to $750 or higher for a registered dog. Like everything else, you will get about what you pay for and sometimes a lot less if you aren't careful.

The best age to buy a mature dog is four to five years. He has settled down by then, had considerable experience and should know his business if he is ever going to. Once a dog is past six, his market value begins to decline, though if he is healthy and well cared for, he still has several good years left. Such a dog will be completely settled and perform with the thoroughness of a real professional, though he may lack the drive and indefatigability of youth. The beginner who wants a mature dog would do well to consider buying this older type, for he will be cheaper and a real pleasure to hunt with.

Before buying the mature dog you should by all means see him perform. The most satisfactory way is to visit the seller and observe the dog worked by its master. In this way you can not only appraise the dog's merits but see how it is handled and learn the commands which it knows and which may be quite different from yours.

Having a dog sent on trial is the next best way but not entirely satisfactory. It takes from two to four weeks for a dog to be accustomed to a new master and environment. No trial is this long, and if you don't like the dog and return it you will have to pay the shipping expenses both ways, which these days may amount to a quarter or half the price of the dog. I have bought and sold many dogs over the telephone. In answering ads on superior dogs this is often necessary because they are soon gobbled up, but one usually has a line on the dog or knows the owner to be reliable.

One very important point to remember in buying a dog over one year of age: pay to have a reputable veterinarian check its health before closing the deal. Don't take the seller's word. The dog may have something unknown, and the five- or ten-dollar fee involved is well worth it. Insist that the vet check for heartworms. Dogs coming out of the South are particularly liable to have contracted this disease that prevails in hot climates. Mosquitoes transmit it by stinging an infected dog and proceeding on to others. Microfilaria or larvae eat into the heart and mature there into large worms of wirelike texture. If they don't kill the dog, they seriously impair his working activity. In advanced cases the dog becomes logy and loses his vigor after half an hour or less of hunting. A simple blood test can determine whether the animal is infected. A dog should never be bought with heartworms. The treatment is dangerous and expensive. And it must be done, otherwise the dog is a carrier of the disease wherever he goes and useless as a hunter.

If you plan to train your own dog, you have a choice of buying either a young dog or a puppy. The former is between six and eighteen months of age, and for the man who will be training his first dog I strongly recommend this kind. At such a stage you can see pretty clearly how much talent the dog has and what you will be getting in the way of size, temperament and hunting desire. If of the pointing breed, he should be almost solid on point, have had some yard and field training, possibly even been hunted over to a limited extent. A spaniel or retriever should be fetching a bumper on sight and from tall grass where he will have to hunt a bit to find it, also show a fearless desire for water retrieving and not be gun-shy.

A started dog is always a good bet as your first attempt at training. These are only sight-pointing, but with a little work they will soon be finding and pointing birds.

A hound should be starting and working his game eagerly, giving good voice and not running much, if any, junk.

Dogs of this age are called "started," that is, they know their names and have begun their lessons. You can begin training immediately, simply picking up where the previous owner left off. Of course the more the dog can do, the more he will cost, but you will save considerably over the price of a fully trained dog. A started dog ranges from $150 to $300, depending upon his ability and breeding.

Dogs of this category come up for sale quite often because they do not have the temperament suited to make a field-trial champion. Owners will dispose of them when it is thought they will not quite be able to knock off the top prizes. For hunting and amateur trials they are superior and offer the most advantages for one's first venture into training. Generally a professional handler or amateur breeder is the man who has such a dog for sale, and here again it is particularly important to see before buying. No gun-shy or spooky dogs wanted, no awkward, loping camels. They should be showing their wares at this stage, and with a little searching you can find a good one.

The other dog which may be bought is the puppy, always lovable, friendly, into trouble, out of it, a care but also a reward. Of all the ways to buy a dog this is probably the least sound, yet most challenging. It's like buying a grab bag. You never know what you're going to get, still, more puppies are sold every year than all other ages combined. I don't know why, but the deeper you become involved with dogs, whether for hunting or field trials, the more inclined you will be to buy a puppy or raise a litter of your own. Puppies are taunting bundles of mystery, not unlike race horses. A certain percentage will be sourballs, untrainable, untractable; a certain percentage will be good, and a tiny percentage will be great. Nobody can predict this with any degree of consistency; that's why, logically, one is a little daft to buy a puppy. Yet we will go on doing it, for there is a thrill in walking over to a litter of eight-week-olds prancing and barking and wrestling in their enclosure. You notice the tough one, the friendly one, the gay one, the aloof one, the runt. You know there is an outstanding one among them and you are sure you can pick it.

Here are some suggestions for buying a puppy in case you've never done it.

1. Buy a registered puppy. Your chances of obtaining a good one are much better, also the resale value is much higher.

2. Make certain the mother and father are hunting or field-trial dogs. The grandparents or great-grandparents are not close enough. A little later we will explain how to recognize field blood when reading a pedigree.

3. Buy from a recognized breeder, either professional or amateur, who runs in field trials or who hunts a lot.

4. Pick the puppy that appeals to you! He or she should be alert, merry and sound. There are a lot of tricks old-timers go through to pick a puppy, but in the end their judgment is no better than yours. I have seen so many good puppies ruined and poor ones made into superior dogs by their upbringing and training that I feel it doesn't make much difference which one you pick unless you're looking for a champion, and that's a matter of luck.

5. Ask for a health record of the pup—i.e., the shots it has had, when and if it has been wormed. This is invaluable information to your vet. The pup will probably have had only temporary serum. If permanent shots have been given, this will save you ten to twenty dollars.

6. Find out what the puppy is being fed. It it is different from what you customarily feed, change the diet slowly over a week's time.

7. Insist upon the registration papers when you pay the owner. If he doesn't have them ready, hold back 25 per cent of the price until they are forthcoming. Likewise, he will hold back the papers until you have paid him in full.

8. Insist upon a written guarantee against hip dysplasia. This congenital disease will not become apparent until the pup is six months old, then only by X ray. If your young dog develops it, he must be destroyed as he is useless for field work. It is absolutely hereditary, consequently the

Puppies are always lovable.

breeder is obligated either to replace the pup or give you your money back. Obtain a written guarantee, no verbal agreement.

When I first started in with hunting dogs I decided never to buy a puppy that wasn't champion-sired. I have violated the rule often, but it still has its advantages. Almost invariably the dog will possess something extra in the way of ability. If he doesn't turn out to be quite what you want, he'll have a good resale value on the strength of his pedigree. As long as you have him you can say with pride that your dog has a famous father, even when he bites the mailman. Also you have a better chance of obtaining the great dog, in which case value as a stud or brood matron is powerfully increased.

The rule has one slight disadvantage. You may come up with the power-house dog that is a bullheaded, rampaging ball of fire which climbs out of his run or dives through the picture window to go hunting. All I can say is that if it happens, sell him quickly to a field-trial fan at a good profit and buy another one.

While on this subject, let me say that not all dogs are good ones. Generally you can tell whether or not a puppy has "it" when he's six months of age. If he is shy or frightened of backfires and noises or shows little enthusiasm in hunting, get rid of him. Don't let sentiment sway you into trying the impossible. Field training is based on the premise that the

dog will have a deeply ingrained desire to hunt. This desire is molded—
sometimes by restraint, sometimes by encouragement—into practical application. But if there is no desire to begin with, the task is hopeless.

As previously stated, I strongly recommend buying a registered dog.
The registered dog today is generally far superior and much more exciting
to hunt over than the "paperless" meat dog. He can also be run in field
trials whereas the unregistered dog cannot, that is, trials that amount to
anything.

There are several registries for dogs of hunting bloodlines. The principal
one is the Field Dog Stud Book maintained by The American Field
Magazine, 222 West Adams Street, Chicago, Illinois. A registration or
pedigree from this source is almost certain to represent active field stock.
Pointers and English Setters form the vast majority of this registry,
although field dogs of all the pointing breeds, retrievers and spaniels are
sometimes included.

The American Kennel Club, 221 Park Avenue South, New York, N.Y., also
registers dogs of field breeding, mostly retrievers and spaniels and just about
all the Beagles and Bassets. Since AKC also registers all the show stock

When choosing a puppy, pick the one that appeals to you.

in these breeds, a buyer must ask the breeder to see the dog's pedigree. The easiest way to tell field blood on an AKC pedigree is to look for champions. Those having simply Ch. in front of their names are bench champions; those having F.T.Ch. as a prefix represent field blood, this indicating Field Trial Champion. If the pedigree contains only bench champions, don't expect the dog to be a great hunter. If it has dual champions or field champions, the chances are the puppy or young dog will be at home afield.

In the case of hounds there are several registries, the main ones being the United Kennel Club for Coonhounds, the Foxhound Kennel Stud Book for Foxhounds and the National Coursing Association for Greyhounds. There are several others for individual breeds, but most hounds work for a living anyway. They aren't pretty enough to live on their looks.

Do not be misled by a Working Certificate. This paper, issued to Labrador Retrievers and Springer Spaniels, says that the dog named has completed a land-and-water retrieving test. It doesn't say whether this was done meritoriously or ignominiously, only that it was done, thus it has little or no worth. A Certificate of Merit is something else. This is awarded to a retriever performance of high quality that doesn't place among the first four winners. In other words it amounts to fifth position, and the owner can be proud of it.

As for choosing between the sexes, it's a matter of personal preference. Generally the bitch will be less rambunctious, a shade easier to train, more loyal, closer-working. The dog will be bolder, more aggressive, bust into cover and water better, make a flashier showing. The big difference is that the bitch comes into season usually twice a year for approximately twenty-one days each time. During most of this period she cannot be hunted safely and ought not to be run in field trials. In one-course trials it's forbidden. Spaying solves the problem, but it has its drawbacks. The bitch loses half her value, she is harder to condition, and if she happens to turn out to be worth while breeding, it is impossible. There are pills and shots which reputedly change the ways of Nature. They are discussed in the next chapter.

One last point which must be re-emphasized in buying a dog or puppy. If you happen to obtain a poor one, don't hold on to him. Undoubtedly he'll be a lovable slob that's a pal of everybody and the roof will fall in when you announce to the family that he's no good. But if he can't find birds or won't take to water enthusiastically or doesn't run a line well, get rid of him. Don't let sentiment sway you. Sell him for whatever you can get and try again. Remember, if you can love a poor dog, you'll love a good one ten times as much, and he'll reward you with ten times the amount of pleasure.

Chapter 8

Care of the Mature Dog and Puppy

It is important not only to take pride in your dog but to take care of him. He is completely dependent upon you for everything, so remember—the better your care, the better his health.

Probably a good eighty-five per cent of the field dogs are kept in kennels. This doesn't mean that one cannot be made into a house dog. He most certainly can, young or old. The puppy is probably easier to housebreak but any old Setter or Labrador that has braved a few winters in a doghouse will learn quickly once he's tasted the plushness of an oriental or the comfort of a fire. More and more throughout suburbia the working field dog is becoming a house dog or at least a compromise of it. He is brought into the house at certain times of the day or evening by his master for enjoyment, then kenneled at night. Still, the owner must know a lot about and practice kennel management.

THE KENNEL

The run or kennel should be cleaned at least once a day, preferably twice in the summer so flies will not congregate and annoy the dog. Droppings should be placed in a box or metal barrel, preferably sunk below ground, and a dissolving chemical applied.

Fresh water should be available at all times in a pan that will not tip over, or, even better, in a pail suspended from a kennel post at dog's shoulder level. At this height he cannot urinate in the drinking water, as some will do out of nervousness. Stainless-steel pails are about six times more expensive than galvanized pails in initial cost but well worth the difference. They can freeze solidly without bursting and are most easily cleaned.

The doghouse should be waterproof and face south. Kennel bedding should be changed at least once a month. Straw or cedar shavings are the best. The latter drives off fleas and doggy odors. In those areas that have cold winters, make the bedding deep so the dog can burrow into it, and even a shorthaired dog will make out fine in temperatures well below freezing. A good winter bedding is two inches of cedar shavings and six inches of straw.

INTESTINAL PARASITES

As you clean out the kennel each day, watch the dog's stools. Much can be learned about the general condition of a dog, especially whether or not he is plagued with intestinal parasites—roundworms, hookworms, whipworms and tapeworms. The stool should be solid and well formed. Once in a while something will be eaten that loosens the bowels, but if they are not generally firm, chances are worms of one or more types are present.

Intestinal parasites kill more dogs than any other disorder. If they don't do it directly, they do it indirectly by lowering the resistance to other diseases. Treatment should begin only after the type of worm has been diagnosed. For this, stool samples must be taken to a vet. He will treat the dog or you can administer the pills yourself. There are several remedies on the market. A veterinarian or pet store can supply them. For roundworm treatment there are powders which can be added to the food, and they are very effective.

Worming a dog successfully is not as simple as it sounds. You may get all the worms in the dog but you won't get all the eggs, and ten days later they will hatch and reinfest the dog. Also, if the dog is kept on a dirt run or a hard-surfaced concrete or asphalt run that isn't kept clean, he will automatically reinfect himself. Worm eggs will lie active on the ground for upward of six months. A dog steps on one, it adheres to his pad, and sometime during the day when he licks his feet he is reinfected. Tape and roundworms are relatively easy to control, but hook and whipworms are the most difficult and pernicious. Now, however, shots have been developed for both hookworm and whipworm which are highly effective. The only problem is that they are expensive, hence are not generally used except in puppies and in cases of severe debility in adult dogs. But they can be lifesavers.

The best inexpensive system I have ever found to combat worms was given me by a wise kennel man. It calls for a dog to be wormed three times in quick succession, each two weeks apart. This takes care of the worms and just about all the eggs which will have hatched. The dog is then wormed every two months for one year, at which time he should be clean of parasites and the ground on which he lives should be free of eggs. Earth kennels can be treated for worm eggs by working salt or borax into the surface. After a rain is a good time. In any event, stool samples should be taken to a vet three times a year for a check.

To worm a dog, back it into a sitting position tightly between your legs. Hold the mouth open with your left hand, the head slightly elevated. With the pill held between the thumb and index finders of the right hand, dip it in some water or oil so it will slide easily, then push the pill as far to the back of the dog's mouth and down the throat as possible. Withdraw your hand quickly, close the dog's mouth with both hands and hold its snout up firmly at a forty-five-degree angle until the dog swallows.

Worm pills are administered according to the weight of a dog. To determine this, pick up your dog, step on a bathroom scale, then weigh yourself separately and subtract the difference.

The worming procedure outlined below isn't simple but it works. Keep a log of your schedule and stick to it. Almost all puppies are born with worms of one type or another, depending upon what the mother has. Most frequent are roundworms, then hookworms. I lost almost an entire litter of champion-sired puppies once from hookworm simply because I didn't know enough to worm the mother before she whelped. They were born with her parasites. Puppies should be wormed as soon as they can swallow a small pill—about two weeks after birth.

WORMING SCHEDULE

Puppies up to three months: Piperazine tablets for roundworms; two or three shots for hookworm by veterinarian.

Puppies at six months: worm three times, two weeks apart.

Mature dogs: when hook- or whipworms are positively identified, worm three times, two weeks apart; for tapeworms, a special remedy with its own directions is used.

Brood bitch: worm three times—one month before breeding, two weeks before breeding, two weeks after breeding. This is very important for protection of puppies.

WORMING PROCEDURE

Feed normally at 4 P.M. and remove all water at that time. Do not put any grease in the food, as it tends to protect the worms.

Administer the pills at 9 A.M. the following morning and at 11 A.M. give a warm beef broth (about a cupful of any canned kind). At 4 P.M. give more warm soup with half a cup of regular food mixed in. Nothing more this day, not even water.

Next morning return the water and feed as usual.

HEARTWORM

Of all canine parasites, this is the most serious. Until recent years, heartworm was confined to Florida and the hot Gulf Coast states. Now it has spread to just about every area of the country that has mosquitoes of a certain type. As explained earlier, the disease is transmitted by mosquitoes stinging an infected dog and proceeding on to others. Microfilariae—the microscopic stage of the larvae—get into the bloodstream, move to the right ventricle of the heart and there mature into worms four to eight inches in length. Eventually a mass of worms begins to restrict the passage of blood through the right side of the heart and to the lungs, thus the dog tires markedly after ten to twenty minutes of exercise. Another sign is a chronic cough. Eventually the dog can die of heart failure.

To date no single treatment has been devised which will kill both the adult heartworms and the microfilariae. Thus the dog must undergo two treatments, and only a veterinarian can do the job, preferably one who specializes in this field. To kill the adult heartworms, arsenic (there are other drugs too) is injected in two or three large doses into the bloodstream. This kills the worms all right, but then come the problems of the body's absorbing them and the destruction of lung tissue with the consequent threat of pneumonia. The dog must be kept completely inactive and under constant watch by the veterinarian. After he has recovered from this he is then treated for the microfilariae, a much simpler and safer procedure.

Any dog carrying heartworm should be treated or destroyed. Otherwise he remains a carrier of the disease, imperiling the health of other dogs wherever he goes, and he will soon become useless as a hunter anyway. Obviously one should try to avoid a dog with heartworm like the plague, but this isn't always easy. If you live in the South or run your dog in a field trial in the South, hunt there or have him trained there, he runs the risk of contracting the disease, particularly during the warm or hot months.

The best precaution against heartworm is to use a pill called Caricide on your dog after each venture south, or at regular intervals if you live in the South. Heartworm doesn't happen overnight. It takes three or four months for the microfilariae to reach the heart and begin to mature there. With Caricide they can be killed at the larva stage before they reach the heart, but it is up to the individual to treat or have his dog treated promptly. A vet can supply Caricide or similar drug for the job.

In severe cases of heartworm the heart, through surgery, has been successfully opened and the worms removed, but this is a touch-and-go operation.

Not only is heartworm treatment expensive and dangerous, but it often seems to leave the dog with a poor nose afterward, certainly for the first six months. I know of two cases where this has happened to great field-trial dogs. They gradually worked out of it but to this day they will often completely mislocate a bird or run right over it.

Have your dog checked periodically for heartworm, and take precautions against it. It's a deadly disease.

A HEALTHY DOG

If your dog skips a meal, especially during the heat of summer, don't be too concerned. If he doesn't eat the next day, check him over immediately. The ways to tell a dog's condition are by his coat, clarity of eye and brightness of mouth. Turn up the lip and note the color of the gum and inside of lip. It should be a lively pink, even red. If it is dull or white, the dog is anemic, probably from worms or improper diet.

When he is standing, lift up a handful of skin in the middle of his back and let go of it. It should snap back into shape. If it creeps back slowly, the dog is dehydrated and needs immediate medical attention. When eyes are mattery and dull, it generally indicates worms. If the nose begins to discharge and the dog refuses to eat, check his temperature immediately with a rectal thermometer. Normal for a dog is 101.5 degrees. If it is much above this, get him to a vet at once.

CARE OF EARS

If a dog begins to shake his head and scratch his ears, chances are he has ear mites, tiny organisms which burrow deep into the ear and can be very dangerous if allowed to go untreated. Lift the ear and examine the inside. If a dark-brown discharge is evident, turn the dog over on his side on the ground or floor and wipe out the ear as deeply as possible with a dry cotton ball. It will be sensitive, so proceed gently. Next pour a little solution of half peroxide, half water, into the ear and again wipe it out. Take a swab of cotton and carefully clean the ear crevices. Once the ear is dry, sprinkle a little canker powder inside or apply any of the canker remedies on the market and work the ear externally so it will spread around. Ears should be checked regularly, particularly on longhaired dogs, and treatment administered as necessary.

CARE OF TEETH

The dog's teeth were designed for tearing rather than for masticating food. This becomes obvious when you see him place both front feet on a big bone and tear off the meat. A dog hardly ever chews his food. He bolts it down, often swallows great chunks whole. All food is digested in his stomach by means of sulphuric acid. There is no need for concern over the dog that downs his food before you can turn around. However, if he is fed mushy, soft dog food over a long period of time his teeth will become coated with tartar and must be cleaned by a veterinarian who will scrape off this yellowish-gray deposit.

If dogs are fed large bones or dry biscuit, their teeth will be kept almost free from tartar. For those who don't approve of feeding bones to dogs, there are some excellent substitutes on the market. A little baking soda on a damp rag will, when worked over the teeth gently, keep them clean and in excellent shape.

Occasionally a dog will break a tooth or wedge a sliver of bone or wood between his teeth. This is most easily noticed by the manner in which he will eat his food. He may try to pick it up with his tongue or lips or roll it in his mouth. Whenever this is noticed, his mouth should be inspected immediately for the cause. A dog's teeth almost never decay, but they do break off or wear down, particularly if the dog develops the habit of collecting stones and carrying them about in his mouth. He should always be discouraged from this.

As for the puppy, he begins to shed his first, or milk, teeth at around four to five months of age. At this time his mouth is sore and he may look around for things to chew on. I have a friend who throws his puppies of teething age a reject leather hide which he buys from a tannery. The pups have a great time playing with it, dragging and tugging on it, chewing and pulling their milk teeth in the process. A specially processed rawhide bone is also good, as is a big shinbone or knuckle.

INOCULATIONS

There are four virus diseases for which a dog should be inoculated—distemper, hepatitis, leptospirosis and rabies. The first three are deadly to dogs, the fourth to humans. Vaccines for distemper, hepatitis and leptospirosis do not always provide complete immunity, but they certainly help. If your dog doesn't have a rabies shot and bites someone, he will, in most states, be impounded for up to ten weeks for a medical checkup and you pay the bill. Let your veterinarian administer the shots. A good schedule is as follows:

Puppies three weeks old: inoculate with temporary serum which gives about two weeks' protection against distemper, hepatitis and leptospirosis. Repeat in two weeks.

Puppies three months old: inoculate with permanent vaccine against distemper, hepatitis and leptospirosis. Do not use serum three weeks prior to this permanent shot, as it will not permit full immunity to take place.

Puppies six months old: rabies shot. This is recognized by law as effective for one year.

Adult dogs: rabies shot annually and dated tag riveted to collar.

Adult dogs: annual booster shot for distemper, hepatitis and leptospirosis.

Never allow any dogs but the mother near puppies. It's impossible to know what they may be carrying, and when a litter contracts a serious disease, the big, strong, beautiful pups will die first. Most kennel owners will not allow customers to handle pups for fear they may carry a contagious disease from another kennel.

Keep records on the dates of all injections and type of vaccine used. This is particularly valuable information to a new owner or another vet in the event that you move.

SHIPPING YOUR DOG

Whenever a dog is to be shipped from one state to another, a health certificate, secured only from a veterinarian, is necessary. Most states also require a rabies shot. Regulations of the particular state to which the dog is being sent can be found out by phoning the local rail or air terminal. I strongly advise sending by air, providing arrangements can be made for someone to meet the dog at the receiving end. The transportation is much more quickly and effectively accomplished. The airlines will provide a shipping crate in the event you don't have one.

The best shipping crate is the aluminum type or one made of light plywood. If the dog is sent by rail, a container of water should be securely fastened to one corner of the crate and some food must also be included. I buy a small box of dry dog food and wire it to the inside of the crate, then tear off the top. The dog can eat when he desires.

On the matter of health certificates, legally you should have one whenever you drive across a state boundary with your dog in the car. I have never been stopped and asked by police, but they have the right to do so. Very often at Coonhound trials out-of-state owners are required to have health certificates for their hounds in order to compete. Generally this is not true of bird-dog or retriever trials.

POISONING

If your dog suddenly has a fit, charges blindly into a wall or does some other crazy thing, he may have been poisoned. A young dog will sometimes get hold of rat poison on bread or eat a poisonous mushroom, in which case he will probably go into convulsions or have a fit. Rush him to a vet for treatment. If this isn't possible, you must induce him to vomit by some means. A good big dose of salt and water or mustard and water poured down the dog's throat will usually work.

Lead poisoning can also affect a dog. This occurs to chewers who start gnawing on a doghouse painted with leaded paint or any object, usually wood, which has been so treated. I had it happen to a good dog once who, out of boredom, pulled the shingles off a barn kennel and ate them. The reaction was slow. He became listless, dragged himself about. I didn't realize what had happened and never treated him. He was three months getting over it. The proper treatment is to induce vomiting to clean out his stomach, then administer a good dose of castor oil to clean out his intestines as soon as possible.

MINOR ACCIDENTS

Minor accidents often occur to field dogs. Thorns and briars become imbedded in the skin and cause infection if not removed. Cuts from barbed wire and tree stumps must be cleaned out with an antiseptic and cared for. Scarlet oil is excellent for this, but it is a mess around clothes and furniture and is best used only on kennel dogs.

When the end of a hunting dog's tail becomes raw from being whipped through the brush, it must be bandaged for protection, sometimes even cauterized. Neglect can lead to serious infection, even gangrene. I have known several Pointers and Setters that had to have their tails docked in order to cure the infection, and in some cases the dog himself will eat his tail off in an effort to cure it.

For minor medical attention you should keep on hand some cotton and gauze tape, wound-dressing powder, eye ointment and the like. Store them in a hand grip in the car whenever you go off for a day's hunt. They'll be invaluable, maybe even save the life of your dog in an emergency.

TATTOOING

Hunting dogs are constantly being stolen, particularly in the fall of the year. Thieves make a business of driving through neighborhoods and picking up loose dogs, then transporting them to another state and selling them. Police will seldom intervene in a stolen-dog case unless positive identification can be established. Markings will not do, an old scar or split ear will seldom stand up, but a tattoo will forever suffice.

A thief may pick up a dog with a tattooed ear but he will think twice about keeping it because he can be apprehended five years later if he possesses a dog with your registration number in its ear. Also, in breeds of solid color like the Weimaraner, you cannot run your dog in a championship if it has not been tattooed.

Tattooing is a simple but momentarily painful thing so you had better have some assistance, preferably three people to hold the dog on the ground, and be sure he is muzzled before starting. Use the last three or four digits of his registration number. The entire number is even better if you want to go the trouble of two impressions.

Disinfect the ear and tattoo needles first. Test it on a piece of paper first to make certain you have the digits correctly arranged. Apply a mild anesthetic like Anbesol to the underside of the ear. Try to select a spot where no large veins show. The tool is like a pair of pliers, but it is not necessary to squeeze so hard as to have the needles pierce the entire ear. In fact this is dangerous because you may puncture a vein and end up with a hematoma. The surface has to be punctured but little more. After this has been done, wipe off the blood and rub the tattoo ink into the perforations. That's all. When it heals, the numbers will remain for life. The loose skin on the inside of the rear leg can be tattooed instead of the ear, if that area is preferred.

THE BITCH IN HEAT

Caring for the bitch in heat is no great problem, but it is mentioned here because one must make adequate provision for the situation before it occurs. During the three weeks twice annually that she is in season, she should be isolated, with adequate care taken that no dog can reach her and that she cannot escape. It is uncanny the effort which will be exerted both ways here. I have seen dogs bite through heavy wire and climb impossible fences, bitches gnaw and scratch through wooden doors, to reach each other.

If the period occurs during the hunting season your veterinarian can give a shot which will temporarily postpone it. Also there are pills that can be placed in the food daily to eliminate the odors which attract the male. However, unless the bitch is a close-working, completely obedient animal, I would not recommend hunting her, though she may be kenneled in a run adjoining a male without his becoming aroused. As for those products designed to keep males away by repulsive scent, they do stink but boys will be boys and I wouldn't rely upon oil of citronella to change the ways of nature.

Chapter 9

Feeding

The changes in this field have been incredible!

I remember when my father made his own dog food by boiling corn meal in a large pot. It would last three or four days and each night he'd scoop out some and add bread, meat and scraps, whatever was available. Dog feeding was not only a chore but nutritional guesswork. Diarrhea, the mange, colds were common, but we had country cures for them all. As a kid, I was often given chicken bones to carry out to our best setter as a treat, and when my father went hunting all day he'd shoot a rabbit around noon, skin it and feed it raw to the dogs for lunch. I don't know how, but all the dogs seemed to live.

The change began when one day the feed man brought a bag of something called Old Trusty. The name was reassuring even though the manufacturer and contents were unknown. At least we didn't have to cook any corn meal after that. Scraps and water were added to a panful of the stuff and given to the dogs.

As the years went by, more brands of dog food appeared. It became a huge business and companies built experimental kennels, researched and tested their ideas on brood bitches, puppies, old dogs. Millions were spent in developing the present-day product, a complete and perfectly balanced diet in forms of kibbles, pellets and meals.

Until recently I took this balanced diet and added fresh or canned meat, cooked vegetables and leftovers, occasionally bought beef liver and heart for extra nourishment. I carefully added vitamins at times and always a spoonful of fat or cod-liver oil. From years of weighing and measuring and personal experimenting I developed pet theories about diets summer and winter, what supplements were necessary. This was all fine until one day recently I discovered that everything I had been doing was obsolete.

I visited a friend who raises setters and had beaten me a couple of times at field trials. He was out in the kennel yard dumping pellets into a bucket when I arrived. "Be right with you," he said. "I'm just feeding my dogs for a couple of days." He hung the pail up inside the run and replenished the water supply beside it.

"Two days!" I gasped. "What do you mean?"

"It's the self-feeding system. No trouble, no worries. The finest way to take care of a dog. In fact, the dog takes care of himself. You just put the feed in front of him."

The next hour was one of the most enlightening and jarring of my dog life. He scuttled all my fond ideas on dog feeding, diet, supplementation, even rearing puppies. To be honest I wouldn't have believed the man if I hadn't known him to be a Ph.D. with considerable more dog-food dabbling experience than I would ever have. I looked at his dogs. They were just as healthy as my pampered ones or more so, and he had had them from three months to nine years.

The ideas behind the self-feeding system are simple but revolutionary. Science broke down the canine body, studied the nutritional relationships to its composition, discovered the point of balance between amino acids, vitamins, minerals, energy, etc., that the body relentlessly tries to maintain regardless of amount or type of intake, then devised a formula for keeping the body in its harmony. The dog food they came up with is complete, which means it supplies all of a dog's nutritional needs *in their proper balance*. This latter cannot be overemphasized because it means that the food already comes as near as possible to the dog's point of balance and any additions of any kind simply create an unbalance which requires more work by the body to regain its equilibrium.

When a dog is placed on the self-feeding system, five important factors are accomplished: first and foremost, the dog has a sound diet designed to achieve the above explained balance; second, by eating a little at a time throughout the day rather than the entire amount at one meal, the dog digests the food more thoroughly, absorbs the nutritional content more completely, eats less in the long run; third, the chore of feeding dogs is greatly reduced; fourth, the dry food is chewy, hence the dog's teeth stay remarkably clean; fifth, self-feeding helps overcome kennel boredom. With nothing to do many kenneled dogs grow restless and often develop the habit of eating their own excrement. I always argued that bones helped pacify them and prevent this near unbreakable habit from starting. Now my friend argues that the feed takes the place of the bones. The dog simply gets up, walks over and takes a nibble.

There are other advantages also. The bitch in the last two weeks of pregnancy requires about twice as much food. By the old system you give her a little more and hope it's enough or not too much, but when she's self-feeding, she simply increases her intake exactly in accordance to her needs. When the puppies are weaned, she drops back to normal consumption. Long and continued experiments at dog-food research centers show that this is exactly what happens. Graphs plotted for every bitch are nearly identical.

Puppies are weaned on mush made from the balanced mixture soaked in water or milk, although the latter is not necessary, and by six weeks they are eating the hard mixture just like old dogs. And since puppies require nearly twice the intake per pound of body weight as do mature dogs, these little rascals can eat to their hearts' content. No vitamin supplement needed, no extra calcium or anything else.

Researchers have, in hundreds of cases, divided litters of puppies at weaning age, raised half on special high-calcium and vitamin formulas, the other half on regular self-feeding diet with no supplements. Inevitably the latter was equal to, if not better than, anything raised on fashionable formulas. It was discovered that feeding puppies calcium in amounts 'way above that supplied by the mother was not as wise as had long been thought. In many cases it led to rickets and spur deposits. The result of feeding excess amounts of vitamins has not yet been determined, but it may safely be said that the minimum damage is allowing those weaker puppies that should not and would not ordinarily survive to mature and perpetuate themselves. This is a detriment to any breed.

I know it is hard to believe, but experimentation has brought full proof. The working dog regulates his own intake, consuming more during months of training, less during months of inactivity. Interestingly, it has been found that a dog, unlike a human, does not draw from an immediate intake of food but from already established reserves. Thus the night before a field-trial event the feeder should be removed, for a full stomach will serve little purpose other than to bog down the dog while running. No dog overfeeds himself, for the simple reason that the food is not as palatable as when meat and gravy are mixed in. It is dry and hard, which is why water must be kept beside the feeder at all times.

The question which pops up is, if this is such a fine system, why hasn't everybody adopted it? Well, people can't really believe it until they see the results. Also, the average dog owner, despite his griping, seems to enjoy mixing pooch's supper each night; this is the one time a day he has to pet and play with his dog. Also, he doesn't cotton to the idea that his best pal can be fed like a cow and still survive, let alone probably do better. The change will come slowly. Professionals are the ones who are switching over simply because of the hours of work it saves. From them the public will begin to learn. I myself have not yet changed but am preparing to do so and will utilize the feeding time for training. I cannot see a single fault to the plan, only that it is based on principles so radical that they go against my falsely acquired beliefs. Who ever heard of feeding a dog something he didn't particularly like, not giving him meat or a bone or delicious table scraps when they are left over! Who ever heard of raising puppies without supplementary vitamins and calcium, not even milk!

The first reaction is to throw up one's hands and walk away. But the best proof is that it works. The only two problems I can see are: first, the balance point of one dog may be different from that of another, but I am told that the difference is so slight as to be negligible; second, how to feed the sick dog. The best way is to return to a highly palatable diet, then reintroduce him to the self-feeding system after he has recovered.

For those cases where the owner of a stud dog or brood bitch wishes to add Vitamin E, the pill is easily administered by hiding it in a tiny bit of chopped meat the size of a marble. It has never been conclusively proved or disproved that Vitamin E affects the reproductive processes of animals, but many people believe it helps and wish to add extra amounts to the diet. In cases where extra coat sheen is desired, dogs may be fed slight vitamin supplement and fat through the same process.

In adapting the self-feeding plan, it is important not to change over too quickly. Don't stop today with your present diet and start self-feeding tomorrow. It won't work or will be too drastic on your dog. To begin, you must, first and foremost, be certain that your present feed is a complete dog food. If not, change to one that is. If it is not a complete dog food, then the dog will not be getting a complete diet. Those which are complete will so advertise and the word will appear somewhere on the package.

Get the dogs used to it in their old diet routine first. You start the self-feeding plan by simply hanging a bucket of feed in the run with water beside it. The food must be sheltered from sun and rain. Then gradually cut down on the tasty food you ordinarily put into the regular meal—meat, vegetables, scraps. Plan it so that at the end of two weeks these will be completely eliminated. You are then feeding nothing but wet meal, and the dogs will be eating the dry meal consistently. The last step is slowly to withdraw the water you are placing in the food until you are feeding completely dry food. This should take no more than another week. After that the dogs are on their own.

Will this system ever catch on? Undoubtedly it will, because the whole future of dog-food research is based on it. Imagine if you could buy a dog food that would eliminate distemper, hepatitis and leptospirosis, the three main canine diseases.

In case you don't want to rush into this system, and I wouldn't blame you at all, a few words about the "old-fashioned" mix-it-yourself way are in order. First of all, feed a good complete food—kibble, meal, pellets, whatever—and add to it table scraps, raw or cooked vegetables and fresh or canned meat. In the summer I throw in raw cut-up tomatoes or cooked squash; in winter I grind up raw carrots which I raise and store in sand for this purpose. All dogs like fresh meat and I prefer this to canned because it is chewy. For years I have fed breast of lamb, a cheap cut of about one-quarter fat, one-quarter soft rib bones and gristle, and one-half solid red meat. A local butcher saves it for me at from ten to twenty cents a pound, which is cheaper than canned dog meat. I weigh it out and cut up half a pound per dog, add it to the basic food and vegetables. I vary the flavor by using gravy or broth from a cooked tongue—if it's not too salty—as a mix instead of always using water. If you use canned or frozen meat, it is important to add fat to the diet to avoid eczema and other skin irritations. I always add it anyway. The ideal plan is a teaspoon of cod-liver oil one day and a tablespoon of grease drippings the next, per dog. Beef, pork, chicken and bacon drippings are all suitable. The cod-liver oil is a fine source of A and D vitamins and should be purchased by the gallon. Ease up on the fat in hot weather, increase it in the winter and whenever the dog is being worked hard. It is interesting to note why fat should be added when horse meat is fed. Horse meat is high in protein and to balance this intake and utilize it, the fat carbohydrates are necessary. Thus the balanced food again seems more logical. However, keep your additions below 25 per cent of the total ration by weight.

Some people will shudder, but I like to feed dogs bones. The right kind—large shins and knuckles—cannot possibly do any harm and will help keep the dog's teeth clean. Otherwise a vet will have to do it because a diet of mush will soon coat them. The argument against bones is that, when chewed, they splinter and are liable to lodge in the throat or pierce the stomach or intestine walls. I do not recommend chicken or pork bones, although many's the generation of Southern hound which has lived on little more than this diet. Dogs love to chew and bones are pacifiers of the first order, great for passing those long hours in the kennel when boredom lies heavy.

My last point about food concerns hand-feeding the orphaned pup. Occasionally, just after a little one is born, something will happen to prevent the mother from caring for her pups. Perhaps she will succumb to an accident or not have a normal milk supply or require emergency surgery. Whatever the reason, you will have to take over and hand-feed the pups if you want any to survive.

I did it once and shall never forget it. I bought an old brood bitch, one of the few remaining daughters of the famous Pointer champion Fast Delivery, and bred her to a fine young dog with the intention of getting one last litter. I conditioned her to perfection, gave her the best of care during pregnancy only to discover that at whelping time she could not give birth because of old and weak muscles. My vet delivered the first two by hand and thereafter that part was solved. Then he informed me that she had no milk, that the eight puppies would have to be hand-fed and not to be disappointed if the entire litter was lost, because saving fifty per cent would be sheer luck. Well, I'm the kind who takes a dare to heart. With quiet vengeance I set about the task of feeding them once every hour around the clock from plastic toy baby bottles. By the end of the third day I was in a state of near-collapse but all were alive. I then fed them every two hours from 6 A.M. through midnight. At the end of a week it was every three hours; in two weeks they were eating gruel and on their way. All made it, but I have never gone through such a sleepless, groping tangle of formulas, tiny bottles, gulping, contrary little beasts in my entire life. The result? Well, there were three winners in the litter, one with fourteen field-trial victories by the end of his derby year. Needless to say, it was worth the effort. Since I did this, further experiment has revealed that hourly feedings are not necessary. It was believed that puppies cried because they were hungry. Now we know they cry because they are cold. Thorough feedings every six or eight hours for newborn orphaned pups are satisfactory—*providing pups are kept warm.*

All newborn puppies, whether orphaned or not, should be kept at 90 degrees for the first week of life, 85 degrees the second, 80 the third, and gradually reduced thereafter. If the puppies are in a room, raising the temperature to 90 degrees is not satisfactory because heat rises and the floor or corner where the pups are will remain cold or chilly. Heat which comes from beneath is twice as effective as heat from above.

The best way is to use a heating pad. There are large-sized ones specially made for puppies. I suggest you put it on the floor of the whelping pen or house before the pups are born. Place a good strong piece of half-inch-square-mesh wire over it and nail the wire to the floor. This will prevent the brood bitch from tearing it all to pieces while making a nest for her puppies, in which case you will not only lose a valuable mat but possibly electrocute the puppies. Be sure also to have the electric wires leading to the mat either hidden or under wire screening so these cannot be scratched or chewed. A blanket or soft cloth can be placed over the wire screening and the puppies put on top of that.

Remember, heat will save orphaned pups a lot better than frequent feedings. Give them heat from below, feed them fully every six or eight hours and you won't have too much trouble. There are several excellent ready-made formulas on the market for feeding orphaned pups. If you can't obtain one, use the formula below. Eyedroppers are all right at the start, but you'll want something bigger than that in a few days. Baby bottles with small nipples are good, also toy bottles. After you feed a pup, put in a cardboard box or behind a divider in the whelping pen so you can tell which have been fed and thus not skip any.

Formula for Infant Orphaned Pup:

   One cup evaporated milk
   One cup water
   Two tablespoons of Karo
   Two egg yolks

Directions:

   Shake thoroughly and heat to body temperature. Feed every six or eight hours and *keep puppies warm.*

Chapter 10

Kenneling and Housing the Field Dog

Since the vast majority of field dogs are kept kenneled outside, it's important to discuss various ways of housing them.

Certain basic concepts should prevail in any kennel layout you construct. For example, the runs should be long and narrow rather than square or rectangular. A dog gains a great amount of exercise running up and down his run. He will be better off if his run is four feet wide and twelve feet long rather than eight feet square, though the perimeter is the same in both cases. He will be far better off if his run is four feet wide and thirty feet long because he will have that much farther to travel up and down, up and down, for his exercise. An active field dog will keep himself in pretty good condition just running up and down his run, provided it is long enough.

Another way to gain this distance is by means of a trolly—a long length of wire or cable stretched between two anchors. Most people think of a dog trolly as stretching between two trees at a six- or eight-foot height above the ground. For a field dog of any size or strength this is a very impractical device. If one good lunge doesn't snap it, one week of good lunging certainly will.

The best way to build a trolly for a field dog is to stretch a piece of wire or cable along the ground and anchor each end by means of a "deadman." For this, a hole about two feet is dug in the ground, the end of the wire is attached firmly to a piece of pipe or log which is placed in the bottom of the hole, then stones and earth are piled over it. With a good job an elephant can't pull it out. Number 8-gauge wire or quarter-inch cable should be used. It will hold any dog I've ever seen.

When you use this system, slip a stout two-inch ring onto the wire just before you sink the last deadman. This takes the place of a pulley and always slides freely. With a good six-foot chain snapped to the ring, the dog has an excellent run at almost no expense. The doghouse can be placed anywhere along the length of the wire, preferably at one end at a distance so the dog can enter but cannot wrap himself around the house and become entangled. Length of the wire can be regulated by the space

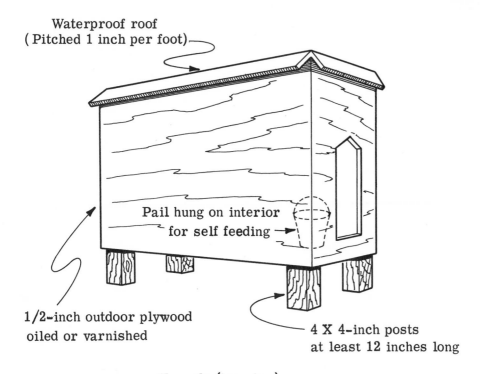

Waterproof roof
(Pitched 1 inch per foot)

Pail hung on interior
for self feeding

1/2-inch outdoor plywood
oiled or varnished

4 X 4-inch posts
at least 12 inches long

Kennels (top view)
20 to 30 feet long

House

House

House

6, 5, or
4 feet wide

Gates to swing in

Wire: chain-link or 2 X 4 galvanized 12 1/2- gauge

A good kennel layout and doghouse.

available, but not much more than forty feet should be used. Otherwise a dog can apply too much pressure at the center of the wire and bow it considerably. Any high grass should be cut down so the ring slides back and forth freely, though in a week's time the dog will have worn the area practically bare. This is the cheapest and one of the most effective runs that can be built. The dog has his own area, a good long stretch to run back and forth on. No chance for fights, no quibbling in sharing a dog-house, and because each dog is isolated he does not easily catch or transmit disease. Only two things against it. In northern winters of snow and ice, the wire tends to freeze in, giving the dog no latitude to move until it is freed. Also, I don't like to chain a dog unless I have to.

To build an enclosed-run kennel, the base or floor must be constructed first. There are three types of bases—the very porous, like sand or gravel, the hard surface, like concrete or asphalt, and just plain bare ground.

Bare ground is the simplest and least effective. Uusually it does not provide adequate drainage, and it's a veritable haven for worm eggs, particularly those of the vicious hookworm. I would keep away from this if at all possible. When you must use a dirt run, apply a good quantity of hand salt or borax to the earth every six months and work it into the ground at least six inches.

Though you may see a lot of concrete or asphalt runs, any veterinarian, even though he uses them, will admit they are far from satisfactory. Veterinarians use them out of necessity because they can be hosed down quickly and thus sanitized quite effectively. All other factors are against them. They are very hard on a dog's feet, particularly an active dog who goes up and down the run a lot. And most dogs that spend a lifetime on concrete show it. They end up being down in the pasterns, what would be equivalent to weak or sagging ankles in humans, and weak legs or feet in field dogs make them about useless. Concrete and asphalt are also extremely hot in the summer and cold in the winter. And the dog that lies down constantly on concrete soon wears the hair off all his bony parts.

The porous base of gravel is far and away the best. Here drainage is assured. Worm eggs are washed down and out of harm's way by rain or hose into the gravel where they cannot contaminate the dog. There is a little "give" to gravel which makes it much easier on the legs of a dog, also the gravel is tough enough to harden the pads and feet of a dog so he's just about ready to hunt when you take him out of the run. It must be leveled with a hand rake occasionally when the dogs pound it out of shape. You will lose a few stones in the process of daily cleaning and each year may need an extra bushel or two of gravel, but the advantages are far greater than those of the concrete run, particularly in northern climates where the frost will often break up a slab of concrete in winter.

Some people prefer sand because the droppings are easier to pick up, but I don't think it makes nearly as effective a run as gravel.

The earth run is, of course, the simplest to build. The concrete run requires more preparation, especially in cold climates. Where the frost line is deep, about four inches of concrete, preferably reinforced with chicken wire or the like, should be poured over eight inches of crushed-stone sub-base. This requires digging a one-foot-deep pit, then working upward. An asphalt run should be built the same way. In both cases the surface should be finished off just as smoothly as possible, because roughness or cracks are ideal harboring places for germs and worm eggs. A hard-surface run must be well pitched for immediate drainage.

To build a gravel run, the same one-foot excavation is necessary but the sides of the pit should be lined with wire or a thin cement block to keep dogs from digging out. When this is completed, put down two inches of lime, which will cut urine smells for years. Next goes down six inches of crushed stone about one inch in diameter; on top of that, six inches of bank-run gravel which has been thoroughly washed. This makes the finest base that can be constructed for a kennel. Stone sizes may, of course, vary according to local supply. In some cases perhaps all gravel will be used,

The base of the kennel is most important.

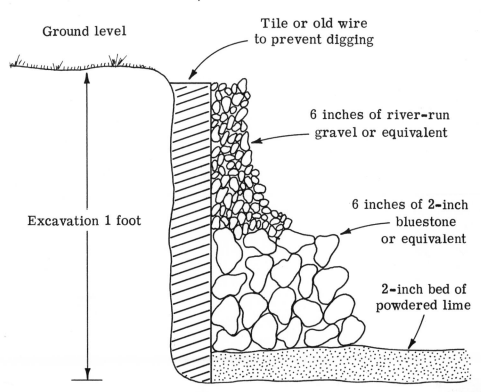

Ground level

Tile or old wire to prevent digging

Excavation 1 foot

6 inches of river-run gravel or equivalent

6 inches of 2-inch bluestone or equivalent

2-inch bed of powdered lime

but sharp-edged quarry stone that will cut a dog's feet to shreds must naturally be avoided.

As for the construction of the sides of the run, several possibilities exist. Wooden or steel posts can be sunk or driven into the ground and wire attached to them. In dirt runs the wire should carry at least three inches below ground. In concrete and asphalt runs, steel posts can be set before the run is poured. In this way they are solidly braced forever. Posts should be six to eight feet apart and each corner braced. Often pipe is run top and bottom between posts to give the wire more security. On any dog run, wire should always be hung on the inside of the posts; the pressure of the dog bouncing on the wire is then placed on the posts instead of the scattered clamps.

For the gravel run the best idea for the sides is the panel system. Several companies manufacture them in various heights and lengths. These panels consist of steel pipe frames with chain-link wire stretched to them. A series of them can be set up, with gates, and they make a neat run. With the proper bracing they are strong and secure as any run that can be built. Their initial cost is relatively high but no higher than the professionally built dog run, and because they are portable you have the advantage of taking them along with you if you ever move—only a new base need be built, so this amounts to a considerable saving.

Another of the panel systems which can be built at home, and much more cheaply, consists of wood and wire. I built one of these myself and found it most effective. I used 2×3s for the framework, made them 6 feet high and in some cases as long as 35 feet. It took four men to lift them into place and they will never be very transportable, but they'll hold any dog and are ideal for gravel runs; inexpensive too. The best wire for wooden panels like this is 12½-gauge 2×4 mesh. Larger dogs like retrievers, bird dogs and hounds require a six-foot-high fence, preferably with a top over it.

In recent years, because of the ever growing concern over heartworm in the South, owners have more frequently been enclosing their entire runs with screen wire. For this a frame must be built, and usually the roof is of corrugated galvanized metal while the sides are covered tightly with screen wire. This is a good idea but it necessarily restricts the size of the pen, otherwise cost becomes prohibitive.

Beagle people very often keep their hounds on wire. There is great controversy about this and I myself would not recommend it because I don't believe a hound or any dog is as sure-footed on wire as on solid surface, consequently he inevitably limits his self-exercise. This, in my opinion, is why so many Beagles on wire are overly fat. In theory, the great advantage of a wire run is that it requires little or no cleaning up. The droppings are supposed to fall through the wire and once or twice a week you can go around with a rake and scratch them away. The trouble is that all the droppings don't fall through. The wire must be supported by under-bracings and if the dog happens to hit one of these, the result stays there. For temporary housing at field trials, small wire runs are perfectly adequate, but I wouldn't use one otherwise.

While on the subject of droppings, I suggest that each dog owner construct some sort of box or barrel into which the daily cleanings from the run can be dropped. For one dog, a box on the surface of the ground may be used. For more than one dog, a metal drum should be buried in the ground and the eliminations placed in it. There is a most effective chemical which organically digests dog droppings. It's called Lim'nate, and the manufacturer supplies complete directions on how to construct the box or drum digester. This solves an otherwise annoying problem.

As for doghouses, an old wooden cider barrel has long been and still remains the favorite of many for sheltering a dog. It should have a good coat of paint so it's watertight, and, when on the ground, be securely propped so it can't roll around. Cider barrels are not easy to come by any more and they don't make very glamorous structures architecturally speaking.

There are many doghouses on the market that can be purchased reasonably. They come in several sizes, shapes and models. If I chose one or built one, the three most important factors that I'd consider would be the proper size, the right roof, and ease of cleaning.

As for size, a dog should be able to stand up and turn around in his home but not much more. In the South a little larger size would be better because it will be cooler in the summer. In the colder northern regions a smaller size would be better so the dog's body heat will be more closely contained.

In my opinion, the roof of a doghouse should be pitched only enough for drainage. It should not be high-peaked or in the shape of an A-frame. Dogs love to jump up on something in their kennel and have a look around. The top of their doghouse is ideal for this. Up and down they go, all day long, to have that look around, maybe curl up for a sun bath. The exercise involved is wonderful. On a steeply peaked house they can't do it. Many dog owners put a table in the run just so the dog can jump up on it and have a shady spot underneath in the summer, but if the right doghouse is used, the table isn't necessary.

I am still amazed that so few doghouse manufacturers bother about building one that is easy to clean. They build them cute, solid, insulated, but try to clean one and see what gyrations you have to go through. What is an easy-to-clean doghouse? Very simple. Either a side or the back is hinged so it swings away from the bottom and you can reach inside with a rake or hoe to scrape out the bedding with no obstacles to block you. The ideal doghouse is hinged so the whole house tips away from the base. Then one simply takes a broom and sweeps away the old bedding, and the inside of the house can be easily disinfected.

A doghouse should face south or in the direction of the least amount of wind. Many come with baffle panels, which cut down on the drafts and breezes. One of the slickest setups I know of is the Air Force guard-dog kennels in Texas. Here each dog has his own graveled area. His house stands on a round post about two feet off the ground and turns freely with the wind like a weather vane, consequently the entrance always faces downwind. The dog is on a fifteen-foot chain attached to a ring around the post which supports the house, thus he can never become twisted in his chain. The only thing I have against the plan is that most dogs on a chain rarely get enough natural exercise.

If you build your own doghouse, here are some tips. Use half-inch *outdoor* plywood. Use brass screws, not nails, to put it together. Don't paint it with lead paint, but with spar varnish or any other finish that takes the weather. Nail a 1×2 molding around the edge of the entrance hole; if your dog likes to chew, this is where he'll start. Design it so it cleans easily. Hinging the top may sound convenient but it isn't. Put legs on the house so it will stand at least a foot, preferably eighteen inches, off the ground. Also, make it large enough to hang a pail on the front inside corner for self-feeding.

Chapter 11

Training

If you have the time and patience to devote, there is no greater pleasure to be gained from a field dog than to train him into a good hunter yourself, then reap the rewards of your efforts. Yes, it takes some knowledge, but it's mostly common sense. If you have the desire to try, I urge you to do so by all means. Even if you don't completely succeed and have to resort to professional help, the dog will be easier to finish, hence money will be saved.

There are many rules about training. The first one centers around why most field dogs are kennel dogs rather than house pets. It's much more difficult, sometimes impossible, to train a dog that is merely a pet. Training consists of channeling desires and talents. This is done mainly by restriction. When a dog leads an unrestricted life as a house pet he has little or no desire to learn, at least not quickly. He wants to play with the kids or run over to the neighbor's for a smell of the hydrant. On the other hand, for the kennel dog to be released from his restricted life and go for a run in the fields is, after a few sessions, the greatest treat he can be given. His concentration and hunting desire are thus channeled and brought to the fore.

This doesn't mean that kennel dogs should not be brought into the home. There is nothing better. Dogs need to associate with people from the beginning of their lives. They should be taken for rides in a car at an early age. They should be around children, around noise, clanging of pans, backfires, whistles, but whenever a training session begins, the dog in training should know it's serious business, yet he should love it.

In recent years a great fad for training dogs at a young age has arisen. This is fine. Dogs should learn from the very start what they can do and what they can't do. There are many advantages to beginning the training of a dog when he is four to six months old. If he is taught right, taught slowly and taught carefully, his lessons become reflexes for life.

On the other hand, there are equally as many pitfalls. Almost inevitably the owner begins to expect too much. The moment the puppy shows a flash or two of maturity and ability, the owner begins to push him beyond his capabilities. When the usual puppy blunders occur, he punishes him too severely. A puppy can take mild correction but not severe discipline. A puppy should not be too obedient. If he is forced to be, he soon loses initiative and incentive.

The old rule of thumb says that one year in a dog's life equals seven in a human's life. Thus, even the two-year-old dog is in the middle of rash youth. Inevitably his enthusiasm overrides his knowledge and a mistake is made. If you can catch yourself and realize that your dog is only a youngster and treat him accordingly, then by all means start training him early.

A few suggestions:

1. For fall hunting buy a puppy born in January or February. Be prepared to start serious training in July. By fall you will have a well-started pup that won't do everything but will provide you with a lot of fun.

2. Bitches are generally more precocious as puppies, learn faster than males.

3. The quick-learning dog is not necessarily the best. Usually it's highly intelligent but possesses a lot of nervous energy and becomes over-competitive or temperamental later. The slow starter often turns out to be a superior dog.

4. Large dogs within a breed are usually slower-maturing than the smaller ones. Sometimes they don't acquire their mental and physical coordination until they're three years old.

5. Remember that not all dogs turn out to be great no matter how well bred they are. There is wise variation even within a litter.

6. You must have patience to train dogs. It's done by repetition from one stage to the next. When your dog makes a mistake, seventy-five per cent of the time it will be your fault because you taught him wrong or allowed him to proceed along lines that created a fault.

7. Don't train your dog for an hour once a week and expect him to know a quarter as much or work one tenth as well as the man who trains his dog each day for fifteen minutes.

8. Use one-syllable words for all commands, no running conversations. Give your dog a call name like Rex, Sam, Jake, and make sure it doesn't rhyme with any of your commands, like Joe and "Whoa!" or Rum and "Come!"

9. Once you begin training, don't let your field dog roam or self-hunt. He will never learn anything.

10. If a dog makes a mistake and you have to punish him for it, don't call him to you and spank him. He'll think he made a mistake by coming to you, and two or three such incidents will cause him to run in the other direction when you call. Go to him and reprimand him on the spot where he misbehaved, then make him do it properly. If you can't get to him to

correct him immediately, forget it. Spanking him five minutes after it happened accomplishes nothing.

11. Make pals with your dog. Be his best buddy. This brings out the desire to please in him. When he makes a mistake and you reprimand him, he'll be crushed. Above all, when he does something correctly, praise him lavishly, pat him, even hug him. He'll learn to distinguish between right and wrong.

12. In training, strive to control the dog without dominating him. He should hunt freely, yet there are times when he must be obedient. He can't chase a farmer's chickens or cows or sheep. He can't chase deer. He can't run across the neighbor's freshly seeded lawn or urinate on his prize rosebushes. If you are going to allow these things, please don't take up field dogs.

13. Don't attempt to train a dog if you have a temper. You cannot possibly succeed.

There are two types of training: basic yard training, which is pure and simple obedience, and field training, which teaches the dog how to handle game properly. All field dogs should be taught both phases of this. Remember, the better you yard-train your dog, the easier he will be to field-train.

Some people make an elaborate project out of yard training by including too many commands. My own personal opinion is that dogs recognize and heed commands as much by the tone of voice as by the word itself, and I eliminate all commands that are not necessary. For instance, teaching the command "No" is ridiculous. It rhymes with the basic bird-dog command of "Whoa," which is vastly more important. "No" is a negative command like "Down" used to keep a dog from jumping up on your clothes. Instead of these two I teach a guttural "Ah-ah-ah!" A dog quickly learns that when I say "Ah-ah-ah!" he'd better stop whatever he's doing, be it barking, jumping, chewing a leg on the dining-room table or chewing a bird in the middle of a retrieve. The same command is applicable, so why clutter a dog's mind with several negative commands? It's an entirely different sound from all my other commands. It's given in three sharp repetitions. The dog, after a couple of paper lickings, learns to stop immediately whatever he's doing and look at you for orders. I even use the command when a dog starts to loop behind in his running pattern. My dogs know when they hear the command they're doing something wrong and they'd better change around and start doing it right. Try this command. It eliminates a lot of useless hollering, and with a little practice you can make it heard for several hundred yards.

The basic yard commands are Sit, Come, Heel, and Whoa. I never teach the command "Sit" to a pointing dog because invariably the dog, when the slightest restraint is put on him, will begin to sit. It looks awful and a field-trial judge will throw him out for it. Retrievers and spaniels are the only field dogs that need to be taught to sit. This is necessary in their field work. The command for spaniels is "Hup," an old English expression. In field-dog work the command "Sit-Stay" is seldom used. Stay is superfluous; if the dog sits, he automatically remains where he is and you should be able to walk off and leave him.

Take the puppy afield several times before yard-training him. If the weather is good, short explorative walks beginning at the tender age of ten weeks will accomplish much. The pup will sniff around, roll into gullies, yelp at thorns and cry when he becomes separated from you. Call him, don't go to him, and he will soon learn to keep up. Continue these walks through the third, fourth and fifth months so he looks forward to them. Try to get him into game, and don't worry if he chases wildly, better if he does. At six months you can start yard work. Of course there are many things you should do in the meantime. You can take him by car to the fields where he runs and he will learn to love riding. From the kennel to the car you can lead him. Don't restrict him if he lunges and tugs eagerly. That's great.

The first bit of restriction a puppy will feel will be his collar. Put it on and let him try to scratch it off. Next comes the lead. If it's used at a young enough age, the pup automatically grows into it. Next comes the stake-out chain. I have a six-foot chain with a foot-long stake that I drive into the ground. I snap the puppy to it and let him fight it for ten minutes. In three days' time he knows that he can race only six feet without being jolted to an uncomfortable stop. Already he's learning.

Early in life you can begin teaching him to retrieve. All pups love to carry objects around in their mouths and you need only encourage this trait to have a fine natural retriever. While the pup is still waddling around, take him to a quiet, sheltered area where there are no distractions. Let him sniff around a few moments to get used to the new place, then toss him an old sock that has been knotted in the middle. He should pick it up playfully and carry it around. Take it gently from his mouth and toss it four or five feet away and encourage him to bring it to you. Do this several times until his interest begins to wane. The moment this happens, stop for the day and put him away.

Later, as he grows, you can take a bumper (the small boat type filled with kapok) and attach several wings (pheasant, pigeon or quail, even chicken) to it by rubber bands or tying. This will simulate a bird and you can toss it into the grass and let him search for it. Just be certain he brings it to you when he finds it. If he wants to run and romp with it, put a long rope on his collar and make him come to you. Gently persuade him, don't horse him in. Almost any field dog will learn this in a few lessons, even hounds. I know of several Beagles that were made into excellent retrievers of pheasants and rabbits this way.

As your dog becomes proficient at this and if he is a retriever or spaniel or bird dog, make him hold until you send him. The best signal for this is a touch on the ear. It will take patience and maybe a little pressure, but it will be worth the trouble for later training.

The puppy almost never gets hard-mouthed. If he shows signs of it, take a foot-long piece of broom handle and wind baling wire along the whole length. Put this inside the sock or attach a couple of wings to it. When he goes to pick it up and bites down hard on the wire, his teeth will hurt and he'll soon handle it gently.

Gun-shy dogs are 98 per cent man-made, not born that way. To prepare the dog to accept the sound of shot is simple enough, and the earlier you start, the better. Whenever I feed puppies I make a lot of noise, rattle pans and especially clap my hands. By the time they're twelve weeks old I have them so I can shoot a cap pistol and they'll come running to be fed. This is certainly an easy way and well worth the trouble. I've never had a gun-shy dog in my life.

A dog can be cured of it and there are many trainers who take them on a guaranteed basis, but with any forethought there is no need for its ever occurring. However, I would suggest using a light-gauge gun, a 20-gauge or .410, if you hunt over a puppy. The muzzle blast of a 12-gauge has scared me plenty of times, even temporarily deafened me, so give a puppy that is the same age as a seven-year-old boy a break.

TRAINING THE POINTING BREEDS

Yard Training

Pointing dogs need know only two commands—Whoa and Come. If these were taught properly, all others could be forgotten. I also teach Heel because there are times when I need to use it, like crossing a road or going through a farmer's yard. Also it fits perfectly into the training sequence. I teach Heel, Whoa and Come in that order, each depending upon the other, and it can be pretty well done in two weeks. One thing, please: when yard-breaking your dog, don't take him out of the kennel and start to work on him. Let him run five or ten minutes to get the steam out of his system.

Put your dog on a lead and make him heel at your left side as you walk forward. Keep the lead snugged up tightly in your left hand and hold a light three-foot switch in your right hand. If the dog tries to move ahead of you, touch the end of his nose with the switch. If he lags behind, give a couple of jerks on the collar. If he's a big, powerful dog and particularly obstreperous, put a chain choke collar on him. The average dog will be heeling well in three nights, but don't proceed to the next step until he is doing it very well on the lead. Don't demand perfection. This is boring for a young dog or puppy. He is bound to wander a mite now and then after a tantalizing smell. Pull him back, repeat "Heel!" but don't demand too much perfection.

After he is heeling well, you can start teaching the command "Whoa!" which is the most important for bird dogs. Put the dog at heel and move out at a brisk walk. After twenty paces, say "Whoa!" crisply, stop in your tracks and jerk up and back on the lead so the dog is forced to stop beside you. Pet him once to give him confidence, then continue and repeat, over and over with patience and a pat each time he does it right. Once the dog learns to stop and stand still when you say "Whoa!" you can slowly begin to edge yourself in front of him, facing him. The first time or two he will want to move too, but you must repeat "Whoa!" and restrain him by maintaining a tight hold on the lead above his head with your left hand.

After a few times of this he will let you circle about him while he stands still. Always praise him when he doesn't move, and admonish him with your voice if he does. If he sits down, pick up his hind quarters. Don't lift him by the tail. Place a hand under his belly. High-strung dogs inevitably want to sit when you walk behind them. In some cases you may have to hold them up the first few times, but they'll soon catch the idea.

Once the dog learns to stand still while you walk around him, you can proceed to the next step, which is to move ahead of the dog several feet while saying "Whoa!" over and over and raising your right arm like a policeman stopping traffic. The idea here is to teach the dog to let you move ahead of him. When he is on point, he won't keep inching up as you go ahead of him to flush. If he is allowed to inch up on point, he will soon begin to crowd his bird, inching a little closer and closer until he flushes it, then he will chase and have a gay old time and you will be left with a handful of problems. This way you avoid them.

If your dog insists on moving ahead as you move ahead, go back to him and say "Whoa!" sharply. Raise his head by the snout and tap him or slap him on the chest between the front legs, also tap him under the chin, then back away, facing him with your arm upraised. He will soon learn to stay put. Remember, the lead or check cord is still on him. You simply drop it on the ground beside him.

Once he has reached the point where he will walk at heel, stop when you say "Whoa!" and allow you to circle around him and move ahead of him, you are ready to teach the command "Come!" For this start walking with him at heel, whoa him and keep on walking yourself until you are the length of the rope ahead of him. Drop down on one knee and call him.

Chances are he won't budge, but with the check cord in your hand you can tug him lightly and make him come. In no time at all he will be doing it enthusiastically. Next step is to take him afield and practice the commands of Whoa and Come until he does them fairly well. Remember, he is still only a puppy. Don't demand perfection yet.

Again, let him run first before you begin to feed him commands to obey. After his puppy energy has worn down a bit, put a check cord on him and start to work on Whoa and Come. Apply the Whoa command when he is moving toward you and you have a chance to raise your hand and stop him. Don't try it when he's barreling along at top speed going away from you and expect him to stop on a dime. Same with the command Come. Apply it when he's approaching you. The first few times he'll goof. If he doesn't pay any attention, step on the check cord or give it a good jerk. He'll start remembering then. With the yard work completed you can concentrate on field work.

Field Training

Your dog is now about seven months old. You have had him afield many times. He handles fairly well—that is, he will generally keep ahead of you, quarter the heavy cover and cast to likely objects in open country—hedgerows, clumps of bushes, etc. When you want your dog to move in a certain direction, you gain his attention by calling his name, then walking in that direction and motioning with your arm at the same time. He is gaining strength, stamina and eagerness to hunt although he is still chasing birds, possibly flash-pointing. You are now ready to teach him how to handle game. In a month's time you will have succeeded if you work him twenty minutes each morning or evening.

First you must find at least a ten-acre field that has cover six inches to a foot high, thus when you plant birds in it they will be concealed but the dog can get a good scent from them. In the beginning you will work him on those days when there is a little cross wind to supply the scent to him. If you can find a field that lies out in a circle or horseshoe and takes ten or fifteen minutes to complete, so much the better.

For field training you will need the following: a 25-foot ⅜-inch nylon check cord with a snap on one end, a roading or chest harness, an 18-inch iron stake painted white or yellow so you can see it easily in the grass, a pair of forty-cent cotton gloves, a cap pistol and a .22 blank pistol, two sieves each five inches in diameter, a pair of live quail (check to see if your state requires a license to possess live game) and a source for buying live pigeons. Buy sieves that can be bolted together, face to face, because you will be putting a quail inside this for your bird planting.

The system for field training carries from sight pointing to scent pointing.

A fine trailer for field trialing or hunting. It carries four dogs, water, guns and all equipment.

Some dogs have more natural "point" in them than others, but this method of training teaches them all to point.

Take a live pigeon, preferably one with some white markings so it is more easily seen, and tie a one-pound weight carefully but securely to one of its legs. Toss the pigeon in a bare spot in a field where he is absolutely visible. Put the roading harness on your dog so when he lunges and you restrain him, the pressure is on his chest, not on his neck where the collar would put it. Attach the check cord to the harness. Tie a knot in the end of the check cord so you can stop him if you have to. Be sure to put on the forty-cent gloves because a nylon rope burn is painful. Put the iron stake in your pocket and begin to work your dog toward the pigeon, encouraging him to hunt with your voice but making sure to hold tightly to the check cord. Work the dog into the wind if there is any. Chances are he will see the pigeon some distance off and try to lunge to grab it. This is a key moment in training. *Under no condition let him catch it.* Restrain him with the check cord, try to quiet him a few seconds by petting his sides and raising his tail. Then slowly let him creep up on the bird to within eight to ten feet. Absolutely stop him at this distance. Calm him again. He will be bug-eyed now, especially if the pigeon moves a bit. Keep saying "Whoa" calmly to him and petting him. After a few seconds, jam the stake into the ground beside the dog, about a foot deep and at an angle like a tent post. Slip the check cord around behind it, and by letting the line play carefully through your hand you can move ahead of the dog and still keep him held there. This system is used when you have to work alone.

Move in very slowly ahead of him, repeating gently "Whoa." When you reach the pigeon, pick it up, weight and all, and toss it twenty or thirty feet ahead of the dog. I usually do this near a stone wall and throw the bird over the wall. It makes a natural barrier and you then have some control over the dog because he will go crazy trying to chase. Hold him back, though. Return to him, try to calm him, pull out the stake and let him go sniff the spot where the bird was standing. After a few moments you can go hunt the bird. Hold him tightly by the check cord and make certain he doesn't catch it. If he does, it's your own fault and you will have created several serious problems. Don't lick him, though. Just take the bird away from him and put him in the run until another day.

Assuming that you and your dog find the bird again, hold him back, encourage him to point it at sight, put the stake in beside him, move ahead of him and repeat the simulated flush by throwing the bird. Ten minutes of this for three consecutive days will have the average dog sight-pointing solidly. As he begins to gain scent of the pigeon you can throw it in grass that lightly hides it. Work him always into the wind so he can catch good scent and point it. Now after you flush you should shoot the cap pistol. The slight pop will not bother him. Remember, you are not letting your dog chase.

As soon as the dog begins to point the pigeon by scent, switch to the quail in the sieve. This little gadget I thought up to avoid leaving my scent when I planted a bird. I discovered that clever dogs soon gave up racing around for bird scent; they simply followed my trail to the bird and thus found it more quickly. The sieves with the quail in them I can toss to left or right as I walk along. It also avoids the task of planting birds by rocking them. I don't care who you are, you can't plant birds without having at least twenty per cent of them fly away. Even worse is the dog that points the scent of the planted bird, sees it and dives in to grab it. If you lick him for this you will quickly ruin him by making him bird-shy or what is known as a "blinker." With the sieve system, if he dives in, he gets only a mouthful of wire.

Thus far you have bought only one or two pigeons. Now you will need more, for you will let a few fly away free, later start shooting them for the dog. Try to keep ten or fifteen on hand.

Put the sieve with the quail in a lightly concealed place where the dog will obtain a good scent but can't see it. Work him with the check cord upwind into the bird. Guide him into it so he catches scent and points.

Style him up. The more you touch and handle him on point the more mannerly he will become around game. Put the stake in the ground, walk in, holding the end of the check cord, and kick around in the immediate vicinity of the sieve, then bend over and toss out a pigeon. Let it fly away as though it were a bird flushing. Shoot the cap pistol while the dog stands watching it, hypnotized. He will not even notice the sound but will try to race after it. Go back to him, calm him and try to get him to stand in one place. Before you let him move on, go pick up the quail in the sieve. He will not know what you are doing. Let him run off, then plant it again and repeat the process.

Releasing two pigeons a day is plenty of bird work. At the end of a week he should be handling this phase of his education perfectly, dragging his check cord loosely without you on the end of it, pointing and holding while you go in and throw out a pigeon, holding until you go back to him and touch his ear to send him on. When he does it right, praise him; when he does it wrong, admonish him with your voice. If he creeps up as you go into flush, put the check cord back on the stake and hold him there. He shouldn't get closer than three or four feet from the quail in the sieve. If he does, pick him up by the collar and an arm under the belly and carry him back bodily to five feet. Set him up in the line of scent and say "Whoa!" to him a bit harshly. Now is the time to get the bugs out of him. If he is allowed to make a mistake, it soon becomes a habit and then you have problems.

Up to the time you began this field work you should have been keeping up his retrieving lessons with the bumper covered with wings. You might refresh his memory a little at this point because he will soon have to retrieve.

Kill a pigeon by hand and let it lie overnight for the next day's training session. Plant the sieve and quail, and get the dog to point it. Now, instead of releasing a live bird, you are going to throw out the cold, dead pigeon. Throw it well up in the air so the dog can see it, but throw it only fifteen feet or so in front of you, no farther than the length of the check cord. Remember how you've been sending your dog to retrieve? Go back to him now and send him, only make sure the check cord is free of the stake and that you have hold of the end. He will go to the bird and pick it up. This is another *key moment*. Be certain he brings it to you directly. Don't let him chew it, mouth it or play with it. Don't jerk him in with the rope either, but use it to make sure he comes directly to you. This is the point where 95 per cent of the dogs are made hard-mouthed because the bird is either alive and the dog squeezes it to kill it, or else it's shot to a bloody pulp and the dog wants to eat the meat.

After he brings you the bird, make a fuss over him, pet him and throw it

This eight-month-old Pointer of the author rigidly sight-points a pigeon. Be sure to talk gently to the dog and calm him by petting as you restrain him.

Check cord is run behind stake in ground, permitting handler to move ahead of the dog.

Handler picks up weighted pigeon with clipped wing. Note that dog has not moved from his tracks and high degree of intensity is maintained.

Simulating flush, handler tosses pigeon into the air. A month after this point you can shoot live pigeons over your dog and have him retrieve them like an old pro.

out again. This time shoot the cap pistol and let him retrieve it the second time.

Use the dead bird for a couple of days, then kill another one. Each time he points, throw the bird a little farther out, also switch from the cap pistol to the .22 blank pistol. In a week's time he should have this down pat. You are now ready to shoot live birds over him. Use a light-gauge gun to start with, 20-gauge or .410, and take along a buddy who is a good shot to shoot the first two or three while you hold your dog to give him confidence.

The procedure is exactly the same. Plant the quail in the sieve, work him upwind into it. When he has pointed, go to him and style him up, repeating "Whoa" quietly but confidently. Take him by the collar and pet him. Signal to your friend to walk in, kick around the sieve. He will throw out a pigeon so the dog can see it fly, and he will shoot it. You will calm your dog, then send him to retrieve it. For the first few times, leave the check cord on him to make certain he retrieves promptly.

After you have shot ten or fifteen pigeons over your dog and had him retrieve them, he is on his way. To teach him to back, you will need another dog, but he can learn it in a couple of sessions. Wild-bird hunting is different from planted-bird hunting, so you can expect him to make some blunders, but he will learn with time and experience and in the end provide years of outstanding shooting.

TRAINING RETRIEVERS AND SPANIELS

These two groups are combined in this section because for the practical side of hunting their training is the same. For field-trial work it is a different story, but that is not our interest here.

Yard Training

The three basic commands for retrievers and spaniels to learn are Sit or Hup, Heel and Come. The bird-dog command of Whoa is not taught here. If you have a retriever pup, start teaching him to sit from the moment you get him. If you have a Springer or Cocker Spaniel, you teach him the same thing just as early only you call it "Hup."

To teach the retriever or spaniel to sit, take him to a quiet spot, preferably fenced in, where there are no distractions. Place one hand under his chin and with the other one push his rump down, while you repeat "Sit!" or "Hup!" as the case may be. Hold him there firmly for a few seconds and keep repeating the command. If he stays seated when you release him, wait over him a few moments, then praise him. Move him about a little and repeat. Try it ten or twelve times the first session, a little longer each

Retrievers take to their trade early by natural instinct, but with a little time and patience any young dog can be taught to retrieve with eagerness.

time thereafter and he'll soon have the knack of it. The retrievers, being bigger and tougher than spaniels, will need a little more persuading perhaps, but it comes easily. Once the dog has learned to sit or hup in one place, he should be made to do so in many other places—around the family car so he doesn't jump on it trying to get in, around guests so he doesn't jump on them, and especially at meal time or tidbit time when he is about to be fed. Field dogs should not be rewarded with food for good efforts as show dogs are. A friendly tone to the voice and a pat on the head are far more effective.

Some people like to teach the command "Stay." As I said earlier, it's unnecessary. You can accomplish the same thing with "Sit" simply by raising your hand like a policeman stopping traffic, backing away and making sure the dog stays there. If he doesn't, pick him up bodily and plank him back down where he was and repeat the command with arm raised. A tap under the chin of a spaniel and a good wallop on the chest of a retriever will usually finish the job.

Remember to be gentle with a spaniel. They are sensitive dogs and can't take much abuse or shouting, whereas a Lab or Chessie will require a small thrashing and plenty of cussing from time to time.

Once the command "Sit" or "Hup" has been mastered, the next step can be the command "Come!" This is done with the dog in the sitting position and the trainer several feet out in front of him. For the first few times a check cord may be necessary. Soon he will be responding with glee. Remember to reward him when he does his job well.

For field-trial work, spaniels and retrievers work by whistle, but for practical hunting, voice commands are much easier and more effective. Since we are not dealing with the field-trial dog here but only with the practical hunting dog, we won't go into that more advanced stage of training.

Spaniels and retrievers are usually taught to retrieve and hunt for game before they learn their yard commands. In other words, the desire to retrieve and hunt is brought out in them before they are at all restricted. In this way they get out and search much better instead of hunting at too restricted a range.

After a few times out, the average spaniel or retriever will begin to quarter almost instinctively. The trick is to teach him that he must stay within gunshot range, around 30 or maximum of 40 yards distant. This is best accomplished by working in an open field where the handler can see the dog and the dog the handler with ease. If the dog tends to range too far out, he will have to be turned. When he reaches the 35-yard point, shout his name, turn and walk in the opposite direction, and make sure to give him an arm signal when he looks at you.

The puppy which is started young in the field—that is, at five or six months—will almost invariably be dependent upon his handler. When he sees the boss turn and start to walk away, he will follow in a hurry. Thus, to teach quartering, the handler must walk a zigzag course himself, but the dog will soon develop the habit of turning when his name is called or when he sees the arm motion. Don't ever deceive or trick a dog in any part of his training, otherwise he will grow to doubt your commands.

Let the spaniel develop on his own. Don't try to push him. If he doesn't stretch out far enough, just keep working him each day. He'll gradually widen his pattern with time and experience. Don't work him too long at one time or in too heavy cover. This quickly dampens the spirits of any young dog. Fifteen or twenty minutes is enough in the beginning.

A retriever is a tougher dog. Generally he will range on the wide side and care must be taken not to let him develop this into a habit. If he becomes headstrong and doesn't turn when called, put a good long check cord on him and step on it a moment after you call his name. When he bounces to a stop, wave him in the opposite direction. He'll soon learn to listen.

It will pay to carry a blank pistol along and fire when the dog flushes game. Fire after he's chased ten or fifteen feet. Don't let him chase birds clean out of sight. This develops a bad habit. Call him back after fifty feet and make a fuss over him. If he doesn't listen, put the check cord on him and stop him that way. Don't require that he be steady to wing and shot —that can come his second year—but neither should he be wild and unmannerly. The flushing dog, whether spaniel or retriever, must be under control at all times and it's best that he learn this from the beginning.

Once the dog has learned to sit or hup in almost any situation you can begin to utilize his early retrieving lessons. These should have begun from the moment you obtained the puppy. An old woolen sock knotted in the middle serves as an excellent starter. Tease the puppy a little with it, then toss it three or four feet away and urge him to go fetch it. Make a game of it and soon the puppy will be playing along. Limit these sessions to five or ten minutes, and the moment his interest lags, stop for the day. Gradually change to a sock full of feathers, then to a cold, dead pigeon.

As the dog grows, the day will come when he won't want to retrieve. Don't worry about it, try something else. We all have our off days, so do dogs. If he doesn't want to complete his retrieves, try running away from him as he comes toward you. If he doesn't take to the transition from the sock full of feathers to the dead pigeon, tie a couple of pigeon wings to the sock.

Once the dog learns to remain steady while you throw out a dead pigeon, shoot, then send him to fetch it, you have him well on the way. From there you throw live pigeons out in front of him, drop them and send him to retrieve. Then you plant the pigeon out in a field and work the dog into it. When he flushes it, try to get him to sit or hup as the bird flies. This is best done with two people, one to restrain the dog by the check cord, the other to shoot the pigeon. A few times of this and the dog will learn what is wanted, and he will be happy as long as he is allowed to fetch the bird.

When you plant the pigeon, best results come when it is not buried too tightly, that is with its head under its wing. The dog can grab it too easily, rather than flushing it. Dizzy the pigeon by whirling it around, toss it into the grass and it will usually stay there long enough to serve the purpose.

As the dog advances it will pay you to go to a game preserve and shoot some pheasants or chukars over the dog. Another good system is to use a quail recall pen with a covey of fifteen or twenty birds. Let out half of them and they will return to the others after you have worked your dog. Or, if you want to shoot them for your dog they are much less expensive than pheasants and when you miss one, chances are he will return to the others for use another day.

In the event that your retriever or spaniel does not learn to fetch naturally, there is a system of force retrieving which can be taught. However, it's not as simple as it sounds, and the rank amateur will do much better working with the natural system.

Most retrievers and spaniels take to water easily. But under no condition should you ever pitch one in bodily for the first time. This can make him water-shy forever. The best way to introduce any dog to water is to exercise him during the summer for a few minutes and when he has become well heated, lead him down to the water's edge. Chances are he'll wallow in right away. You can take off your boots and socks, roll up your pants and wade in yourself. This encourages the dog no end. After two or three times of this, bring along his favorite retrieving dummy and toss it just a couple of feet into the water so he can wade in and reach it. Gradually extend the distance until he begins to swim for it. After that you'll have trouble getting him out of water.

Try tossing bumpers into deep water, along banks, into marsh grass— every possible situation that your dog may encounter in his retrieving. Always work him into the wind so he catches scent easier. As he progresses, use two or three bumpers at once so he learns to mark and remember his falls.

Retrievers more than spaniels are often required to make blind retrieves. This happens particularly when duck hunting. The dog may be in the water fetching when you drop another one in a different direction. Any duck dog should take a line that the gunner gives him, go out and hunt the area indicated, whether it be land or water or, most likely, marsh.

Teaching a dog to take a line is not as difficult as it would seem. It is done principally by tracking. That is, the handler walks out twenty yards, drops the bumper, then walks back over the same line. The first few times it should be done on bare ground so the dog can see the bumper. Each time he sends the dog he should make a definite motion with his arm in front of the dog as though drawing an imaginary line. Gradually the handler walks farther out, into concealing grass, to drop the bumper and the dog learns to follow the human scent to the bumper. Once this is accomplished, the handler can toss the dummy a few feet in a direction that the dog does not see, then send him. In time the distance is lengthened until he is making blind retrieves of fifty to a hundred yards.

Actually, flushing dogs do not need a great deal of training to be hunted over, but the more they have, the better-mannered they will be in the field and the more gunning pleasure they will bring.

TRAINING HOUNDS

Not enough people yard-break their hounds. There's no need to teach all the obedience commands but any field dog should know "Come" and "Heel." Hounds are no exception. Frequently the hunter starts game himself and he must be able to call his hound in to pick up the line. Beyond that, every dog should come whenever he is called. For this the command "Sit" is sometimes taught as a preliminary to "Come." It is a way of holding the dog in one spot at least until he learns his commands. For this the check cord is again the persuader. "Heel" is valuable in many hunting situations such as returning to the car, crossing a garden or road, going through a barnyard.

Also, teaching the Beagle or Basset to retrieve is most worthwhile. He will bring in crippled or lost game to the hunter and save many footsteps as well as disappointments. The best way to teach this is to start with the young puppy and encourage him to bring in a knotted sock as previously described. After a few patient sessions he should be responding. Force retrieving does not work well with hounds. The natural system is about the only way.

The easiest method to teach a Beagle or Basset to hunt rabbits is to run him with another of his kind, but this isn't necessarily the best. It can make for a very jealous hound, and the faults of the old dog may rub off on the youngster.

A good way is to take the pup either by himself or with his brothers and sisters into rabbit coverts. Try to start a cottontail and call the young dog over to the line of scent. Generally he will follow it with slight encouragement. After a few times of this the young hound will usually open of his own accord.

Another method that a lot of Beaglers use is to release a cottontail in a wire enclosure of perhaps 100×100 feet and put the puppy inside the enclosure and let him run the rabbit both by scent and by sight. If the Beagle catches and kills the rabbit, all the better. This generally excites him enough after two or three times to strike out boldly on his own.

Once he is started, his advancement will depend upon how much experience you can give him. The more times you hunt him the better he will be. Don't make the sessions too long. The moment he shows signs of tiring, pick him up.

It's a good idea to develop a whistle that will attract his attention when you want him to hark in to you. In time he will learn to know its meaning and the moment he hears it he'll come running to pick up the trail you've found. Don't be in too great a hurry to shoot a rabbit for him. Better that he have a chance to run a while and learn how to work out checks. When and if you see him back-trailing, grab him by the collar and take

Beagles harking in on a line. Young dogs learn quickly from the older and more experienced ones.

him back to the check. Just be sure you're right. Some clever old rabbits deliberately double back to hide their track. If he starts to pottering or fussing, take him on and find a new bunny.

As he improves with experience, he will gradually take to working pheasants. Once you get to know your Beagle or Basset, you'll be able to tell by his voice what he's running. Make a pet of him. Encourage him when he's right, be firm but not heavy-handed in correcting his mistakes. Above all, don't push him too much but let him have his head and learn.

The larger hounds like Coonhounds and Foxhounds are trained mostly by hunting them with older dogs that are well broken and know what they're doing. For the Coonhound a live coon is often used to lay a trail for young dogs to follow. The coon is chained up a tree, out of reach of the hounds when they come charging up. One thing to avoid is letting a young, inexperienced Coonhound move in on a coon that has just been shot out of a tree. He may get mangled enough so he won't want to have much to do with coons thereafter.

For Coonhounds and Foxhounds there are several "drags" on the market which are scented to lay an artificial trail, and they're very effective.

One of the great banes of hound men is junk—that is, having the Coon-

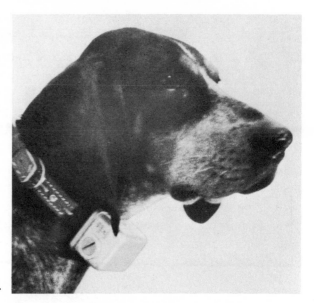

The electronic shocking collar.

hound or Foxhound run deer, squirrels and other off-scents. On the market now are several breaking scents which, when applied either as a nasal spray or on a pad attached to the dog's collar for a period of time, so annoy, even nauseate him, that he never has the desire to run that particular scent again. They are quite effective.

At this point we come to the new electronic devices that may be used in dog training. There are three: the electric collar, suitable for training all types of field dogs; the electric leash, a variation of the collar; and a remote-control bird releaser for pointing dogs only.

The electric collar is quite a gadget, expensive but highly effective if properly used, also the ruination of a dog forever if improperly used. It works this way. The leather collar, containing a small receiver that delivers electric impulses, is attached to the dog's neck. The handler carries a transmitter about the size of a camera. When they go to hunting and the dog makes a serious mistake, the handler presses a button on the transmitter which sends a radio wave to the receiver on the dog's collar and he receives a good shock of electricity, harmless but highly effective.

The device is deadly for breaking a dog of bad faults like chasing deer, livestock or poultry, fighting, bolting, barking, chasing cars, etc. It is not to be used as a constructive training device—that is, to teach your dog to point. It is effective after you have taught your dog what you want done and he refuses to do it. It is suitable for bird dogs, hounds and retrievers but not recommended for spaniels because they are inclined to be soft, and this delivers a real jolt. The better models have a high- and low-shock control.

The electric collar is no toy, and the handler must know a lot about training in order to use it properly. For example, if he uses it to make his dog come in and the dog happens to be pointing out of sight, he may forever ruin him. It can be used only when the dog is in full view. The device is expensive, $150 to $250, depending upon the model and the range, so it is best bought by a group who can split the cost. Within the group, the one man who knows the most about training should use it.

The electro leash is a training device similar to the shocking collar, only instead of a transmitter, the handler carries a check cord which has an electric wire running to the dog's collar. By squeezing the box at the end of the rope he can give the dog a jolt of electricity. This is a highly effective device for obedience training. A dog can be taught yard work in a quarter of the time it ordinarily takes and he remembers his commands effectively. The difficulty is in starting with too young a dog and demanding too much obedience. No dog much under a year of age can take it. In field training the electro leash has many applications but again it requires the wise and experienced trainer to know when to use it and when not to use it. They range from 10 to 50 and 100 feet, between $25 and $50 in price, depending upon the length.

The remote-control bird releaser is a training device for pointing dogs. It consists of a box into which a quail or pigeon or pheasant can be placed. The box is then hidden in the field. A special collar containing a tiny transmitter which emits radio waves within a radius of just a few feet is attached to the dog and he is allowed to work upwind into the bird in the box. As he catches scent he should stop and point. If he keeps creeping up, the collar he wears will trigger the mechanical latch on the box and eject the bird. There is no shocking involved. It simply teaches the dog not to crowd his birds and is very effective in this respect. The distance that the trap will spring can be decided in advance at any distance such as 3, 6, 12 feet, but it should allow the dog to catch good scent. So many dogs, after they catch scent, keep moving up until they get too close to the bird and it flushes. This quickly eliminates the habit.

One last word of caution in training any field dog: don't expect too much of him his first year. It is valuable to teach him as much as you can, but so often he will be perfect around the yard and then appear to lose all training when hunted over in the beginning. This is where patience comes in. He has to be disciplined so he knows what is wanted and expected of him, but don't lose your temper. Even though he performs well at the end of his first hunting season he will probably have to be trained quite a bit at the start of his second year to brush up on his manners. But to see a well-trained dog work afield is always worth the effort, particularly if it is your dog and your effort.

Chapter 12

Field Trials and the
Future of Hunting Dogs

Hunting is man's oldest form of providing for himself. In our time it has become a sport enjoyed by millions of people across the length and breadth of our country. Like any sport, sooner or later competition arises. In the case of the hunting dog this competition takes the form of the field trial.

Throughout this book there has been constant reference to field trials. Suffice to say here that this type of competition is the chief reason for the general over-all improvement of our hunting dogs in the last twenty-five years. As field trials grow in size and numbers, the competition will bring even further improvement in the quality of the field dog and the methods of training him.

Because field trials are exciting, they attract all kinds of people and each

Two Pointers break away for an open all-age stake. Handlers, judges and gallery must ride horseback to keep up with them.

breed of dog, be it Pointer, Shorthair, Labrador, Beagle or whatever, draws a certain type of following. The wide-going Pointer is owned and handled by a lean breed of man who must be an excellent horseman, able to ride hell-bent-for-leather at times, handle his dog by singing, shouting, cussing, instinct and a good pair of eyes. He's a rugged individual who borders on being an outlaw like the dog he owns. God preserve the thinning ranks of both.

The closer-working dogs of the pointing breeds and spaniels are owned and handled by more normal people, particularly in those cases where

National Retriever Champion Bigstone Hope takes a line from D. L. Walters to fetch a duck in a field trial.

husband and wife enjoy going to a field trial in a picnic atmosphere where each can perform with the dog. They can walk the course on foot, enjoy the great outdoors and see a fine field dog do the job he was created for.

The retriever people love to watch the intricate work of a blind retrieve or a tough triple from an embankment or the comfort of a camp chair. At a retriever trial there is not much moving about, very little noise. It is like being on the eighteenth green at a golf championship. Toward the end you

Breakaway for a Beagle stake. Field trials are held almost every weekend of the year across the country.

can cut the tension with a knife, and an owner or handler will be visibly shaking as his dog moves to the line.

Deep within the souls of hound people is a thirst for music, for this is what makes most people follow a pack of Coonhounds or a brace of Beagles in a field trial. This and a thousand other points which go to make up the competition—the way the hound runs his line, picks up the checks, the stories the old-timers tell, the side bets between excited contestants who are sure they're going to win.

As field trials grow and the population expands, it would seem that sooner or later one or the other would have to give way. Already we are seeing the beginnings of this, particularly in the Northeast, where large tracts of grounds are fast disappearing. Yet the result has been that the character of field trials has changed—that is, the dogs work closer and hence require less land to hunt.

Many states are making the acquisition of land a part of their conservation program. These tracts are used for field trials each weekend of the spring and fall, then are opened for public hunting during the regular season. Connecticut has its Pelton's Pastures at East Windsor. New York has superb grounds at Baldwinsville, where several championships are held each year. Many other states have similar projects either operating or under contemplation.

At this time there is plenty of land left but we have certainly reached the point where we must make plans for the future. Each hunter should join some organization which has a long-range goal of protecting his right to hunt and/or compete in field trials. Alone he stands little chance of moving the machinery necessary for action, but a group can make itself heard and urge a particular state to acquire a parcel of land for such use. Without the beginnings of this action now, the long-range future of the hunting dog is definitely limited.

Some men are keenly aware of this, to the extent that they have placed their plantations in the South in perpetual trust for use as field-trial areas. The Ames plantation in Grand Junction, Tennessee, home of the annual National Championship for Pointers and Setters, is an outstanding example of this.

As for the future of the hunting dog himself, there is no reason in the world why he won't continue to flourish if we watch out for him and cherish him as men have done previously. The progress he has made in the last two centuries, even in the last two decades, has been almost phenomenal. Most important, by his ability and beauty, the American hunting dog is providing an ever increasing host of people with more happy hours of recreation, healthy sport and worth-while memories than any other animal. May it always be so.

PHOTO CREDITS

Pete Czura, frontis, 6, 9, 17, 21, 33, 38, 69, 126, 131, 134, 139, 140, 142, 146, 147, 148, 151, 153, 155, 157, 172, 209, 227, 228, 229, 231, 243, 300, 305, 309

German Wirehaired Pointer Club of Wisconsin, 47, 49

Evelyn Shafer, 52, 55, 82, 84, 87, 98, 102, 112, 200, 244, 308

Paul and Harriet Daniel, 187

William Brown, 92, 95, 105, 253

Gibson-Nail, 182

Clarence Goering, 56, 59, 60

Paul E. Nelson, 182

Herb Levart, 27, 262

Ed Bakal, 187

John O'Brien, 188, 191

Joe Clark, 193

Larry Mayer, 221

Dale Henry, 238

Cardinali Studio, 26

Erasie Studio, 219

Fred Nobs, 294

Lee Supply Co., 306

Michigan Conservation Dept., 213 (right)

Anderson Independent, 213 (left)

Purina Dog Care Center, 106, 109, 110, 174, 196, 198, 205, 211, 310

Gaines Dog Food Company, 177

American Field, 70